Preface

A Question of Faith covers all three years of the Junior Certificate Religious Education Syllabus. Each chapter title is directly linked to the syllabus. It is comprehensive and precise throughout and **covers both Higher and Ordinary Level**. The Higher Level material is clearly marked with pink pages.

The book is both fresh and challenging and backed up by a **modern student-friendly design** and vibrant photographs and artwork. The language level is carefully chosen to ensure the information is accessible to all students.

Different styles of questions are used throughout the chapters to help the student prepare for the examination. It is also useful to help non-exam students to focus on the questions at home and in class.

All **Key Concepts** are defined clearly in each chapter. They are also redefined at the end of each section. This is very useful for the section on short questions in the exam.

As experienced teachers the authors are aware how important it is to give choice and they have included all the **World Religions** in *A Question of Faith*.

An invaluable section on **The Journal** is also included to help the student focus on what is expected in the exam. The Journal is worth 20% of the overall mark in the exam.

Lori Fields-Whelan and Niamh McDermott are both teachers of Religion at Manor House School and Loreto College, St. Stephen's Green. They have worked as Associate Trainers with the Religious Education Support Service. They have also worked in the role of Chief Advising Examiners with the State Exams Commission at both Higher and Ordinary levels.

The Educational Company of Ireland
Ballymount Road
Walkinstown
Dublin 12

www.edco.ie

A member of the Smurfit Kappa Group

Design: Outburst Design
Cover: Outburst Design
Illustrations: Kim Shaw
Editors: Robert Healy, Antoinette Walker

Photos courtesy of: Jeffrey Healy, Corbis, Getty Images, Alamy Images, The Irish Times, The Young Social Innovators

Printed in the Republic of Ireland by: ColourBooks

The authors and publishers wish to thank the following for permission to reproduce copyright material and/or for their help in producing the book: Ali Selim; Reena McDermott; Sr. Thérèse Larkin I.B.V.M.; The Chief Rabbi's Office; Reverend Ann Wallace; Imam Yahya M. Al-Hussein; Laura Seery; Sr. Margaret Cashman; The priests and parishioners of St. Mark's Church, Tallaght; Trócaire; Saint Vincent de Paul; The Dublin Mosque, South Circular Road, Dublin; The Young Social Innovators; Liam Lawton; The Christian Brothers; Antoine de Saint-Exupéry for *The Little Prince*; Garth Brooks for *Unanswered Prayers*; Paul Simon for *A Bridge Over Troubled Water*; The Glencree Centre for Reconciliation

In the case of some copyright pieces, the publishers have been unable to contact the copyright holders but will be glad to make the appropriate arrangements with them as soon as they make contact.

Note from the authors:
We would like to dedicate this book to our parents, Margaret and Paddy Fields and Tony and Lee McDermott, and to our ever patient husbands Donogh Whelan and Kieran Dufficy.

SECTION A
COMMUNITIES OF FAITH

SECTION B
FOUNDATIONS OF RELIGION: CHRISTIANITY

Contents

SECTION C
MAJOR WORLD RELIGIONS

SECTION D
THE QUESTION OF FAITH

SECTION E
THE CELEBRATION OF FAITH

SECTION F
THE MORAL CHALLENGE

SECTION A

COMMUNITIES OF FAITH

AIMS

- To explore the nature and pattern of human communities.

- To identify the characteristics of communities of faith/churches.

- To examine these characteristics as they occur in communities of faith/churches in local, national and international examples.

HIGHER LEVEL ONLY
- To explore the concepts of leadership, authority and service in communities of faith/churches.

In this chapter,
you will become familiar with
the following concepts:

- Co-operation/lack of co-operation
- Sharing
- Communication
- Roles
- Community breakdown

Chapter 1:

Community

Belonging to a Community

Community – A community is a group of people who have something in common.

We all belong to many different types of communities. A **community** is a group of people who have something in common. Read the following story and see what it tells you about community.

Just Another Day

Ben's alarm clock went off at 7 am as it did every Monday morning. Having quickly dressed, he raced down the stairs to eat the bowl of hot porridge he knew his Mam would have ready for him. His twin sister Katie was already halfway through hers. Meanwhile, his Dad was telling his Mam about an important meeting on that day. For a few minutes all the family sat and chatted about the party they had been to the day before for their Granny's birthday. Ben and Katie in particular had had a great time catching up with all their cousins. After breakfast the twins quickly left the house to catch their bus to school.

On the bus Ben sat beside his friend James. Since they were babies James had lived next door to Ben and they were great friends. Straight away, James told Ben about all the drama he had missed on Sunday while he was at the family party. In the afternoon Ben's dog Misty had escaped from the garden and all the neighbours had been out trying to help find him. Even old Mrs Kelly had joined the search party and she didn't like dogs! When they eventually found Misty, James's Mam had invited all the neighbours in for tea to thank them for their help.

School that day wasn't like a normal day. It was sports day and along with all the fun there was huge competition between all the first year classes to see which one could win the Best Class Award in the year group. However, when Ben saw his sister with her best friend Isabelle he felt worried. Katie's class, the 1Ms, were really good at sports and everyone was sure they would win the award. In first year Katie and Isabelle were the best cross-country runners. He'd never hear the end of it if their class won!

That evening over dinner Katie told their parents all about the sports day and how Ben's class and hers had won the award jointly. It was very close all day and no one was surprised when the two classes came first. In fact, the whole first year group had a great day. Because Ben was at band practice he didn't get to show his parents the medal he had won for the long jump. In the school band he played the trumpet and even though he

3

loved playing, it took a good deal of practice and hard work. But lots of his friends were in the band so they always had good fun at rehearsals. After the long day on the sports field he was tired, but the band were playing at a concert that weekend and needed all the practice they could get!

Over to You

1. In the story how many different communities did Ben belong to?
2. Do you belong to similar communities? Make a list and compare them to others in the class.
3. What have the people in these communities got in common?

Characteristics of Communities

In the story above the communities mentioned were all examples of local communities. There are also national and international communities. An example of a national community is An Garda Síochána, as they are found throughout Ireland. An example of an international community is the EU, as it is made up of countries from around Europe.

Being part of a community is very important. In their lives people need to feel they belong to a group. But in order for a community to work properly certain things are needed. These characteristics are **co-operation, communication** and **sharing.**

Co-operation

To co-operate means to try and get along with people for the good of the community. Sometimes this means that we have to make sacrifices and be willing to compromise. Being part of a community takes hard work and all the members must co-operate with each other.

Co-operation – Trying to get along with people for the good of the community.

Communication

To communicate means to share ideas with others. All relationships need communication to work. If people do not communicate they do not know how others in the community are feeling. We also need communication in order to share our ideas. This will help the community to grow and improve.

Communication – Sharing ideas with others.

Sharing

To share means to give something to others. In a community we may need to share our time, our knowledge or our talents. If people share in a community, it means that the community can reach its full potential and be the best one it can be.

Sharing – Giving something to others.

Roles in the Community

Woodvale football team is an example of a local community. The members of this community belong to it because they all share a love of the sport. The community is made up of many different people. Each member of Woodvale has their own role to play. A role is the part that someone plays in a community.

Role – The part that someone plays in a community.

Woodvale Football Team

Every Wednesday night the team meet for training and have a match most Saturday mornings at ten o'clock. Their manager Jimmy organises what teams they will play against and he is in charge of who plays at each match. He also gives the players their positions. Before training he has a meeting with the team coach, Tony. It is Tony's job to get the players fit for their matches. Without fail, he makes them practise their tactics and helps them to improve their game.

At their meetings, Jimmy and Tony decide which players will begin the match and who will be substitutes. In addition, they talk about any injuries the players have and what areas the team need to improve on. The goalkeeper for the team is Pat. However, if Pat is injured a defender named Joseph takes his place. Even though Joseph does not like playing in goal he knows he must if Pat cannot do it. Finally, the team captain is David and he plays centre forward. It is his job to encourage the players and lead them on the field.

At the end of last season's league, however, things didn't go to plan…

Jimmy was late for training and so didn't get time to have his meeting with Tony. Because they didn't get a chance to talk, Jimmy didn't realise that the match time had been changed to nine o'clock. At training, Pat announced that he wouldn't be at the match on Saturday. His friends were going away for the weekend and he wanted to go with them. On hearing the news, the team was very angry and more so when Joseph said that he didn't want to play in goal. But there was nobody else to do the job. Training finished and everyone left feeling very annoyed.

Saturday got off to a bad start. Jimmy didn't turn up until half past nine and the match had already started. Joseph had refused to play in goal and one of the substitutes stepped in to do it, but he wasn't very good and the team were already two goals down. Even so, David wanted the team to win and kept trying to score goals. The other players were very frustrated because he wouldn't pass the ball to anyone. Just before half-time one of the forwards was injured. But there was no one to take his place. The other substitute hadn't turned up for the match because he felt his job wasn't important. For all their matches, the substitute hardly ever got to play and he was sick of sitting on the bench every Saturday. The half-time whistle went…

Over to You

1. Name three different roles that people play in the Woodvale football team.
2. What happened when Jimmy and Tony did not communicate?
3. Do you think there was co-operation and sharing shown by all the team members?
4. Do you think David was a good captain? Why?
5. Everyone's role was important. How do we know this?

Community Breakdown

Sometimes in a community there can be tension. In fact, it is not always easy to be part of a community. In the Woodvale football team there was tension between what the team needed and what individual players wanted. For example, Joseph did not want to play in goal but his team needed him there. Sometimes we have to sacrifice what we want for the good of our community. The Woodvale team had forgotten about the need for co-operation, communication and sharing. Unfortunately, it led to the **community breaking down.**

Community breakdown – When a community collapses due to a lack of co-operation, communication and sharing.

Over to You

Write a story about your school community. Mention the different roles that are involved. Show how there is co-operation, communication and sharing in the community.

In this chapter,
you will become familiar with
the following concepts:

■ Commitment
■ Service
■ Vision
■ Leadership

Chapter 2:
Communities at Work

Communities of Faith

Service – Doing
something for others.

Leadership – Guidance
given by those in a
position of authority.

Commitment – Being
dedicated to something.

Vision – What a
community sees as
important and central
to their work

This chapter looks at the meaning and purpose of communities of faith in Ireland today. Together we will examine two such communities, Trócaire and the Society of Saint Vincent de Paul.

- **Trócaire** was set up by the Irish Catholic bishops in 1973. It is involved in many overseas projects on poverty as well as making Irish people aware of global poverty.

- **The Society of Saint Vincent de Paul (SVP)** was founded in 1833 in France by Frederic Ozanam, who was inspired by the life of St Vincent de Paul. Later in 1846 the Society was established in Ireland. Today the Society highlights the growing problems of poverty in Ireland.

We will now look closely at the work of these two communities in terms of their **commitment, service, vision** and **leadership.**

Trócaire

In the Irish language the word *trócaire* means compassion. The agency Trócaire draws its inspiration from scripture and the social teachings of the Catholic Church. In the Gospels we are taught to love one another and to treat everyone equally.

In 1973 the Irish Catholic bishops set up Trócaire to show the concern of the Irish church for the world's poorest people. Trócaire has two purposes:
1. To support long-term development projects overseas.
2. To provide relief when necessary during emergencies.

Today Trócaire is the official overseas development agency of the Catholic Church in Ireland.

Service

At home the job of Trócaire is to inform all Irish people about what causes poverty and injustice. In doing so, it raises public awareness of worldwide poverty. It does this in order to help the public bring about change. Trócaire tries to live out the message of the Gospels each day in the work that it does. Its work is influenced by the experiences and hopes of the poor and oppressed society. The agency helps communities in their efforts to improve their lives, while at the same time it has respect for their human dignity.

Vision

Trócaire envisages a world where everyone's basic needs are met and human dignity is respected. Its vision is one of equality and love for each other. Christ himself heard the cries of the poor and today he continues to long for joy, peace and love. Trócaire hopes for a better world where resources are shared and people are free to write their own destiny. The agency supports all people, regardless of age, gender, religion or politics, in a spirit of unity.

Leadership

Trócaire raises public awareness in Ireland of poverty and injustice abroad. The major and most high profile event to date was the tsunami in South East Asia in December 2004. Trócaire's response was immediate, sending financial aid and technical support to the most needed areas. During emergencies like this one Trócaire co-operates with international Catholic relief organisations and local groups to respond appropriately to the crisis. The needs of the people are put first. In 2006, Nicaragua was the country of focus for the Easter Lent Campaign. The public was encouraged to take action by campaigning and fundraising.

Commitment

Living out the Gospel message is central to Trócaire. It is committed to its work of solving the problems of poverty. Its work is with the poorest of the world yet these people are listened to closely because they are the focus of the work. Their opinions and needs are put first so that the right solutions are found. Trócaire's commitment to the poor of society is continually seen in their fundraising campaigns too.

Whichever country Trócaire is in, it is there for the long-term. It has now spent three decades working in the developing world. Much has been achieved but there is still much more to do. There are no quick-fix solutions to the poverty and injustice of the world. Trócaire believes in helping people to help themselves. As the Chinese proverb says 'Give them a fish and you feed them for a day, teach them to fish and you feed them for a lifetime'.

For more information look up www.trocaire.org

Over to You

1. What does the word 'compassion' mean? Do you think it is appropriate to the type of work described above?
2. What role did the Catholic bishops play in the organisation to begin with?
3. Do you think Trócaire lives out the message of the Gospel today?
4. Do you think Irish people are aware of the world's poverty? How does Trócaire help us in our knowledge of poverty?
5. What do you think of the Chinese proverb above?

The Society of Saint Vincent de Paul

Yours must be work of love, of kindness; you must give your time, your talents, yourselves. The poor person is a unique person of God's fashioning with an inalienable right to respect. You must not be content with tiding the poor over the poverty crisis: you must study their condition and the injustices which brought about such poverty, with the aim of a long-term improvement.

Blessed Frederic Ozanam 1813–1853

Society of Saint
Vincent de Paul

Leadership

The above words are clearly the message that the founder of the Society, Frederic Ozanam, wanted to leave behind to its members. The Society is a Christian organisation, working with poor and disadvantaged people. It continually seeks to respond to the call of its founder and its patron St Vincent de Paul in order to bring the love of Christ to those that need it in society. The organisation is an international one that helps people in need in about 100 countries worldwide. In Ireland there are about 1,100 branches throughout the country.

Vision

Many join the organisation because they want to spread the message of Jesus Christ. They want to put into action this message by loving and serving those that are disadvantaged. Their vision comes from the founder of the organisation to look after the weakest of society, and to love them and God like we love ourselves.

Service

The Society offers friendship and support to people in need. Its volunteers carry out their work in their own free time. Each member takes on a role. Some members visit people in their homes to help them with various things like money management. Other members visit the elderly in hospital, or prisoners in prison, while others organise things for young children to help them in school. Whatever their role is, it is important because so many people depend on their generosity of time and kindness.

In Ireland, even today, there are still many people who believe that poverty is something to be ashamed of. As a result, there is a certain amount of hidden poverty. The Society respects people's privacy and is very confidential in its work and practice.

Commitment

The work of the Society means there is much person to person contact. Therefore they are committed to respect the dignity of all people. As Matthew's Gospel says: 'I was hungry and you gave me something to eat, I was thirsty and you gave me something to drink, I was a stranger and you made me welcome … in so far as you did this to one of the least of these brothers of mine, you did this to me.'
For more information go to www.svp.ie

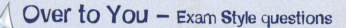

Over to You – Exam Style questions

1. What is the main message of this organisation?
2. What is the vision of the Society of St Vincent de Paul?
3. What roles do their members play?
4. How important do you think an organisation like the St Vincent de Paul is to Ireland and the world?
5. What is hidden poverty, in your opinion?
6. Imagine you are a worker from either Trócaire or St Vincent de Paul. Write out a short speech you would give to students in your school telling them about the work of your organisation and encouraging them to join.

Needs and Wants

As you can see from looking at Trócaire and the Society of St Vincent de Paul there is much poverty in our world today. Sometimes we feel that because we cannot have something we are deprived. However, there is a big difference between **wanting** something and **needing** something. For example, we **need** water, clothes and shelter to survive. These are called basic needs because without them we would die. We **want** the latest iPod because our friends have one and we do not want to be different from the crowd. In reality, we do not need an iPod to survive.

Over to You

Make a list of all the things you need and all the things you want. Which list is longer? Why do you think this is so?

In this chapter,

you will become familiar with the following concepts:

- Denomination
- Religious commitment
- Vocation
- Preaching
- Mission
- Leadership (HL)
- Authority (HL)
- Service (HL)

Chapter 3:

Communities of Faith and Leadership

Major World Religions

There are many different religions found all over the world today. The following are known as the major world religions. Some basic details on each are listed here, but you can find more information about them in Chapters 10–13.

RELIGION	FOUNDER	DATE	LOCATION	SACRED TEXT	BELIEF
Buddhism	Siddhartha Gautama	550 BCE	Northern India	Tipitaka (Three Baskets)	Polytheistic
Christianity	Jesus Christ	33 CE	Palestine	The Bible	Monotheistic
Hinduism	Unknown	2,000 BCE	Indus Valley, India	The Vedas	Polytheistic
Islam	Muhammad	610 CE	Mecca, Saudi Arabia	The Qur'an	Monotheistic
Judaism	Abraham and later Moses	1900 BCE	Israel	Tanakh (Hebrew Bible)	Monotheistic

Communities of faith – Communities that come together because of their religious beliefs.

So far in this section we have looked at what a community is and different types of community. People can be part of a community for many different reasons – where they live, what school they go to or what their hobbies are. But there are other types of communities too. Some people are part of a community because of their religious beliefs. Communities which come together because of their religious beliefs are called **communities of faith.**

Communities of Faith

In this chapter we will explore what it means to be a member of a community of faith and discover the work that is involved.

The Loreto Order

The religious sisters known as Loreto Sisters belong to the Institute of the Blessed Virgin Mary (IBVM), which was founded in 1609 by a 24-year-old woman from Yorkshire called Mary Ward.

It was in France that Mary Ward and her first companions set up their first school. After that she went on to set up schools all over Europe. At the time Mary's ideas about religious life were very radical, so much so that she was forbidden from spreading her ideas by the Catholic Church. However, she did not give up and in 1821 the Loreto order was introduced to Ireland by Sister Teresa Ball.

Read the following interview with Thérèse Larkin, a Loreto sister, and answer the questions that follow.

Q: Thérèse, how long have you been a Loreto sister?
A: I've been a part of the Loreto order for 24 years, basically since I left school.

Q: What inspired you to join this particular order?
A: Really there are two parts to this answer. Firstly, why did I join a community of faith at all? Like others who follow this path I have a vocation. This is a difficult concept to explain. I suppose you could say it's like a calling from God. In my later years at school I developed a more personal relationship with God. I discovered God's love for me and felt a desire to love God in return by spending my life for and with him. You could compare it to that desire in our heads to get married. It was very real and alive. You marry someone because you love them enough to give your life to them. My heart was drawn to God and so I wanted to give my life to him. For me, it was a feeling I couldn't ignore. I didn't make the decision, God called me and I answered. I made the decision to follow the inclination, the invitation I felt within.

Vocation – A calling from God to the religious life.

The second part of the answer is why did I choose this particular order? I went to a Loreto school and so experienced the Loreto ethos or atmosphere during my teenage years. To be honest, I wasn't exactly a top-class honours student. I was an average schoolgirl who would have preferred to be out having a laugh with my friends rather than studying! When I looked at the Loreto sisters I knew I saw strong, independent, down-to-earth women. They were individuals and enjoyed what they did. And they also valued me, even though I may not have been a star pupil.

Q: What kind of work does the order do?
A: We're a very busy order! We work at a local, national and international level. Locally and nationally we have 26 schools in Ireland, so education plays a central part in our work. We're also involved in parish work. At this local level we try to help people to develop their faith. We do this through retreat work and spiritual direction.

We also go out into the wider community as chaplains in schools, hospitals and even prisons. I suppose you could say we go where we're needed. Some of our sisters work as counsellors or social workers. Sometimes now in Ireland our work is not as visible as in the past because of the sensitive nature of the work we do now.

Working with women is very important to us and we have centres for women who need our support. We help by providing them with education courses and generally help to build their self-esteem.

Missionary work is another way we live out our vocation. Sisters have travelled to places all over the world to pray, work and teach. Our most recent mission is in Sudan.

Justice is one of our core values and this can be seen in the fact that we have an office at the United Nations in New York! All that we do comes from the call by Mary Ward all those years ago to care for the faith.

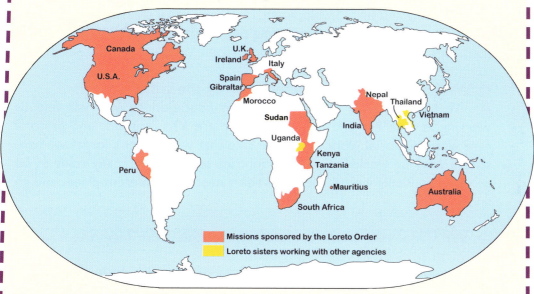

Missions sponsored by the Loreto Order

Loreto sisters working with other agencies

Q: What inspires the sisters to do all this work?

A: Our biggest inspiration is Mary Ward. Her life experience and beliefs make us want to continue the work she started. She asked us to promote certain virtues or qualities. These were freedom, justice, sincerity and joy and they are at the core of our work. We are inspired by the fact that what she set out to do all those years ago is still relevant today. Another influence would have to be Ignatius of Loyola. He was the man that set up the Jesuit order. In 1609 Mary Ward felt God was calling her to follow the rule of St Ignatius and the Jesuit spirituality. (For more on Jesuit Order see www.jesuit.ie.)

Obviously, behind these two influences is something bigger. God is the driving force, the main inspiration. It is through people like Mary Ward and St Ignatius that we come to know who God is.

Being part of a group who believes in and values this kind of life is inspiring as well as being a great support.

Mission – Putting our religious beliefs into practice.

Mary Ward, founder of the Loreto order.

Commitment – Being dedicated to something.

Q: What impact does your work have on other people and communities?

A: Looking at all the different work I described I would have to say empowerment. The work we do affects people, especially women, by giving them power. When I say power I mean the kind of power that gives you the freedom to be yourself. This is often through education. It also helps give people equality. We try to help them to take their place in society. We hope that people we work with (and for) feel cared about and nourished because of their contact with us.

Q: What is your own particular role in the order?

A: Like a lot of Loreto sisters I play more than one role. My main role is that of vocations director for the Loreto Sisters in Ireland. This means that together with a team I work on promoting our way of life today. I inform people about the order. As a result of this, I help and guide women who are considering joining the order. This may include praying with them, bringing them on retreat or to certain Loreto events. My other work is in the area of counselling and faith development. My professional training in these fields offers me the privilege of supporting people through difficult moments in their lives and the joy of accompanying people on their spiritual search.

Q: What other roles are undertaken by the sisters?

A: We have a lot of sisters working in education so you will find us working as teachers and principals. There are also chaplains and pastoral care workers. Social work is another role that we fill. Don't forget we have sisters working worldwide in 25 countries so there are many roles to be carried out. Really we try and see what is needed in different places and go and do it.

Q: What do you think are the challenges that face the Loreto order in today's world?

A: I suppose the biggest challenge is the culture in which we live and trying to live out our **commitment** in that world. We want to constantly try and keep up with the times, whether it means being computer-literate or aware of the political situation around the world. People's perception of religion is a challenge too. They tend to stereotype people with a religious vocation. Overall, I would say the biggest challenge is going out and trying to make the world a better place.

For more information go to www.loreto.ie.

Over to You

1. Why did Thérèse choose to join the Loreto order?
2. After reading the interview, do you think that she is happy to be part of the order? Why?
3. Do you think Thérèse has an interesting job?
4. Would you describe Thérèse as a person of faith and why?
5. Do you think the Loreto order does good work?

The Church of Ireland

The Church of Ireland is an important community of faith in Ireland. It is a Protestant church but has much in common with the Catholic Church. It is also sometimes called the Anglican Church because it is part of an international group of churches known as the Anglican community. However, it is important to note that the Church of Ireland still has its own independence. Read the following interview with Reverend Ann Wallace to find out more.

Reverend Ann Wallace

Reverend Ann Wallace

Q: How long have you been a minister in the Church of Ireland?
A: I was ordained a deacon in 1995 and made a priest the following year.

Q: What inspired you to take the step from lay person to minister?
A: I have been influenced and inspired by many people. My father was a musician and church organist so I have always been involved in the musical life of the Church. When I left school I trained as a commercial artist, then married a farmer and became a mother of four and eventually a grandmother of six! For a long time I had wanted to participate in the Church's liturgy and so I studied for three years to become a diocesan lay-reader, which I found very fulfilling.

Then in 1990 the Church voted in favour of allowing women to become priests and bishops and I knew the chance had come to follow my vocation. With the approval of my bishop and after three years of study, I was finally ordained.

Q: What kind of work does your Church do at a local level?
A: It tries to identify with the wider community by taking part in local organisations. Recently, we have begun to work with asylum-seekers and refugees. Many in our parish are also involved in social services, heritage projects and sporting organisations.

Q: What is the motivation for this work?
A: In a world which has become very impersonal we want to show that the Church is not just a big organisation but is made up of individuals who care.

Q: What impact does this work have on other people and communities?
A: I would hope that our Church is seen as serving God and showing his

love through our interaction with and treatment of people of all faiths and none. The very best thing about being a priest in Christ's church is the privilege of being beside people at the most significant moments of their lives. This could be baptizing a baby, or sitting with the family of a loved one who is dying, or guiding a couple through their marriage vows. Sometimes just sitting and listening can help others and I feel blessed to have been called to the priesthood. I hope my work helps others in a positive and spiritual way.

Preaching –
Spreading the
message of God.

Q: What is your own particular role within the Church?
A: I am the assistant priest working with the rector of a large rural parish. This involves leading services, preaching and celebrating Holy Communion. I also work in faith development and chaplaincy in schools. Another role I have is to visit the sick at home and in hospitals and bring them the Eucharist if they wish.

Service – Doing
something for others.

I am also a member of a prayer group who meet regularly to pray for those in need. I am on the parish committee and the primary school's board of management. Finally, I am chaplain to the Mother's Union, a worldwide Christian organisation committed to family values and helping with the challenges of family life. It also organises marriage preparation courses.

Q: What kind of other roles do people take on in the Church community?
A: Because there are six churches in our parish group there are two select Vestries (parish committees), so there are 30 or 40 people who are members of these. Then there are all those who volunteer to teach Sunday school, work with youth organisations and clubs, clean churches, arrange flowers and care for graveyards. Others play music for church services, do scripture readings and produce the parish newsletter. Without all these dedicated volunteers parish life would not be as alive as it is.

Denomination –
Belonging to a
particular branch
of a religion.

Q: What do you think are the challenges that face the Church of Ireland in today's world?
A: The challenges are much the same as those that face other Christian denominations. We have to try and make the Church seem interesting and attractive to people. In today's world this is a difficult job as a lot of people are just not interested. We also want to help people develop their spiritual sides, even if they don't feel they want to be a part of the Church community.

Over to You

Exam Style questions
1. Who or what inspired Ann Wallace to become a priest in the Church of Ireland?
2. What does her job involve?
3. From your reading of the interview do you think Reverend Wallace enjoys her work and why?
4. How does this interview show what the terms 'vocation' and 'mission' mean?

Higher Level

Leadership

Every group or community needs certain things if it is to work properly and reach its full potential. We know that characteristics such as co-operation and communication are important. One way of ensuring that these characteristics are present is through strong leadership. A leader is someone who guides their community. They are given a position of authority. Authority is the official power that a leader possesses. Today there are many different types of leaders in our world.

Leadership – When a leader guides his or her community.

Authority – The official power that a leader possesses.

Noel Conroy
Garda Commissioner

Mary McAleese
Irish President

Alex Ferguson
Manager of
Manchester United

Over to You

1. Name three leaders you come in contact with regularly.
2. Describe a time when you acted as a leader.
3. Name a leader you admire and explain why you think they are a good one.

Styles of leadership

Throughout our lives we come in contact with many different types of leaders. Some of these would include family leaders, team leaders, school leaders and religious leaders. Each of these leaders may have different styles of leadership. This means that they lead their communities in different ways.

Three of the most common styles of leadership are:
1. Authoritarian
2. Democratic
3. Free reign.

Authoritarian leadership – When the leader tells the members of the community what to do without asking for their opinion.

Democratic leadership – When the leader encourages the members of the community to be involved in the running and decision making of the community.

Free reign leadership – When the leader hands over control to the members.

Authoritarian leadership

Authoritarian leadership is when the leader tells the members of the community what to do without asking for their opinion. In this style of leadership the leader has all the power. They make all the decisions for the community. When used correctly it can be effective as it gets things done and avoids mistakes. However, it does not work for all communities. If not used correctly, it can lead to a bossy leader and an unhappy community.

Democratic leadership

Democratic leadership is when the leader encourages the members of the community to be involved in the running and decision making of the community. This kind of leader shares information with the members. The leader may have to make final decisions but only after they have asked the opinion of the members. This style of leadership can be very effective in helping to give the members confidence and allowing them to develop. However, it may not work if there is no trust between the leader and the members.

Free reign leadership

Free reign leadership is when the leader hands over control to the members. In this case the leader takes a very 'hands off' approach. The members have a huge amount of freedom and are often left to solve problems on their own. This style of leadership can work well as the members feel important and valued. However, it can lead to trouble in a community if there is no structure and members do not feel supported.

Up for Discussion

Which type of leadership style do you think would work best in the following communities and why? A prison warden / an office manager / a youth group leader?

Leadership in the Church of Ireland

Every community of faith is organised and run in a different way. In the Church of Ireland there is a very democratic style of leadership. It comes from the bottom up rather than the top down.

The joint leaders of the Church are the Archbishop of Armagh and the Archbishop of Dublin. Their role is to be the official voice of the

**General Synod =
House of Bishops and House
of Representatives**

Diocesan Synod

Select Vestry

Annual General Vestry

Church of Ireland and to lead their members by example. They consult with the other bishops and represent the Church on many international bodies. Rev John Neill is the Archbishop of Dublin and Primate of Ireland. The Archbishop of Armagh and Primate of All-Ireland is Reverend Alan Harper.

1. Every lay member of a parish over 18 years of age is entitled to attend and vote at the Annual General Vestry of the parish.
2. This general vestry elects the Select Vestry (parish committees), which is responsible for the running of the parish.
3. Every third year the General Vestry elects the parish's lay representatives to the Diocesan Synod.
4. Every third year the Diocesan Synod elects the clergy and laity who will represent the diocese on the General Synod.
5. This governing body consists of two houses: the House of Bishops and the House of Representatives, which is made up of clergy and laity.

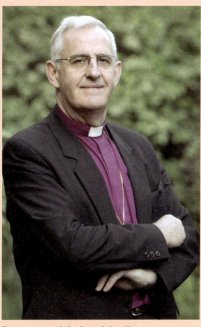

Reverend John Neill

The leadership of the Church involves both laity and clergy and everyone's views are represented. Leaders are elected in a very fair way. When a parish becomes vacant the bishop calls a meeting of a board of nomination. This board is made up of clergy and laity representing both the diocese and the parish. The board selects a person for the role and this must be supported by two-thirds of the members. If the bishop approves, he makes the appointment and the new rector takes up their position.

Leadership in the Roman Catholic Church

The Roman Catholic Church is the largest Christian church in the world. As Christians they are followers of Christ because they believe that Jesus Christ died to save mankind. The mission of the Catholic Church is aimed at the whole world and does not exclude any country or race. The word catholic means 'universal'. The Catholic Church is a community of believers. Every Sunday they are invited to attend Mass where a community prays together.

In the Catholic Church everyone has a role to play. People serve God in different ways.

Pope

Cardinals

Archbishops

Bishops

Priests

Lay people

Pope Benedict XVI

The Pope

Pope Benedict XVI is the current Pope of the Catholic Church. As Pope he is head of all Catholics worldwide and serves God this way. He lives in the Vatican in Rome, which is the headquarters of the Catholic Church. All Catholics believe that the Pope is St Peter's successor on earth. At the beginning Peter was given the task of leading the whole church. Jesus told him 'You are Peter and on this rock I will build my community' (Matthew 16:18). When a Pope dies his successor is one of the cardinals.

The cardinals

Cardinals are given their position by the Pope. They are the chief advisers to the Pope on all religious matters.

The archbishops and bishops

The archbishop is the religious leader of the whole country. Sometimes he can be head of a province or a group of dioceses (archdiocese). In 2004 Dr Diarmuid Martin became Archbishop of Dublin and Primate of Ireland. Dr Seán Brady is the Archbishop of Armagh and Primate of All-Ireland – this is for the island of Ireland.

The bishops have a very important leadership role in the Church. The bishop is the religious leader of a diocese. The island of Ireland is divided into 26 dioceses. Find out the name of the diocese in which you live.

Dr Diarmuid Martin

One of the many roles the bishop has is to confer people at Confirmation. Another role involves working with other bishops and discussing important religious matters. Three times a year they attend an Episcopal meeting in Maynooth College in Co Kildare.

Dr Sean Brady

The priests

The priest is the religious leader in the parish. He celebrates the sacraments of baptism, Eucharist, last rites, marriage and reconciliation with his people. Often the priest visits people in their homes. His own home is among the people in the parish.

Do you know the name of your parish? Do you know the name of the priests in your parish? How many priests are in your parish?

The lay people (laity)

A lay person is someone who is not ordained to the priesthood or religious life. They are baptized members of the Catholic Church. The lay person plays an important role in the Church by reading at Mass, giving out the Eucharist or helping with the parish centre. Lay people also play an important role in schools and at work. The Society of the Saint Vincent de Paul is an example of a lay organisation in the Catholic Church. You will have read about this organisation in Chapter 2.

Over to You

Exam Style questions

1. What does the term leadership mean?
2. Explain one style of leadership that may be used by a leader?
3. Describe the leadership structure in a community of faith you have studied?

In this chapter,
you will become familiar with the following concepts:

■ Ecumenism
■ Interfaith dialogue
■ Sectarianism
■ Religious conflict
■ Tolerance

Chapter 4:

Relationships between Communities of Faith

Before we begin this section, have you ever heard of any of the above words before? Can you give examples of sectarianism, religious conflict or interfaith dialogue in the world?

Inter-faith dialogue in action

Religious conflict in the Middle East

Sectarian Violence

Ecumenism

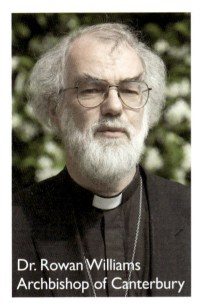

Dr. Rowan Williams
Archbishop of Canterbury

Christians believe in God and see Jesus Christ as the son of God. Christians believe that he died on the cross so that humankind could be saved. Christians read the scriptures and believe it is the word of God. Yet Christian Churches have different beliefs about who their leader is, the number of sacraments and the true meaning of the Eucharist.

For many years Catholic, Protestant and Orthodox Christians worked against each other. This has now changed as they communicate with each other and join in ceremonies together. They listen to each other's viewpoints and share ideas with each other. Ecumenism is the name given to the attempts that Christians are making to understand and respect each other and to grow more as one.

Ecumenism – The attempts that Christians make to understand and respect each other and to grow more as one.

Patriarch Bartholomew
Archbishop of Constantinople

Many people are involved in ecumenism. Co-operation between all the Christian Churches is vital to the success of the movement. This movement is not trying to make all Christians the same, but asking them to work together and understand and respect each other's differences. In the month of January every year there is a week set aside for Christian unity. Catholics and Protestants are invited to attend an ecumenical service together where prayers, hymns and readings are used to symbolise the unity of the Christian Churches and not their divisions.

Taizé: An Example of Ecumenism

Brother Roger of Taizé

Each year thousands of young people travel to a small town in France called Taizé. Young people from all walks of life come to this place to deepen their faith. They meet other people from all over the world and pray with them and the Brothers that live in Taizé. The Brothers belong to different Christian Churches: Catholic, Protestant and Orthodox. Despite the different denominations, everyone gets on well together there. Essentially, Taizé is a place that gives every visitor a place to pray and think about their lives.

In 1940 the Taizé community was founded by Roger Louis Schütz-Marsauche from Switzerland. Later he became known as Brother Roger. It was his dream to set up a community of people who would share a similar life of prayer and work together. Today this community is a sign of peace and reconciliation. The most important aim of the community is to work for Christian unity. All the Brothers work for a living and do not accept donations.

In Taizé everyone helps with the cooking and the cleaning. Groups gather together to pray and to learn about the Christian faith. Prayer is very important in Taizé. People come together three times a day to pray and to sing. There are also discussion groups where people gather together and talk about their lives. Listening is an important element and it is not surprising that so many lifelong friends are made in this small town.

For the last 65 years Taizé was built and led by Brother Roger. He was deeply loved by all who met him and he made a lasting impression on those around him. Tragically, he was stabbed to death in 2006. Today his death leaves a legacy which is felt in churches all over the world. Taizé is a whole approach to Christian life and worship and, although Brother Roger has died, it is likely that Taizé will go on for a long time to come.

Over to You

Exam Style questions
1. What is Ecumenism?
2. Why do people work for Ecumenism?
3. Briefly outline one example of Ecumenism you have studied.
4. Imagine you are organising a Christian Unity Week, design a poster you would use to explain what it is and to advertise it.

The future of ecumenism

The Christian Churches are all very different. However, the ecumenical movement respects these differences between the Christian Churches and does not wish to destroy what is unique to each Church. For this reason, the purpose of the movement is twofold:

1. It promotes mutual respect and understanding between all Christian Churches.
2. It encourages all Christians to co-operate with each other and so spread the love that Christ has for each of us to one other.

Pope John Paul II promoted Christian unity by claiming that we are children of God and therefore have a place as Christians in the Kingdom of God.

Sectarianism

Whenever we hear the word sectarianism we immediately are reminded of the Troubles in Northern Ireland. Sectarianism is the hatred of someone because of their religious beliefs. Since the 1960s there has been much sectarian violence in Northern Ireland, resulting in the injury and death of many Catholics and Protestants.

Sectarianism – The hatred of someone because of their religious beliefs.

Sectarianism can have many negative conquences. People can become afraid, angry and suspicious of other people. They can forget that their religion tells them to love others.

Religious conflict – When a lack of trust and deepening hatred towards other religions leads to problems in society and is difficult to heal.

David Trimble, Bono and John Hume.

The causes of sectarianism are deep and complex. Communities become divided and this leads to tension everywhere. There is a lack of trust and a deepening hatred towards each other. This is religious conflict at its worst and it is difficult to heal.

Today Catholics and Protestants live in a more happy and peaceful Northern Ireland than before. This religious tolerance is mainly due to the efforts of many political leaders – John Hume, David Trimble, Gerry Fitt, Tony Blair, Garret FitzGerald, Charles Haughey, Bertie Ahern, Gerry Adams and many others.

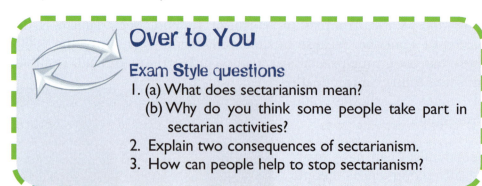

Over to You

Exam Style questions
1. (a) What does sectarianism mean?
   (b) Why do you think some people take part in sectarian activities?
2. Explain two consequences of sectarianism.
3. How can people help to stop sectarianism?

Religious Conflict

Read the following words of the song *Through the Barricades* by the 1990s band Spandau Ballet. What does the song have to do with the Troubles of Northern Ireland?

Mother doesn't know where love has gone
She says it must be youth
That keeps us feeling strong
I see it in her face, that's turned to ice
And when she smiles she shows
The lines of sacrifice.

And now I know what they're saying
As our sun begins to fade
And we made our love on wasteland
And through the barricades.

Father made my history
He fought for what he thought
Would set us somehow free
He taught me what to say in school
I learned it off by heart
But now that's torn in two.

And now I know what they're saying
In the music of the parade
And we made our love on wasteland
And through the barricades.

Born on different sides of life
We feel the same
And feel all of this strife
So come to me when I'm asleep
We'll cross the lines
And dance upon the streets.

And now I know what they're saying
As the drums begin to fade
We made our love on wasteland
And through the barricades.

Oh, turn around and I'll be there
Well there's a scar right through my heart
But I'll bare it again
Oh I thought we were the human race
But we were just another border-line-case
And the stars reach out and tell us
That there's always one escape.

I don't know where love has gone
And in this trouble land
Desperation keep us strong
Friday's child is full of soul
With nothing left to lose
There's everything to go.

And now I know what they're saying
It's a terrible beauty we've made
So we make our love on wasteland
And through the barricades
Now I know what they're are saying
As our hearts go to their graves
We made our love on wasteland
Oh, oh oh through the barricades.

Here is another example of religious conflict in Northern Ireland.

Fr Aidan Troy: A Symbol of True Courage

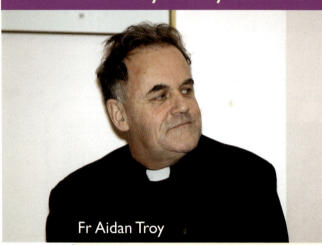

Fr Aidan Troy

In September 2001, a small group of Protestants attacked young Catholic schoolgirls from the Nationalist Ardoyne area of North Belfast on their way to Holy Cross primary school.

These little girls were subjected to sectarian abuse and violence as they walked to their school. It went on for 12 weeks as the eyes of the world watched and people prayed that a solution would be found.

Ordinary Catholics and Protestants could not understand why some people would act in this way. Members of the Protestant community wanted people to know that they did not approve of what was happening.

At first Fr Aidan Troy knew very little about the North. But within months of his arrival in the Catholic Ardoyne community, he witnessed one of the most disturbing incidents in the North's recent history. Yet he believed the rights of the child should be put first.

As the police and the cameras of the world looked on, the little girls and their parents were pelted with balloons of urine and stones, sectarian abuse was shouted at them and even a pipe bomb was found.

The children themselves never held any hatred towards the people that did this. Every morning Fr Troy joined the children and their parents on the walk to the school. After 12 weeks a resolution was found. Looking back, Fr Aidan Troy felt that he was not the courageous one, the children were.

Over to You

1. Does the newspaper article shock you in any way?
2. How do you think these little girls felt as they left their homes each morning?
3. Why do you think an event like this caught the hearts and eyes of the world?
4. Do you think Fr Aidan Troy deserves his title – a Symbol of True Courage?
5. Imagine you were one of the children on the walk to school. What feelings do you think you would have towards those that shouted at you and your parents?

Interfaith Dialogue

We have looked at what ecumenism means. Interfaith dialogue is something similar, but there is an important difference that we must remember. Interfaith dialogue is communication and understanding between people from different major world religions, not just the Christian Churches. In today's multicultural Ireland interfaith dialogue is more important than it has ever been.

Interfaith dialogue – Communication and understanding between people from different major world religions.

The World Council of Churches

The World Council of Churches (WCC) is a group that aims to bring about peace and understanding between different faiths. Most of what they do is based around ecumenism but in recent years they have expanded their work to include interfaith dialogue.

They have a special team that deals with inter-religious relations. It promotes contact between Christians and people from other faiths. Their aim is to build trust and face common challenges together through dialogue. During the past few years they have organised a number of Hindu-Christian, Christian-Muslim, Buddhist-Christian and Jewish-Christian dialogues. As well as discussing religious topics, they also share ideas on justice and peace issues.

People from all different religious backgrounds are beginning to see more and more the need to build relationships between them. Dialogue has led to practice. One example of this is in the Middle East where a group called Clergy for Peace brings together rabbis, priests, pastors and imams to work for justice and peace in this troubled area. Interfaith dialogue is not about making all religions the same. It is more about respecting and celebrating the differences between them.

World Day of Peace, 1986

An excellent example of interfaith dialogue was one which began in a place called Assisi in Italy in 1986. It was organised by Pope John Paul II as part of the World Day of Peace. He invited all the leaders of different religions to come together to work and pray for peace in the world.

Pope John Paul II at the World Day of Peace in 1986.

Each religion was given their own space to pray in their own way. When the groups came together each leader gave a speech about peace. Each religion listened to the prayers of the others. Perhaps Pope John Paul had remembered the words of St Peter when he was talking about all the different religious beliefs of people: 'I truly understand that God shows no partiality, but in every nation anyone who fears him and does what is right is acceptable to him.'

Over to You

1. What is the difference between ecumenism and interfaith dialogue?
2. Why is interfaith dialogue so important in today's world?
3. What does interfaith dialogue aim to do?

Tolerance verses Intolerance

Tolerance – Respect and communication with one another.

The key to solving sectarianism is through tolerance. Tolerance is about respect and communication with one another. If the lines of communication are open between two groups, dialogue can occur and so a solution may come about. It is important to foster and spread tolerance in young people in schools. This is because they will then grow up with an attitude of mutual respect and dignity, not only of themselves but of each other.

Intolerance – A lack of respect and communication with one another that leads to problems.

Intolerance can lead to problems like the ones mentioned above – ignorance, disrespect and hatred can all be fostered at a young age. It is important to educate all people together so mutual respect and dignity can be passed from one generation to the next. In order to prevent sectarianism happening, people get involved in ecumenism and interfaith dialogue. They do this to promote peace and justice and because they feel it is what their leaders and God would want.

Over to You

Write an article for your school magazine entitled 'Sectarianism – what is it and how do we stop it?'

Section A – Key Definitions

Authority:	Being responsible for others/having power.
Church:	A community of believers.
Commitment:	Being dedicated to something.
Community:	A group of people with something in common.
Community breakdown:	When a community collapses due to a lack of co-operation, communication and sharing.
Communication:	Sharing and discussing ideas with others.
Co-operation:	To help others and make compromises for the good of the community.
Denomination:	Belonging to a particular branch of a religion.
Ecumenism:	Christian churches working together to achieve unity and understanding.
Gospel:	Good news/New Testament books.
Identity:	The unique characteristics of a person or group.
Inter-faith dialogue:	Different world religions working together to achieve understanding and respect.
Inspiring vision:	That which motivates people to believe in something.
Leadership:	Guidance given by those in a position of authority.
Ministry:	The work a person does within their community or faith.
Mission:	Putting our religious beliefs into practice.
Preaching:	Spreading the message of God.
Religion:	Belief in and worship of a God or Gods.
Roles:	The parts people play in a community.
Sectarianism:	Hatred or discrimination of another person because of their religious belief.
Service:	Doing something for others.
Sharing:	Giving of yourself to others.
Tolerance:	Accepting others regardless of their beliefs.
Vision:	What a community sees as important and central to their work.
Vocation:	A calling to serve God.

SECTION B

FOUNDATIONS OF RELIGION: CHRISTIANITY

AIMS

■ To explore the context into which Jesus was born.

■ To identify the Gospels as the main source of knowledge about Jesus.

■ To examine the meaning of the life, death and resurrection of Jesus for his followers, then and now.

HIGHER LEVEL ONLY
■ To have an understanding of the meanings attached to the new titles for Jesus.

In this chapter,
you will become familiar with the
following concepts:
- The Holy Land
- The Roman Empire
- Messianic expectation
- Ancient Judaism

Chapter 5:
The Context of Jesus' Birth

The Holy Land

This map shows some of the most important places associated with the life of Jesus.

The Holy Land – The region where Jesus lived, preached and died.

Galilee, Samaria and Judea	The three provinces of Palestine.
Bethlehem	The birthplace of Jesus.
Nazareth	The town where Jesus grew up.
River Jordan	The river where Jesus was baptized.
Sea of Galilee	The place where Jesus met his first disciples.
Jerusalem	The town where Jesus was arrested and put to death and where his resurrection took place.

The region where Jesus lived, preached and died became known as the **Holy Land**.

The Roman Empire

Palestine was under the control of the Roman Empire at the time of Jesus. With Rome as its centre, the Roman Empire stretched to Spain and France in the west, the Alps in the north, Greece, Turkey and the Holy Land in the east, and across North Africa and the Mediterranean Sea in the south.

Even though it was small, Palestine was an important area. It was split into three different provinces: Galilee in the north, Samaria in the middle and Judea in the south. In order to rule their lands well the Romans appointed a governor or procurator in each province.

At the time of Jesus, Pontius Pilate ruled over Judea and Samaria. Galilee, seen by Rome as the least important area, was governed by Herod Antipas. At the hands of foreign rulers, the Jewish people had suffered a long history of hardship. They had moved from place to place in search of a land they could call their own but without success. The Jewish people were therefore not happy to be ruled by the Romans. They wanted their own independent land. Being under foreign rule meant that they had to obey Roman laws and pay heavy taxes to the Romans.

The Roman Empire – All the lands that Rome ruled at the time of Jesus, including the Holy Land.

However, as a compromise the Jewish people were allowed to follow their own customs and practise their own religion. The Roman rulers were not interested in how the Jewish people practised their religion and lived their day-to-day lives. Their interest was in the Palestine land because whoever controlled the roads in and out of these areas gained power and wealth.

Messianic Expectation

The Jewish people believed strongly that they had a special relationship with God and were his Chosen People. They had experienced a troubled past, which you can read more about in Chapter 11. For many years they longed for a united and prosperous kingdom like the one they had when King David ruled them. King David had ruled them from 1010 BCE to 970 BCE. He was Israel's greatest king and a faithful follower of God.

Ever hopeful, they waited for a messiah that God would send to save them. They saw the Messiah as a great military leader, a king-like figure, strong and powerful. The Messiah would be the anointed one who would lead them to freedom. In the meantime they prepared themselves for his coming by following the laws set down for them by the prophet Moses. (To learn more about Moses, go to Chapter 11.)

Messianic expectation – The Jewish people were awaiting a messiah, who would free them from Roman rule and establish a new Jewish kingdom.

Over to You

1. What does Messianic expectation mean?
2. What did the Jews long for?
3. The Jews prepared themselves for this coming. If you were a Jewish person at the time, how would you prepare for this coming?

Ancient Judaism

Ancient Judaism refers to the history of the Jewish people, including their politics, culture and religion.

Ancient Judaism – The history of the Jewish people, including their politics, culture and religion.

Political and religious structures

Throughout history, politics and religion have gone hand in hand in many countries. Palestine at the time of Jesus was no different.

There were four important groups of people who had very strong opinions about issues such as the coming of the Messiah and Roman rule.
1. The Sadducees   3. The Pharisees
2. The Zealots   4. The Essenes.

The Sadducees –
A small, powerful wealthy group in Palestine that held the position of high priest in Jerusalem.

The Sadducees

The Sadducees were a small and powerful wealthy group in Palestine and held the position of high priest in Jerusalem. As temple priests they collected the temple taxes that visitors had to pay. For this group the temple was a most important place.

The Sadducees dominated the Sanhedrin, which was the ruling council of the Jewish religion and the highest law court in the land. Only the written Torah was accepted as the word of God by them. The first five books of the Jewish Bible are known as the Torah. Unlike many other Jews, the Sadducees were happy to be ruled by the Romans because they felt they brought stability and wealth to Palestine. In fact, they felt their losses would be great if the Romans were not present.

The Zealots –
A group of religious Jews who hated the Romans and caused violence.

The Zealots

The Zealots were another group of religious Jews. However, they hated the Romans intensely and wanted them out of Palestine at all costs. In fact, they considered Palestine as a gift from God to the Jewish people. As a result, they killed many Roman soldiers and sabotaged anything they did. They hoped for and were willing to achieve freedom at any price. More so, they believed that the violence was acceptable because it was for a just cause of the Jewish faith. Their hatred was not only confined to the Romans. They hated the Sadducees also because they worked with the Romans. Overall this group caused a lot of unrest among the people.

The Pharisees –
Holy men who were the religious leaders of the synagogues, but not priests.

The Pharisees

The law of God was important to the group known as the Pharisees. They consisted of holy men who were not in fact priests. However, they were the religious leaders of the synagogues. Living in the towns and the villages, they kept themselves apart from the ordinary Jews, who were not as devout as them.

The purpose of the Pharisees was to teach the Jews how to live. They followed the law above everything else. Those who did not live their lives properly, they called 'sinners'. They believed that one day God would send a king or messiah that would free them from foreign or Roman rule.

The Essenes –
A community of monks who lived in remote places.

The Essenes

The Essenes led a very simple life and were basically a community of monks. By living in remote places, they believed it kept them away from corruption. They also believed that they had the correct interpretation of the Torah. In their daily lives, they were very clean and spent much of their time bathing.

The dwelling of the Essenes as seen today

The Sanhedrin

The word Sanhedrin means assembly. In Jesus' time the Sanhedrin was a small but powerful assembly. In Palestine they were the court of law for the Jewish people. However, they were only concerned with the religious laws and had no power to punish people who broke the civil laws.

The group was made up of 70 members and a president and were recognised by the Romans. In fact, the Romans did not want to get involved in the religious laws of the people. Therefore, they were quite happy that the Sanhedrin helped to keep peace in their lands.

Both the Pharisees and the Sadducees were represented on the Sanhedrin. When it came to filling the position of president, there was great rivalry between the two groups. The Sanhedrin even had its own guards for the temple. As you will find out later they played an important part in the story of Jesus' life.

The Sanhedrin – A small but powerful assembly of men who acted as the court of religious law for the Jewish people.

Over to You Crossword

1 (down): Region where Jesus lived and died.
2 (across): The Province in the north of Palestine.
3 (across): This group were willing to use violence to rid Palestine of the Romans.
4 (down): This group held the position of High Priest and co-operated with the Romans.
5 (down): This group followed the law above everyone else and were very devout.
6 (across): The religious court of law for Jewish people.

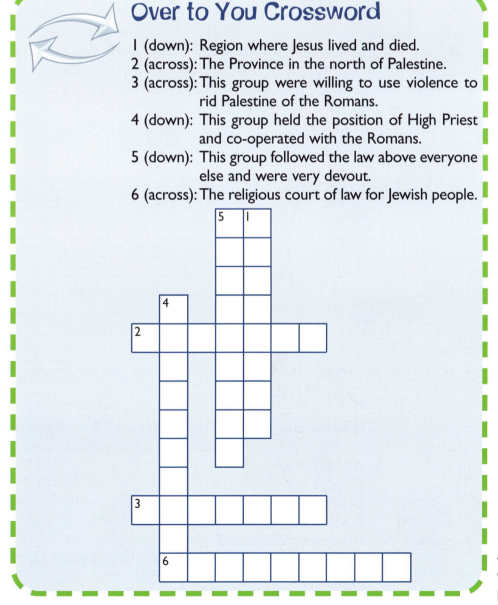

Answers to the crossword on page 43.

Tax collectors

Tax collectors –
Jewish people who collected taxes for the upkeep of the Roman army in Palestine. They were disliked because they worked for the Romans.

In Jesus' time tax was collected to pay for the upkeep of the Roman army in Palestine. This money was collected by some Jewish people called tax collectors. Many Jews worked hard to look after their families, led simple lives in small houses and did not have much money. Naturally, when they were asked to pay these Roman taxes, it caused problems. Soon tax collectors in Palestine were disliked because they worked for the Romans. Also, some tax collectors greedily kept the money they collected for themselves. For that reason many tax collectors were wealthy in Palestine.

However, Jesus recognised the position of the tax collector in society. On many occasions he was criticised because he ate with them and visited them in their homes. One of the most famous stories in the Bible is about the tax collector Zacchaeus.

Over to You

Read the story of Zacchaeus in St Luke 19:1 – 9 and answer the following questions. (You will find this story in chapter 7)
1. Who was Zacchaeus?
2. What kind of man was Zacchaeus?
3. Why did people complain to Jesus when he was going to Zacchaeus' house?
4. Why do you think Zacchaeus changed when he met Jesus?

The temple and synagogue

At the time of Jesus there were two kinds of religious buildings or places of worship for Jewish people to pray:

1. The temple
2. The synagogue.

The temple
The most sacred building of all for Jewish people was the temple in the city of Jerusalem. This was a beautiful building deeply respected by Jews. It was so large that numbers of people would fill it. In the temple there were areas allocated according to your degree of holiness. Women sat in the outer large court known as the Court of Women, while men advanced to their allocated position at the Court of the Israelites. From there only priests that performed temple duties could enter the Court of Priests and the Sanctuary.

At the heart of the temple building was a place called the Holy of Holies. It was hidden behind a veil and entered only once a year by the high priest on the Day of Atonement. Here the high priest prayed to God for the forgiveness of his people.

The Jews saw the temple as a dwelling place for God and it was at the heart of their lives. Many of them visited the temple once a year during a religious festival. Eagerly, they came with their families to pray and worship God there.

The outer court of the temple was called the Court of Gentiles. It was a place of commerce, where Jews changed their money from Roman into temple money. Many of them also brought things like birds and animals to be sacrificed. These were later sacrificed in the Court of Priests.

The Temple – The most sacred building for Jewish people where religious ceremonies took place.

Holy of Holies

Veil of the Temple

Sanctuary

Court of the Priests

Court of the Israelites

Court of the Women

Court of the Gentiles

In St Mark's Gospel 11:15 – 19, Jesus pays a visit to the temple with his family. On entering the temple, he was angry to see what was going on in such a sacred place. At once he threw the people that were selling and buying there out of the temple and overturned the tables of all those collecting money. He told them: 'Does not scripture say: My house will be called a house of prayer for all peoples? But you have turned it into a bandit's den.' Even though the people began to listen to him in the temple, the high priests and scribes wanted to get rid of him because they did not like what he was saying to the people. The scribes were men responsible for interpreting the scripture.

In St John's Gospel, Jesus says 'I am the light of the world'. With these words Jesus enlightened the temple spiritually just like the lamp that physically illuminates the temple and its people.

Over to You

1. Where was the temple located?
2. Why was the temple so important?
3. Describe the layout of the temple.
4. What do you think Jesus was trying to convey when he overturned the tables in the temple?
5. Do you think it is fair to say that he was right in his actions? Why/why not?

The synagogue

The synagogue played an important role in the Jewish faith. At the time of Jesus there was one in every town and village in Palestine. Each week Jews attended a ceremony called the **Sabbath**.

The synagogue –
The building where the weekly ceremony called the Sabbath takes place.

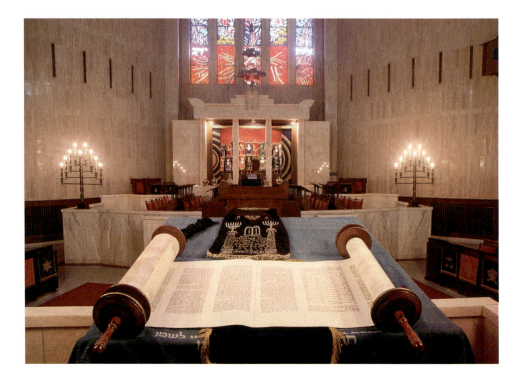

At the Sabbath scripture was read and the ceremony lasted for about one hour. Today the synagogue remains the focus of the Jewish community. In Jesus' time it was a small building that held about one hundred people. Women sat in the gallery upstairs and had a door to enter through, while men sat downstairs and entered through their own door. It was customary for men to sit with their older sons.

During the Sabbath the scroll containing the Jewish scripture was read. The rabbi or head priest then gave a talk on the readings. The scrolls kept in the Ark were treated with great respect as the Jews believed that it was the word of God. The Ark was a special wooden press found at the front of the synagogue facing towards Jerusalem. A candle was lit in front of it, which was never allowed to burn out. This was because it reminded the Jews that God was always close by, looking after them and protecting them. In front of the Ark lay a menorah. This is a candelabrum or special candleholder with places for seven candles.

Over to You

1. How important was the synagogue to the Jewish people?
2. Why do you think men and women sat in different places in the synagogue?
3. What was the Ark?
4. Why do you think the sacred scrolls were so important?
5. How important was keeping the flame of the candle alight?

Answers to crossword on page 39

1. Holy Land
2. Galilee
3. Zealots
4. Sadduccees
5. Pharisees
6. Sanhedrin

In this chapter,
you will become familiar with the
following concepts:

■ Evidence from the oral
  and written traditions
■ Gospel
■ Evangelist
■ Witness
■ Synoptic

Chapter 6:

Evidence about Jesus

Source of Evidence

**Evidence from the
oral and written
traditions** –
How information about Jesus
went from the spoken to the
written word.

Evidence about Jesus comes from the oral and written traditions. These sources include The Bible, historical documents and four gospel writers.

The Bible

We are used to thinking that the Bible is a single book, but as soon as we open it, it becomes very clear to us that it is in fact a collection of books – 72 in total. Some of its stories are quite short while others are long. Some of its books were written at the time of the Roman Empire, while others were written centuries earlier. The material in the stories varies too. Some parts consist of historical material, while other parts contain wise sayings (Psalms) and personal letters. The Bible itself is divided into two parts: the Old Testament and the New Testament.

The Old Testament / Hebrew Scriptures

This part tells the story of the coming of the Messiah. It consists of many books from the story of Genesis, when we were created in the image of God, to the story of the **prophets** who spoke on behalf of God. The most

famous prophets are Jeremiah, Isaiah and Ezekiel. The prophets reminded the Jewish people about the Law of God and warned them against disobeying it. They were told that if they obeyed it, God would look after them. Because they had suffered for many years, the Jews wanted to live in peace and harmony. The Old Testament traces the history of the Jewish people.

Over to You

1. How would you describe the Bible?
2. How many books are in the Bible?
3. What sort of material is found in the Bible? Give examples.
4. What is the Old Testament / Hebrew Scriptures?
5. Draw the books of the Old Testament, labelling them clearly.

Image of the prophet Ezekiel from the Sistine Chapel by Michelangelo.

The New Testament

The **Evangelists**, namely Matthew, Mark, Luke and John, are the four Gospel writers. The word Evangelist means person of faith, and those who believe that Jesus is God. The Evangelists wanted to tell everyone about the Good News. In time, the Good News came to be known as the **Gospel**. The four Gospels are mainly about the last three years of Jesus' life. They focus on the teachings of Jesus as well as his death and Resurrection.

The Gospels of Jesus came together in three separate stages:

1. The actual events that took place during Jesus' lifetime.
2. The disciples preaching about Jesus.
3. The writing down of the Gospels.

Evangelists – Gospel writers and people of faith.

Gospel – Stories of Jesus' life that are found in the New Testament. The word means Good News.

Over to You

1. Name the four Gospel writers.
2. What does the word Gospel mean?
3. What does the word Evangelist mean?
4. What are the three stages of the Gospels?
5. What are the main events of Jesus' life?

1. Actual events in the life of Jesus

All over Palestine (the Holy Land) Jesus the teacher travelled with the **disciples** (the chosen ones). Much of his teaching was based on what God had already told us in the books of the Old Testament. In Matthew's Gospel we are told that Jesus himself said, 'Do not think that I have come to do away with the Law of Moses and the teachings of the prophets. I have not come to do away with them, but to make their teachings come true.'

The Last Supper by Domencio Ghirlandaio showing Jesus and the 12 apostles.

Jesus took the teaching of the Old Testament and brought it to completion. The Old Testament encouraged us to love our neighbours as ourselves and Jesus also encouraged us to do this. He lived out this message of love in his life.

Everywhere he went Jesus taught with authority. When he spoke to people it was as if he knew them inside out. In fact, Jesus made a big impact on everyone he met. Those that hated him recognised a power within him to make strong speeches and work miracles. It was Jesus who was the crucified one, who died on the cross and rose from the dead on Easter Sunday. After the resurrection, he appeared many times to the disciples.

2. Disciples preaching about Jesus

Today Jesus makes a huge difference to our lives because he is living among us. After he rose from the dead and sent the Holy Spirit to the **apostles**, they realised how powerful and good he was. They realised that Jesus was God-made man, the Son of God.

The apostles travelled all over Palestine telling everyone the good news of the resurrection. When told, many people believed and became Christians. The story of the resurrection was told and retold for many centuries. It was passed from one person to the next by word of mouth – this is called the oral stage. This was like in Ireland years ago when *seanchaí* told stories.

When we hear the story of the resurrection, we are reminded that Jesus died on the cross so that we could be saved. God's love for us is so great that he gave his only son for us. Because Jesus is both God and man, his resurrection gives us the strength to one day rise from the dead by the power of God.

Up for Discussion

1. How has Jesus made a huge impression on our lives?
2. What is meant by the oral tradition?
3. How important do you think this phase was?

3. The writing down of the Gospels

As news of the resurrection spread, it was impossible for the disciples to preach in all the areas where there was a demand for them. The apostles were also getting quite old and some of them had died. It therefore became very important to begin the process of writing things down before it became too late.

Witness – A person who is present at the time an event takes place.

The written Gospel would help future generations to get to know Jesus, the Messiah, and the Chosen One. The details of some events, like when Jesus healed the sick, were taken from **witnesses**, that is, those who were present at the time and witnessed the event.

Others that witnessed the miracles performed or the resurrection told their stories and they were written down first hand. When the evidence was given, it was written down and then sorted and examined by the Evangelists. The Evangelists picked out what they thought would be important to future generations. As we have already mentioned the four Gospel writers are Matthew, Mark, Luke and John. Their Gospels are in fact documents of faith.

Some people make the mistake of comparing the Gospels to a history book. If you think about the history book you study for your Junior Cert, it is full of dates and times and everything is in chronological order: Early Christian Ireland, the Middle Ages, the Renaissance, etc. In the Gospels there are no dates and the events of Jesus' life are in no particular order. For this reason Christians often refer to the gospels as a story of faith instead of a precise history with exact dates. Often information is grouped together because a particular topic is being addressed. For example in St Luke's Gospel he devotes some time to parables.

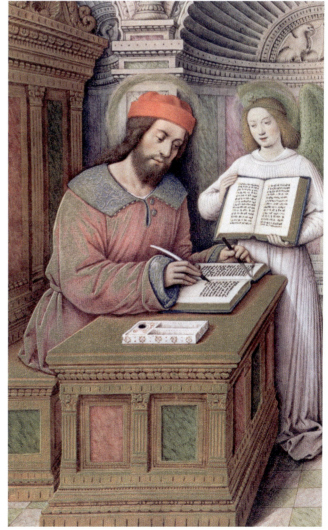

The evangelist St. Mathew writing his gospel.

The Gospel stories are mainly about the last three years of Jesus' life. In fact, little time is spent writing about his childhood. Just like his father, Jesus too worked as a carpenter, yet we are told nothing of this in the Gospels. The Gospels are really documents that provide us with important written information. They provide us with information that Jesus is God. The Evangelists show this to us through Jesus' actions and words. Through the evidence we read, we know that Jesus is God. The four Gospel writers believed Jesus to be God and wanted to tell this good news to all.

Over to You

1. How important was the writing of the Gospels?
2. Do you think it was necessary to write them down? Why?
3. How important do you think evidence is to the writing of the Gospels?
4. What important news do the Gospels give us?

Historical Documents

Most of what we know about Jesus comes from our reading of the New Testament in the Bible. We also get information about Jesus from historical documents written around the first century. Two such examples are written by Josephus and Tacitus.

The historian Josephus

There were many documents written at the time but an important one was written by a man called Josephus around 60 years after the death of Jesus. He was a Jewish scholar and wrote a book about the history of the Jews. In this he described Jesus as a wise man and teacher. Also, he wrote about the crucifixion of Jesus by Pontius Pilate and his resurrection from the dead three days later.

The historian Tacitus

Like Josephus, Tacitus was also an historian. However, he was a Roman and was suspicious of Christianity. In his case, he set down his beliefs about 80 years after the death of Jesus. Among the things he wrote about were the death of Jesus, how he was sentenced by Pontius Pilate and how Christians got their name from Jesus Christ.

Both these men were historians and were concerned with facts and details. They wrote many facts about events that happened and people that were present. Because they were not Christians, they had no personal interest in Jesus, the man or his message. Both documents show that Jesus was a real person who did exist and lived among ordinary people.

Over to You

1. Who were Josephus and Tacitus?
2. How important are their writings?
3. From their writings are you convinced that Jesus did exist?

The Four Gospel Writers

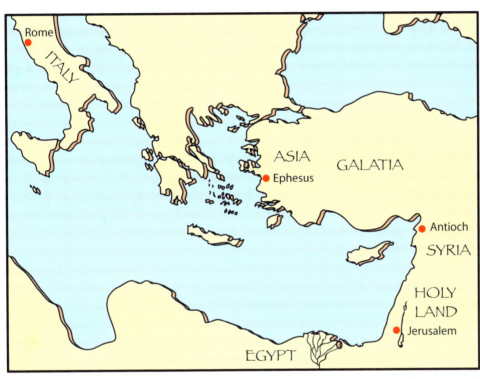

The New Testament introduces us to four Gospel writers. The Gospels are based on the life, death and resurrection of Jesus Christ. These men felt inspired by God to undertake this work. Although there are four Gospel writers, there is only one Jesus Christ.

Gentile – A non-Jew.

The Bible was written so that people, according to Richard of Chichester, could 'Know him more clearly, love him more dearly, and follow him more nearly, day by day'. Each Gospel writer wrote for a particular group:

- Matthew wrote his Gospel for the Jewish Christians and his symbol was the angel.
- Mark wrote his Gospel for the Christians living in Rome and his symbol was the lion.
- Luke wrote his Gospel for the **Gentile** (non-Jew) Christians and his symbol was the bull.
- John wrote his Gospel for the Christians throughout the mediterranean world and his symbol was the eagle.

The Gospel of St Matthew

CE – (Common Era.)

This Gospel was once believed to be the first Gospel written. However, research has shown that it was written after Mark's Gospel, in Antioch where there was a large community of Jewish Christians. It is now believed that the Gospel was written about 85–90 CE. It is clear that Matthew had a wide knowledge of the Jewish religion and the Old Testament. He saw Jesus as the new Moses, the promised one by God. In essence, Matthew taught his followers a new way of living.

The Gospel of St Mark

It is believed that Mark's Gospel was written for Christians around 65–70 CE. At that time Mark was well known to Peter, who was Jesus' closest disciple, so he could listen carefully to what Peter told him and record the information precisely. In this Gospel Jesus is seen as the miracle worker and a teacher. Much of it is devoted to the miracles performed by Jesus.

Mark in his Gospel tells us that Jesus is indeed the promised messiah who suffered at the hands of the authorities in Jerusalem. He also informs us that Jesus had feelings like everyone else.

The Gospel of St Luke

It is believed that Luke's Gospel was written around the same time as Matthew's one. In his case, Luke wrote his Gospel for Gentile Christians. He himself was a Gentile and wanted to spread the Good News about Jesus. Throughout this Gospel, Luke's caring side is evident. He had great sympathy for the oppressed and poor people of society.

Luke's Gospel in particular helps us see that Jesus is the saviour who brings God's love to all people. He also showed Jesus as someone who brings love and forgiveness to all. His Gospel too has a special place for Mary as the mother of Jesus. Another important aspect of this Gospel is prayer. Luke describes Jesus as a man of prayer.

The Gospel of St John

It is thought that John wrote his Gospel around 95 CE. However, this Gospel writer used different sources to describe the story of Jesus. He may have been a follower of one of Jesus' youngest disciples, who was also called John. We do know that Jesus had a special place for this disciple John, because when he was dying on the cross he asked him to take special care of his mother, Mary.

By all accounts John wrote this Gospel for Christians living throughout the Mediterranean world – in Turkey, Greece and Italy. His Gospel helps us to see Jesus as a real human being as he shares our pain and burdens, and is also there in good times to share our joys. He is the real Son of God. Much of this Gospel is spent telling stories that are not found in the other three Gospels.

Synoptic Gospels – Describing events in the Gospel from a similar point of view.

The Synoptic Gospels

The Gospels of Matthew, Mark and Luke are all quite similar and therefore they are known as **Synoptic Gospels**. The word synoptic means 'describing events from a similar point of view'. Sometimes these three Gospels are so similar that one would think they were copied from each other. Both Matthew and Luke use Mark's Gospel as the basis of their own work.

The Gospels of Matthew and Luke are longer than Mark's Gospel. This causes us to ask the question: where did all the extra information come from for them to write their Gospels? Many Bible experts believe that this information came from a document called the 'Q' or Quelle document (*quelle* means source in German). This document is a collection of Jesus' sayings that were recorded at a much earlier stage. No evidence of this document has ever been found. In Matthew and Luke's Gospels the Beatitudes can be found. These blessings are nowhere to be found in Mark's Gospel.

The Fourth Gospel: John

The Gospel of John is different to the other three Gospels as it uses other sources to tell the story of Jesus. There are no parables found in John's Gospel and the kingdom of God is only mentioned once, whereas it has great importance in the other three Gospels. This Gospel focuses more on who Jesus is rather than what he says and does.

Part of the opening lines of John's Gospel are that of a poem: '…who were born not from human stock or human desire or human will but from God himself', showing God's power towards his people. Jesus revealed God to us in a way that an ordinary person could.

There are many 'I am' statements to be found in this Gospel, where Jesus makes the following statements about himself: 'I am the bread of life' (6:35), 'I am the vine' (15:1) and 'I am the light of the world'. When John writes about Jesus in this way, he is identifying Jesus with the God who appeared to Moses in the burning bush. There Moses asked God his name and God answered, 'I am who I am'. Through the various 'I am' statements, John identifies Jesus as God.

In John's Gospel the themes of love and life are also evident. These are gifts given to us by God and ones that we receive so willingly. To love God is to love one another. Jesus brings this gift to those who have faith in him.

Over to You

1. What does the word synoptic mean?
2. Why are the three Gospels, Matthew, Mark and Luke, known as synoptic Gospels?
3. How are Matthew and Luke's Gospels similar?
4. What is meant by the Quelle document?
5. What is so different about John's Gospel?

Over to You – Exam Style Question

Imagine you have been asked to give a talk at a Bible meeting explaining the stages involved in the development of the Gospels from the oral tradition to the written word. Outline the talk you would give making reference to the importance of the gospels in the Christian community of faith.

(Taken from exam papers 2004)

In this chapter,
you will become familiar with
the following concepts:

- Kingdom of God in
   (a) parable
   (b) miracle
   (c) table fellowship
   (d) discipleship
- Vocation
- Mission

Chapter 7:

The Person and Preaching of Jesus

What is the Kingdom of God?

Kingdom of God – A way of Living based on jesus' message of truth, justice, peace and love.

Imagine for a moment a perfect world. What would your perfect world be like?

Read Matthew 20:1–16 to find out how the Kingdom of God was described. Jesus imagined a world that would be full of love for each other, would show justice towards our neighbour and would give peace to our time. Essentially, Jesus wanted love to rule our minds and hearts.

When we read or think about a kingdom, we immediately think of a place or a piece of land. However, the **Kingdom of God** is not found on a map, as it is 'a place' found inside people when they show love to others. It is a way in which someone lives out their life. It is more accurately called the Reign of God – a reign of peace, justice, truth and love.

In the New Testament, Jesus used miracles and parables to describe to us what the Kingdom of God was like.

The Kingdom of God in Parable

What is a parable?

A **parable** is a story with a meaning. Jesus used parables to give us a glimpse of what the Kingdom of God is like. Reading one parable is not enough to understand what the Kingdom is like, however. This is because the Kingdom of God is such a great way of life that no one story does it the justice it deserves.

In general, parables are used to teach us a lesson about life. Jesus used parables for different reasons:

1. To command attention from the disciples.
2. To challenge their growth in faith.
3. To use stories to explain difficult concepts so that they could understand. For example stories about fishermen and tax collectors.

The parables made the disciples and others question their everyday lives and ask themselves were they living a life that was worthy of the Kingdom of God.

Parable – A short story told by Jesus to teach the people about the Kingdom of God. The story is based on earth with a message about heaven.

The Good Samaritan: Luke 10:25-37

Jesus told this parable about a kind-hearted man that helped a stranger at the side of the road.

There was once a man who was going down from Jerusalem to Jericho when robbers attacked him. They stripped him and beat him up, leaving him half dead. It so happened that a priest was going down that road; but when he saw the man, he walked on by, on the other side. In the same way a Levite also came along, went over and looked at the man, and then walked on by, on the other side.

But a Samaritan who was travelling that way came upon the man, and when he saw him, his heart was filled with pity. He went over to him, poured oil and wine on his wounds and bandaged them. Then he put the man on his own animal and took him to an inn, where he took care of him.

The next day he took out two silver coins and gave them to the innkeeper. 'Take care of him,' he told the innkeeper, 'and when I come back this way, I will pay you whatever else you spend on him.'

And Jesus concluded, 'In your opinion, which one of these three acted like a neighbour towards the man attacked by robbers?'. The teacher of the law answered, 'The one who was kind to him'. Jesus replied, 'You go then, and do the same'.

The Samaritans were people that came from the province of Samaria. Although they were Jewish, they were looked down on by other Jews. Their customs and religious practices were different to other Jews. As a result, they were treated as outsiders by many. In Jesus 'time' they mixed freely with non-Jews (Gentiles).

In this parable it is the Samaritan that helps the man at the side of the road, while some religious people just pass him by. Being a good neighbour and friend has nothing to do with the colour of your skin, the clothes you wear or your religion.

Throughout his life Jesus taught us that we should love our neighbour as we love ourselves. The kingdom of God is a place of truth, justice, peace and love. It is the goodness in each one of us. The Parable of the Good Samaritan shows us that it is often the most unlikely person who will come to our aid at the end of the day.

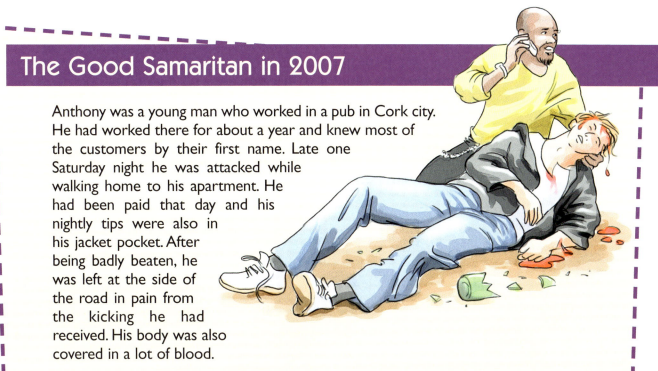

The Good Samaritan in 2007

Anthony was a young man who worked in a pub in Cork city. He had worked there for about a year and knew most of the customers by their first name. Late one Saturday night he was attacked while walking home to his apartment. He had been paid that day and his nightly tips were also in his jacket pocket. After being badly beaten, he was left at the side of the road in pain from the kicking he had received. His body was also covered in a lot of blood.

An hour passed and many cars drove slowly by him, the drivers looking out their window but none stopped to call an ambulance. Once he thought he saw a priest in one of the cars. But then he thought to himself that maybe the priest did not see him. Perhaps he was tired and just wanted to get home or was thinking of the nine o'clock ceremony he would have to give the following morning. Anyway, the priest drove past him.

After a while he heard voices coming towards him. It was a well-dressed couple on their way home from a nightclub. As they passed by, the woman made some comment about how he must be drunk and had fallen on the ground. The man threw a euro at Anthony and laughed as he climbed over him. Many others passed by on foot, but no one stopped to ask what had happened.

Some time later a rough-looking guy came up the road. He too had been out and fell over Anthony. As soon as he saw the blood on Anthony's face and body, he leaned down beside him to talk to him. Straightaway he took his mobile phone out of his pocket and rang 999 to get an ambulance. And then he called the guards. Without hesitation he stayed with Anthony until the ambulance came. During that time he spoke to him softly, telling him that he would be alright.

Over to You

1. Who do you think was the true neighbour, the true friend?
2. Is this story a typical example of today's society? Why/why not?
3. What would you do in a situation like this?

The Parable of Talents: Matthew 25:14-30

Find the parable above in the Bible and read it.

No two people are ever born alike. Everyone has different talents and the extent of our talents varies. Often we think this is unfair and we long to be talented at singing, dancing, or whatever. Jesus told this story to explain to us that we should use our talents wisely.

The Parable of Talents in 2007

Daniel, James and Tom were all very excited about the new youth club and indoor race track that was about to open in Kildare. They had watched the building of the club and Daniel's dad was involved in the overseeing of the race track, as he was a keen runner himself.

All of the boys were talented in different areas. Daniel loved running and longed to represent Ireland in the Olympics at the 100m sprint some day. He also loved basketball and chess. James on the other hand liked indoor soccer and table tennis. In Tom's case, he wanted to learn how to play the guitar, as he liked the instrument and he heard there was a really good teacher going to give lessons at the youth club.

A few months passed and Daniel blossomed at the youth club. He enjoyed his time spent there and made lots of new friends. His running, basketball and chess really improved and the youth club leader complimented him on this. James also enjoyed going to the club. He tried really hard at soccer and table tennis and after a while got even better. He had a real talent for the two sports he played. Overall, he was very happy with himself.

Tom on the other hand was bored all the time and therefore began to cause trouble in the club. Only rarely did he bring his guitar to practice and once when the teacher loaned him his, he broke all its strings. Finally one day, he was asked to leave the youth club.

Tom never used the talent that God had given to him.

Over to You

1. What is the main message of this parable?
2. Why do you think Tom did not use the talents that he was given by God?
3. What are your talents? Make a list of all the talents that you have and how you use them.

The Kingdom of God in Miracle

What is a miracle?

The **miracles** that Jesus performed were signs of his power. In the parables Jesus taught the people something about the kingdom of God, but through the miracles he performed he showed them what he meant. Throughout his life he performed many miracles: he healed the sick, he changed water into wine, he fed five thousand people from a few loaves and fishes and he raised Jairus' daughter back to life.

Miracle – An amazing event performed by Jesus that showed the power of God.

Often the miracles can be divided into three groups:

The miracles of healing: Jesus healed the sick, the blind, the lepers, *e.g. Luke 5:18–26.*

The miracles of nature: Jesus changed something in nature, *e.g. Luke 5:4–9.*

The miracle of exorcism: Jesus removed evil spirits from people, *e.g. Mark 5:1–20.*

Often people find miracles difficult to believe. Even so, Jesus' enemies did accept that he had the power to work miracles. During his life Jesus did not use this power to win over the powerful or to gain acceptance. He worked miracles to reveal God's power and to show his people that the kingdom of God had begun in him.

The calming of the storm: Mark 4:35–41

In this miracle that you are about to read, Jesus shows the power he has over nature and calms the storm. In the boat the fishermen with him were frightened by the fierce winds and waves. Yet Jesus calmed the storm much to the amazement of those that watched.

With the coming of evening that same day, he said to them, 'let us cross over to the other side'. And leaving the crowd behind they took him, just as he was, in the boat; and there were other boats with him.

Then it began to blow a great gale and the waves were breaking into the boat so that it was almost swamped. But he was in the stern, his head on the cushion, asleep.

They woke him and said to him, 'Master, do you not care? We are lost!' And he woke up and rebuked the wind and said to the sea, 'Quiet now! Be calm!'. And the wind dropped, and there followed a great calm.

Then he said to them, 'Why are you so frightened? Have you still no faith?'. They were overcome with awe and said to one another, 'Who can this be? Even the wind and the sea obey him'.

Passage from the Jerusalem Bible

Often life can be difficult for us. We feel alone and afraid and think there is no one watching over us and caring for us when we feel this way. But God is always looking down on us and walking with us through difficult times in our lives. He guides us through many a difficult path and navigates the journey that we should take. When we are faced with tough times and keep our faith, we become stronger human beings.

Over to You

1. What miracle happened at sea?
2. Do you think the fishermen had faith when the miracle happened?
3. Name the different types of miracle. Write a summary on each one.

Healing the leper: Mark: 1:40-45

When Jesus was on earth leprosy was an infectious disease that was incurable. Once someone got leprosy they became an outcast in society. They had to leave their families and move to leper camps because many considered them 'unclean'. Leprosy could affect many parts of the body and often left people deformed.

A man suffering from an infectious skin disease came to Jesus and pleaded on his knees saying, 'If you are willing, you can cleanse me'. Feeling sorry for him, Jesus stretched out his hand, touched him and said to him, 'I am willing. Be cleansed'. And at once the skin disease left him and he was cleansed.

Immediately Jesus sent him away and said to him sternly: 'Mind you tell no one anything, but go and show yourself to the priest, and make the offering for your cleansing prescribed by Moses as evidence to them.'

The man went away, but then started to proclaim freely and tell the story everywhere he went. So much so that Jesus could no longer go into any town openly, but had to stay outside in deserted places. Even so, people from all around kept coming to him.

The Healing of the Lepers
by James Tissot

Over to You

1. What is leprosy?
2. Why do you think Jesus healed this man of leprosy?
3. Why do you think Jesus told the man not to tell anyone about the miracle?
4. What significance did the miracle have on Jesus' life?

The Kingdom of God in Table Fellowship

Table fellowship – Jesus chose to share his meals with all to show that God's kingdom was for everyone.

When we sit down to a meal with our family or friends we share something that is special and unique to that meal. We not only sit down at the table together to eat, but also to enjoy the company present at that time. In some way we are connected to the people that share our meal. Most families share a meal in the evenings or at birthday times, or at anniversaries, and so on.

For Jewish people the most important meal is the Passover. This meal celebrates their escape from Egypt under Moses. At Christmas time in Ireland, the Mansion House in Dublin – home of the Lord Mayor – is open to those that have nowhere else to go to share a meal with others. This meal is important on a day that reminds us of the birth of Jesus Christ, who later died for us so that we could be saved.

Throughout his life Jesus himself shared a meal with many people that were seen as outcasts in society such as tax collectors and sinners. To Jesus **table fellowship** made no distinction between rich and poor, saint or sinner, healthy or sick. Everyone is invited to participate in the kingdom of heaven.

The Story of Zacchaeus

Jesus went on into Jericho and was passing through. There was a chief tax collector there named Zacchaeus, who was rich. He was trying to see who Jesus was, but he was a little man and could not see Jesus because of the crowd.

So he ran ahead of the crowd and climbed a sycamore tree to see Jesus, who was going to pass that way. When Jesus came to that place, he looked up and said to Zacchaeus, 'Hurry down, Zacchaeus, because I must stay in your house today.' Zacchaeus hurried down and welcomed him with great joy. All the people who saw it started grumbling, 'This man has gone as a guest to the home of a sinner.'

Zacchaeus stood up and said to the Lord, 'Listen, Sir! I will give half my belongings to the poor, and if I have cheated anyone, I will pay him back four times as much.' Jesus said to him, 'Salvation has come to this house today, for this man, also, is a descendant of Abraham. The Son of Man came to seek and to save the lost'.

Passage from the Jerusalem Bible

The Kingdom of God in Discipleship

Andrew James Thaddeus Simon John Philip Peter James Jesus Bartholomew Judas Matthew Thomas

In Chapter 5 you looked at a map of the different provinces, towns, rivers and lakes at the time of Jesus. Do you remember looking at the Sea of Galilee on the map? This is where Jesus met his first disciples.

Being a disciple is all about change and wanting to become a better and holy person. The kingdom of God encourages us to be better people so that we can become a follower of Jesus.

Disciples are called to have faith and when Jesus called Simon and Andrew, his first disciples, James and John also followed. This was because they knew Jesus was special and they wanted to follow him too. These four men left what they were doing to follow Jesus. More than anything they wanted to change their old way of life. Also, Jesus needed their help to bring more people into the kingdom of heaven.

Soon Jesus chose 8 more disciples to help him in his work on earth. Jesus the teacher had much to teach them and they had a lot to learn from him. All Jesus wanted these 12 ordinary men to do was to put God first in their lives. Having spent time with Jesus, the disciples saw him as a very holy man. But it was not until he died that they saw him as the Son of God.

Discipleship – Following the call of Jesus in thought, word and deed.

The teachings of Jesus

During his life Jesus taught the disciples many things. He did this through the parables he told and the miracles he performed. Another thing he taught the disciples was the Beatitudes, which were good ways of behaving towards God and other people. He encouraged them all to sit and listen. Through the Beatitudes he taught them to care for each other, to forgive one another and to be prayerful.

It is very clear from the accounts of Jesus that he had a special place for children. When the disciples told the children to leave their master alone, Jesus quickly said, 'Let the little children come to me and do not stop them; for it is to such as these that the kingdom of God belongs. In truth, I tell you, anyone who does not welcome the kingdom of God like a little child will never enter it'. (Luke 18:16–17)

All his life, Jesus taught his disciples to love one another. He wanted them to love all people regardless of race, colour or position in society. In fact, Jesus treated sinners and outcasts like he would everyone else. In particular, he treated women with respect and had a special place in the kingdom of heaven for the poor and downtrodden. No matter what your background is, there is always a place for you in the kingdom of heaven.

Over to You

1. What is table fellowship?
2. Why do you think it was important for Jesus to share a meal with outcasts?
3. If Jesus were alive today living in Ireland, who do you think the outcasts would be?
4. What does it mean to be a disciple?
5. What sort of men were Jesus' 12 disciples?
6. Why do you think Jesus taught the disciples?
7. When Jesus said 'Let the little children come to me' after the disciples pushed them away, what lesson did the disciples learn from this?

The Kingdom of God and Vocation

The word **vocation** means 'to serve'. At the Sea of Galilee, Jesus began to call his disciples, so they were called to serve. Their vocation was to spread the message of Jesus Christ when he was alive and walk with him, and after he died to continue on with his message.

As Christians we are also called to serve.

- **Parents:** Your parents were called to serve when they brought you into the world. The love that your parents have for you is unconditional. When you were baptized, you too became part of the Christian faith. Jesus' love for us is unconditional.

- **Teenagers:** As teenagers you too are called to serve. Many of you may be involved in charity work for Trócaire, Concern or the local St Vincent de Paul Society. You might fundraise in school or through a youth group in which you are involved. Next year you may become involved in the Young Social Innovators group – a group that wants to be innovative and make a change to a particular group in Ireland or abroad. For more information on this go to www.youngsocialinnovators.ie

- **Church leaders:** Pope Benedict XVI also has a vocation as head of the Catholic Church worldwide. He tries to reach out to the downtrodden of society just as Jesus did in his ministry.

Seán Óg O'hAilpín, GAA Hurling Star, with students at the YSI Showcase 2006

- **Individuals:** Fr Peter McVerry reaches out to the homeless of Ballymun in Dublin all the time. He looks after those that are young and tries to get them safe accommodation, so that they can get back on their feet. Through his vocation he is carrying out Jesus' work on earth.

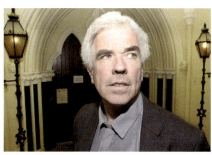

Fr. Peter McVerry

Everyday we are called to serve God. This can be something simple like helping our elderly neighbour with their shopping or visiting our grandmother, who is alone, instead of going out with our friends. Every one of us has a vocation in life. What is important is the way in which we live out that vocation. As God's children we are called to repent and change our sinful ways.

Vocation – A calling to serve God.

The Kingdom of God and Mission

The Movie *Finding Nemo*

Have you seen the film *Finding Nemo*? In this film, a fish called Nemo gets caught in a small net by a diver and is brought to live in a fishbowl in a dental surgery. Nemo's dad who is swimming near by sees the whole event. Deeply upset, he sets out on a mission to find his son. Along the way he faces many difficulties, but he never gives up, as his love for his son is far greater than any difficulty he may face. The two are reunited near the end of the film and realise that each of them needs to listen to the other before heading out on another adventure. The love they have for each other out weighs any differences they may have once felt.

Mission – Something we stand up for because we really believe in it.

Every person has a **mission** in life to respond to the values of the kingdom of God. We must discover this mission for ourselves. A mission is something that we stand up for because we really believe in it. As Christians we are all called to love and serve God.

The kingdom that we long for is a just place where we are all treated with equality. It is a place where we show love, not only to God but to all peoples. It is a place where we are true to ourselves and to others. Finally, it is a place where we find inner peace and forgive those who have hurt us. As Christians we are called to respond to and act on something we believe in – this is our mission.

Over to You

1. What does the word vocation mean?
2. Name someone you know with a vocation.
3. What does the word mission mean?
4. Think of an example from a film or book in which you feel mission is evident. Describe the mission.
5. As Christians what is our mission on earth?

Over to You

Exam Style questions

1. (a) Explain what the word parable means and name one you have studied.
   (b) Why did Jesus use parables in his teachings?
2. Describe one miracle Jesus performed.
3. What do you understand the term 'Kingdom of God' to mean?

In this chapter, you will become familiar with the following concepts:

■ Conflict with authority
■ Sacrifice
■ Martyrdom
■ Memorial
■ Passover
■ Eucharist
■ Resurrection
■ Transformation
■ Presence

Chapter 8:

The Death and Resurrection of Jesus

Conflict with Authority

As we have learned so far, Jesus caused quite a stir as he went about his public mission. We know that he was unlike any other preacher who had gone before him.

People are often afraid of new things that they do not understand. We can all be wary and suspicious. Many great people in the past were treated badly because of this, especially when they came into **conflict with authority**. This includes people such as Martin Luther King and Nelson Mandela who preached a new and challenging message to people.

Dr. Martin Luther King

Conflict with authority – The tension between Jesus and those in power, such as the Pharisees.

Jesus was another important person who preached and encouraged change. While he had many loving and devoted followers, he also clashed with certain groups of people. The groups who felt most threatened by him were those that held positions of power. They did not want change as they thought they might lose their power. Hence Jesus came into conflict with those in authority. As the Son of God, Jesus did not seek trouble with these groups, but he was not afraid to stand up to them either.

Nelson Mandela

JESUS vs THE PHARISEES

My name is Alsom. I am a committed and proud Pharisee. I can only describe my feelings towards this man they call Jesus as anger. He is everything I am not. We Pharisees know how important the law is. We live our whole lives by it. But this man Jesus completely ignores it! He must be stopped before his bad influence spreads to other innocent people.

We don't want to be associated with people who are sinners. Anyone who says they follow God should ignore law breakers. Yet this man, who goes around claiming to know more about God than we do, continually breaks the law! He has healed people on the Sabbath which is against the law. I also saw him and his followers eat without following the rules of washing beforehand. And if that's not bad enough, he chooses to eat his meals with tax collectors and sinners!

But it's not just his actions that offend me, it's the things he says too. You should hear some of those parables he's told. But don't worry, he won't be around for much longer. The Pharisees will see to that!

Over to You

1. What impression do you get of the Pharisees after reading what Alsom has to say?
2. Why do you think the law is so important to them?
3. Read the following Gospel stories about Jesus' clashes with the Pharisees and write them as a story in your own words: Mark 3:1–6 or Matthew 9:9–13.
4. What do these stories tell us about Jesus?

Here is an example of one of the parables that angered Alsom so much. Jesus also told this parable to people who were sure of their own goodness and despised everybody else.

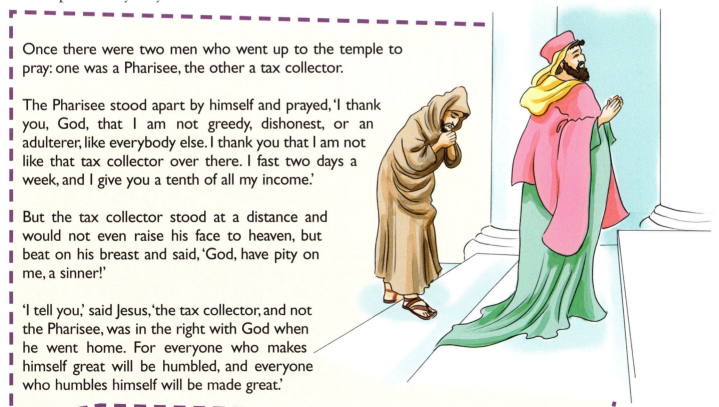

Once there were two men who went up to the temple to pray: one was a Pharisee, the other a tax collector.

The Pharisee stood apart by himself and prayed, 'I thank you, God, that I am not greedy, dishonest, or an adulterer, like everybody else. I thank you that I am not like that tax collector over there. I fast two days a week, and I give you a tenth of all my income.'

But the tax collector stood at a distance and would not even raise his face to heaven, but beat on his breast and said, 'God, have pity on me, a sinner!'

'I tell you,' said Jesus, 'the tax collector, and not the Pharisee, was in the right with God when he went home. For everyone who makes himself great will be humbled, and everyone who humbles himself will be made great.'

69

Up for Discussion

What does this parable tell us about
(a) the Pharisees and (b) Jesus?

Holy Week

There are certain moments in history that will always be remembered. Sometimes it is a particular year such as 1914 when World War I began. Or even just a day like 9/11. For Christians, the events of the week that became known as Holy Week will never be forgotten. They are remembered every year at Easter time when Christians all over the world take part in ceremonies to commemorate them.

Let us go back in time to the place where these amazing events happened. If we imagine what the local newspaper might have said that week, we can follow the story as it happened.

The Jerusalem Herald

Sunday

The streets of Jerusalem were thronged today as people entered the great city for the annual festival of Passover. But this time there was more commotion and excitement among the pilgrims than last year.

A travelling preacher named Jesus of Nazareth entered the city on a donkey. But he is no ordinary preacher. There are many recent reports of this man performing miracles.

It was a strange sight indeed. Crowds of people waved palm branches in the air and shouted 'Hosanna', much like they would welcome a new king. But what kind of king rides around on a donkey?

What will the leaders in the Sanhedrin have to say about this man who some people are calling the Messiah? And what will the Romans make of it all?

Make sure to read the *Herald* tomorrow as this roving reporter keeps a close eye on the story.

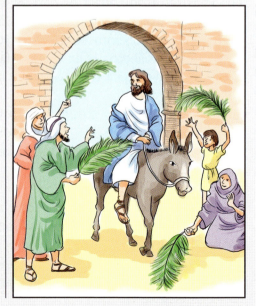

Over to You

1. Why did this day become known as Palm Sunday?
2. The donkey is seen as an animal of peace. Why do you think Jesus chose to arrive on one?
3. How do you think the Pharisees felt after reading this article?

The Jerusalem Herald

Monday

The Temple today was a scene of total chaos and confusion and the man at the centre of it all was none other than Jesus of Nazareth. For the second day running this man has attracted huge attention in our city. By sheer coincidence *this* Jewish reporter happened to be at the scene.

Like many other Jewish people I had gone to the Temple to worship. Obviously, I first had to change my money for Temple coins. Then I had to buy an acceptable animal to offer for sacrifice. As I finished this costly transaction, Jesus appeared in the Court of Gentiles. Readers, I am not exaggerating when I tell you there was steam coming out of his ears!

In a fit of rage he overturned the tables of the money changers and drove out the people who were selling animals. I couldn't hear everything he was saying but I did catch something about turning the Temple into a hideout for thieves!

After he left I saw a group of Sadducees gathered together and they seemed very annoyed at what had just happened.

Read the *Herald* tomorrow and find out how the saga continues.

This event, which became known as the Cleansing of the Temple, meant that Jesus was now in conflict with another group in authority, the Sadducees. Remember the Sadducees were a wealthy group who held the powerful position of High Priest. They controlled temple worship and this brought them money and power.

The Sadducees were quite happy co-operating with the Romans and saw Jesus as a threat to the status quo. After this incident in the temple, they began to work closely with the Pharisees in an effort to get rid of Jesus.

The Jerusalem Herald

Tuesday

Today saw the man of the moment, Jesus of Nazareth, back at the Temple. This time he was not turning over tables but teaching and preaching to all who were there. Obviously, the Pharisees and Sadducees were not happy about this because of all that has happened.

I witnessed a very interesting exchange between Jesus and some of them. They questioned him about paying taxes. Readers, as you know, this is an awkward subject. It was almost as if the leaders were trying to catch him out. If he said it was wrong to pay taxes he would be in trouble with the Romans, and if he said it was right it would be like saying the Emperor was greater than God. His answer, readers, was clever indeed. He said, 'Pay the Emperor what belongs to the Emperor and pay God what belongs to God.'

It seems that this preacher man will not give in. He is afraid of no one. To be honest readers, the more I see of him the more I am impressed by him. Overall he seems calm and a man of peace. The next question is who exactly is he?

Buy the *Herald* tomorrow to see if we are any closer to the truth.

Christ Preaching in the Temple by Criostoforo de Predis, created 1476

Over to You

Imagine you are a Jewish person living in Jerusalem. Write a letter to your cousin in a faraway town, telling him/her of the recent events in Jerusalem.

The story continues...

The reporter of the *Jerusalem Herald* would not have been able to see all that went on behind the scenes that week. While some events like the Cleansing of the Temple were very public, others went on behind closed doors.

On the Wednesday, one of Jesus' apostles, Judas, went and met with the high priests in secret. They struck a deal. In exchange for 30 pieces of silver, Judas offered to help them in arresting Jesus. The Jewish leaders felt they could not arrest Jesus during the day as he would be surrounded by his followers. And at night they knew it would be hard to find him. So Judas' offer was just what they needed.

The Last Supper

Thursday was the day when the event known as the Last Supper took place. It is called this because it was the last meal Jesus ate with his apostles before his death. While the events of the Last Supper had not happened before, there are very important similarities between it and the **Passover** meal.

As Jesus and his followers were Jewish they would have followed the tradition around this time of celebrating a Passover meal. Let us put the two meals side by side and see why the Last Supper was a meal in the Passover tradition.

Passover – The festival celebrated by Jews to remember the events that led them to freedom.

The Passover

The Passover is a celebration of freedom. It is remembering the time when the Israelites escaped from slavery in Egypt after the angel of death had 'passed over' the houses of the Israelites and spared them.

The festival is celebrated by sacrificing a young male unblemished lamb. The blood of the lamb is sprinkled on the doorpost of the house and the lamb roasted and eaten. Unleavened bread and bitter herbs are also eaten.

The meal begins with a blessing. A cup of wine is blessed and drunk. The family then give thanks to God. The head of the family blesses and breaks the bread and shares it out.

The Last Supper

Jesus and his apostles met together to celebrate the Passover meal on the Thursday evening.

Jesus got up from the table and began to wash the feet of his disciples. This shocked the disciples as he was their master and should not have been doing this task. But Jesus insisted. He was showing them that being a disciple meant serving others and giving them a good example to follow when he was gone.

He then told them that one of those present would betray him. The disciples would not believe him but Jesus knew that Judas was the one.

Then he took a piece of bread, gave thanks to God, broke it and gave it to his disciples saying, 'This is my body, which is given for you. Do this in memory of me.' In the same way he gave them the cup after the supper saying, 'This cup is God's new covenant sealed with my blood, which is poured out for you'.

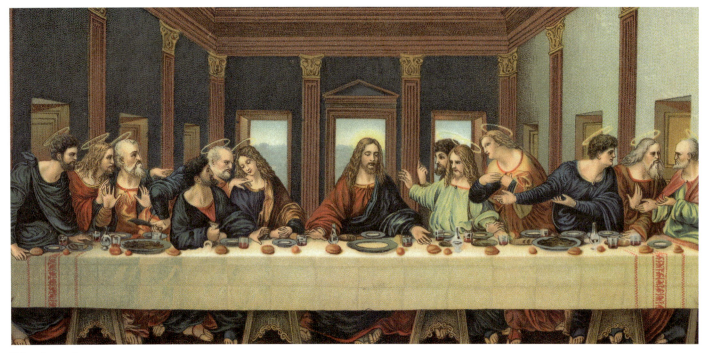

The Last Supper

Sacrifice – To give up something for the sake of others.

Memorial – Something that is done to remember and honour the memory of someone or something.

Eucharist – A thanksgiving meal that is celebrated by Christians.

We can see that the Last Supper is a meal in the Passover tradition because:

1. A lamb is sacrificed at Passover to symbolise the Israelites' freedom. In the Last Supper Jesus is the new lamb that is sacrificed. To **sacrifice** means to give up something for the sake of others. In this case, Jesus would give up his life for us to receive freedom from our sins.

2. The Passover meal is a **memorial** meal. In other words, it is celebrated as a way of remembering the events that happened to the Israelites in their history. However, it does not only remember incidents from the past. It also celebrates what the event of Passover means for the Jewish people in the present. In the Last Supper Jesus asks the disciples to 'do this in memory of me'. So we see that both meals are memorials.

The Passover meal celebrated that night by Jesus later became known as the **Eucharist** to Christians. Eucharist means thanksgiving. It is one of the seven sacraments celebrated by the Catholic Church.

The arrest

After the Passover meal Jesus went to a place called the Garden of Gethsemane on the Mount of Olives to pray with his disciples. All week Jesus had tried to prepare his friends for what was about to happen. He knew that the time had come for him to fulfil his mission on earth. He asked his apostles to keep watch while he went to pray. Once alone, he prayed to his father for strength saying, 'If you will, take this cup of suffering away from me. Not my will, however, but your will be done'.

While he was terrified, he was also willing to do whatever God wanted. But his prayers made him strong and he went back to his friends. On his return, he found them sleeping, as they were tired and confused by the events of the past week. They knew something was going to happen but did not want to believe that Jesus was going to leave them.

Judas betrays Jesus with a kiss

It was at this moment that Judas entered with a crowd. He went up to Jesus and kissed him. This was the sign for the Jewish leaders to make their arrest. Jesus knew what the sign meant. Suddenly afraid, his apostles saw what was about to happen and one of them took a sword and cut off the high priest's ear. But Jesus said 'Enough!' and healed the man. Next the temple guards arrested him and he was taken away to the house of the high priest for his trial to begin.

Over to You

1. How do you think Jesus felt when he went to the Garden of Gethsemane?
2. Why did he choose to pray?
3. Why do you think Jesus healed the High Priest's ear?
4. Imagine you were one of the apostles with Jesus that night. How would you feel?

The trials

After he was arrested Jesus was treated like a criminal, even though he had broken no laws. But unlike most criminals he had to endure two trials. And unlike most criminals he did not receive a fair trial. Firstly, he was beaten and taunted by those who had arrested him. Secondly, his first trial was held at night which was not the common practice.

Christ before Caiaphas
by Bachiacca

Blasphemy – When someone claims to be as great as God.

First trial

The first trial Jesus went through was a religious trial. As we know the Sanhedrin was the religious court at the time. The leader of this was Caiaphas, the High Priest. The Sanhedrin had no authority to put Jesus to death, only the Roman governor Pontius Pilate had the power to do this. So the purpose of this trial was to try and decide what charges they could bring against Jesus that would convince Pontius Pilate to put him to death.

The first thing they accused him of was that he had said he would destroy the temple. False witnesses came forward and told lies about Jesus. But Jesus remained silent. This angered Caiaphas greatly. He wanted Jesus to say something that would help them to convict him. But Jesus' silence ensured this did not happen.

Eventually, Caiaphas asked Jesus straight out, 'Are you the Messiah, the Son of the Blessed God?' Finally, Jesus spoke and said, 'I am and you will all see the Son of Man seated on the right of the Almighty and coming with the clouds of heaven.'

This answer meant that according to their laws the Sanhedrin could accuse him of **blasphemy**. This was when someone claimed to be as great as God. So they decided to hand him over to Pontius Pilate.

Second trial

The second trial took place the next morning on the Friday. This time Jesus was put in chains and brought before Pilate. The Jewish leaders informed Pilate, 'We caught this man misleading our people, telling them not to pay taxes to the Emperor and claiming that he himself is the Messiah, a king.' When they had finished, Pilate asked Jesus, 'Are you the King of the Jews?' Jesus answered, 'So you say'.

However, Pilate did not want to get involved in the religious affairs of the Jews, so he sent Jesus to Herod who ruled the region of Galilee where Jesus was born. All Herod did was to mock Jesus and send him back to Pilate. No matter how hard he thought about it, Pilate could find no reason to condemn Jesus to death, and so he told this to the Jewish leaders. However, the leaders had won over the people to their side.

Every year it was the custom for the Roman governor to release a prisoner on the feast of Passover. Pilate offered the people a choice of releasing Jesus or a violent criminal named Barabbas. But the crowd shouted, 'Kill him! Set Barabbas free!'

Yet Pilate still did not want to condemn an innocent man, so he asked the crowd again but they repeated 'Crucify him!' Afraid the people's anger would cause a riot if their wishes were not met, Pilate handed Jesus over to be crucified.

Over to You

Pretend you are the reporter with the *Jerusalem Herald*. Write an article for the paper, covering the story of the arrest and trial of Jesus.

The death of Jesus

Now the Pharisees and Sadducees had got what they wanted. But before they took Jesus away to crucify him the Roman soldiers scourged him. This meant they stripped him and tied him to a pillar where they whipped his back with leather straps studded with pieces of metal.

Then they dressed him in purple robes, put a crown of thorns on his head and mocked him saying, 'Long live the King of the Jews!'. After that, they beat him and spat on him.

Now began Jesus' journey to his death. He was forced to carry a heavy wooden cross through the streets of Jerusalem to the place where he would be crucified. On his way he was met with different reactions. Some people jeered at him, but others cried and mourned for him. At this stage Jesus was very weak and bleeding heavily from his earlier beatings. Once he fell and the soldiers forced a man from the crowd called Simon to help him carry the cross.

Finally, they reached the place called Calvary (sometimes called Golgotha). Here Jesus was crucified. Crucifixion was a brutal form of death. The victim was nailed and tied to a cross. They were barely able to breathe in this position and were tired and thirsty. The soldiers continued to mock Jesus, even as he was dying in front of them. They told him to save himself if he were really the Messiah. But all Jesus said was, 'Forgive them Father; they do not know what they are doing'.

At three o'clock, darkness covered the land and Jesus cried out in a loud voice, 'Father! In your hands I place my spirit'. These were his very last words. Now Jesus had become a martyr. A **martyr** is someone who is willing to suffer and even give up their life for something they believe in.

Martyr – Someone willing to suffer and die for their religious beliefs.

Jesus on the cross by Niccolo dell Abate

Those who were left behind...

Jesus had gone. How must his followers have felt at this time? His apostles had believed he was their saviour and that he would be with them always. Some of them felt angry because it seemed as if Jesus had abandoned them. Others felt afraid. They worried that the same thing would happen to them because they had been Jesus' friends. Who would protect them? They all felt confused. How would they carry on without him? Who would be their leader now? They felt deep sorrow, as they saw the man they had loved and believed in suffer and die.

Over to You

Imagine you are one of the apostles. Write your diary entries for Holy Week, saying how you felt as you watched the events unfold.

Resurrection

Usually if the central character in a film or story dies it means it is the end. There is nothing else left to happen. But Jesus was not just a character in a film or story. And this was not the end. The events which happened next meant it was only just the beginning.

A man named Joseph of Arimathea went to Pilate to ask if he could take the body of Jesus away for burial. Even though Joseph had been a member of the council who had wanted Jesus crucified, he did not agree with their decision. In fact, he was a good man who was waiting for the kingdom of God to arrive.

The laws at the time stated that the body could not be left on the cross over the Sabbath, which began on that Friday evening. Because it was so late in the day the burial had to be rushed. Jesus' body was wrapped in a shroud and placed in a tomb. The entrance to the tomb was sealed with a large rock. It was agreed that some of the women would return on the Sunday after the Sabbath was over to prepare Jesus' body properly.

Early on the Sunday morning the women, led by Mary Magdalene, returned to the tomb with spices they had prepared to wash and embalm his body. When they got there they saw the rock had been moved and the tomb was empty. The women were scared and confused.

All the Gospels mention that there was a presence in the tomb. Matthew's Gospel tells us that it was an angel who spoke to the women and told them not to be afraid. The angel said that Jesus had been raised from the dead and that the women should go and tell the others.

Jesus appears

The Gospel stories are slightly different in how they tell the stories of Jesus' appearances after his **resurrection**. You can read them fully in the Gospels themselves. However, we can take the following to be a summary of what happened:

Resurrection – Jesus was restored to life three days after he had died.

1. The followers of Jesus were afraid when they saw the empty tomb. They did not know what had happened to the body and even suspected it had been stolen.
2. All the Gospels agree that Jesus approached the people to whom he had appeared. They did not go looking for him.
3. One of the first people Jesus appeared to was Mary Magdalene.
4. The people he appeared to did not recognise him at first because he had been changed in some way.
5. Jesus said to those he appeared to, 'Peace be with you' to reassure them, because they were afraid and did not understand what they were seeing.
6. Their fear was quickly replaced by joy when they realised that their master had not left them after all.
7. Jesus gave those he appeared to instructions to go and do his work.

Read the following account of one of the appearances of the Risen Jesus found in the Gospel of Luke:

The Road to Emmaus

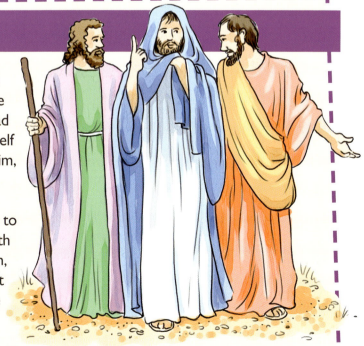

On that same day two of Jesus' followers were going to a village named Emmaus and they were talking to each other about all the things that had happened. As they talked and discussed, Jesus himself drew near and walked along with them; they saw him, but somehow did not recognise him.

Jesus said to them, 'What are you talking about to each other, as you walk along?' They stood still, with sad faces. One of them, named Cleopas, asked him, 'Are you the only visitor in Jerusalem who doesn't know the things that have been happening there these last few days?' 'What things?' he asked.

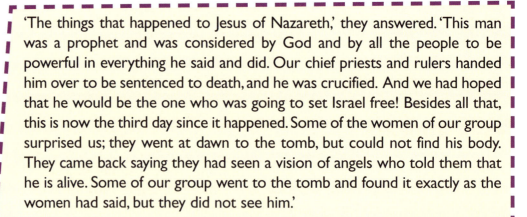

'The things that happened to Jesus of Nazareth,' they answered. 'This man was a prophet and was considered by God and by all the people to be powerful in everything he said and did. Our chief priests and rulers handed him over to be sentenced to death, and he was crucified. And we had hoped that he would be the one who was going to set Israel free! Besides all that, this is now the third day since it happened. Some of the women of our group surprised us; they went at dawn to the tomb, but could not find his body. They came back saying they had seen a vision of angels who told them that he is alive. Some of our group went to the tomb and found it exactly as the women had said, but they did not see him.'

Then Jesus explained to them what was said about himself in all the scriptures. As they came near the village, Jesus acted as if he were going on further; but they held him back saying, 'Stay with us; the day is almost over and it is getting dark.'

So he went in to stay with them. He sat down to eat with them, took the bread, and said the blessing; then he broke the bread and gave it to them. Then their eyes were opened and they recognised him, but he disappeared from their sight.

They said to each other, 'Wasn't it like a fire burning in us when he talked to us on the road and explained the scriptures to us?'. They got up at once and went back to Jerusalem, where they found the eleven disciples gathered together with the others and said, 'The Lord is risen indeed!'

Up for Discussion

Do a role play of the Gospel story above with your classmates.

Transformation – The change that occurred in Jesus after the resurrection, making him alive in a new way.

Presence – Jesus' presence (existence) after the resurrection was an everlasting one.

The resurrection is not an easy thing to understand. To be resurrected means literally to be restored to life. But Jesus was not just brought back to life as he himself had done to others in some of his miracles. The Gospels tell us that Jesus – though he was the same Jesus who had been a leader to the apostles – was somehow different now. He was not a ghost but he was not entirely human either. There had been a **transformation** or change in him. It was as if he were no longer just of this world but also of a heavenly world. He was present among them in a new way. And he promised that this **presence** would continue.

Over to You Crossword

1 (down): Jesus found himself in conflict with this group after he cleansed the temple.

2 (down): The most important events in Jesus' life took place during this week.

3 (down): The name given to the day Jesus arrived in Jerusalem.

4 (down): A Jewish festival that celebrates their freedom.

5 (down): The apostle that betrayed Jesus.

6 (across): A thanksgiving meal celebrated by Christ.

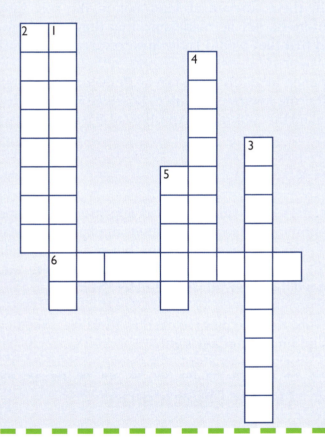

Answers to crossword

1. Sadducees
2. Holy Week
3. Palm Sunday
4. Passover
5. Judas
6. Eucharist

In this chapter,
you will become familiar with
the following concepts:

- Pentecost
- Missionary
- People of God
- Son of Man (HL)
- Son of God (HL)
- New creation (HL)
- Christ / Messiah (HL)

Chapter 9:

Faith in Christ

Events after the Resurrection

As we said in the last chapter, the resurrection marked a new beginning for the disciples. When Jesus appeared to them after the resurrection, they were filled with joy. They had their master back. But Jesus could not stay with them forever, at least not in the way they expected. However, before he left he made sure that they would always feel his presence and that they would know how to carry on his work.

This all happened in an event known as **Pentecost**. The events of what happened after the resurrection are to be found in a book from the New Testament called the Acts of the Apostles, which was written by St Luke.

The Ascension

For 40 days after his death Jesus had appeared to his apostles many times and continued to teach them about the kingdom of God. He also said to them, 'Do not leave Jerusalem, but wait for the gift I told you about, the gift my Father promised. John baptized with water, but in a few days you will be baptized with the Holy Spirit'.

After saying this, the disciples watched as Jesus was taken up to heaven and a cloud hid him from their sight.

Up for Discussion

Do you think the disciples felt different when Jesus left them at the Ascension compared to how they felt when he left them at the Crucifixion?

Pentecost

Pentecost – The event marking when the apostles were given the gift of the Holy Spirit.

After this event the apostles continued to meet and pray together regularly. They were joined by Mary, the mother of Jesus. When the day of Pentecost came, all the believers were gathered together in one place. Suddenly there was a noise from the sky which sounded like a strong wind blowing. Then they saw what looked like tongues of fire that spread out and touched each person there.

All of a sudden they were all filled with the Holy Spirit. Amazingly, they were able to speak in other languages previously unknown to them. The power they received from the Holy Spirit gave them the courage to go out and preach the word of God and baptize in the name of Jesus. That very day about three thousand people were baptized.

Over to You

1. Why do you think Pentecost was such an important event for the apostles?
2. How do you think they felt as they sat in that room and received the gift of the Holy Spirit?
3. Have you heard of the Holy Spirit before? What do you know about it?

Beginning of Missionary Work

Up until Pentecost the followers of Jesus had been afraid to go out and preach in his name. They had seen what had happened to their leader and feared for their own lives. They knew they were seen as a threat by many people and so were afraid of attack. This threat of attack did not go away after Pentecost. But what did go away was their fear.

Missionary – Continuing the work of Jesus on earth.

Before he ascended into heaven Jesus had given his apostles the authority to teach in his name. He said to them, 'Go then, to all peoples everywhere and make them my disciples; baptize them in the name of the Father, the Son and the Holy Spirit, and teach them to obey everything I have commanded you.' After Pentecost the apostles began to do just that. The Christian Church had begun its **missionary** work.

The first Christian communities

Portrait of Saint Peter

All the apostles carried out the work Jesus had asked them to do. But one apostle in particular stood out: Peter. After Pentecost he was the first apostle to stand up and address the large crowds with confidence and enthusiasm. He told them about the gift of the Holy Spirit and explained how they would receive it through baptism. The people listened carefully to him and were baptized. It was these believers who made up the first Christian community.

The Acts of the Apostles tells us, 'They spent their time in learning from the apostles, taking part in the fellowship, and sharing in the fellowship meals and the prayers'. A fellowship is a group of companions who come together because of a shared belief.

So we can see that the first Christian communities were a close and friendly group. They spent time together and shared their knowledge and ideas about God and his son. They tried to mirror the person of Jesus in how they lived together. Everything they had they shared. If one had more than another, they would sell what they had and distribute the money among the rest of the community. In this way no one wanted for anything and all were equal. This was their way of trying to bring about the kingdom of God that Jesus had preached about. And, most importantly of all, they remembered Jesus' words and actions in the Last Supper by sharing their meals.

Clearly, they were a happy and content community and their numbers grew in size every day. As the scriptures say: 'The group of believers was one in mind and heart.'

Over to You

1. Do you think Jesus would have been proud of the work his apostles were doing?
2. Do you think the first Christian community would have been a nice group to belong to? Why?
3. How was this community like the kingdom of God that Jesus had preached about?

A dangerous time

Unfortunately, all was not well. The groups who had been in conflict with Jesus and had played a part in his death were watching the activities of the Christians very closely. They heard the apostles preaching about the resurrection in the temple and had heard reports that Peter had healed a lame man.

Soon after, Peter and John were arrested. When the leaders questioned them about where they had acquired the power to do and say these things, they were surprised by Peter's bold and brave answer. Filled with the power of the Holy Spirit, Peter told them that his power came from Jesus of Nazareth, the man they had condemned to death.

Peter's answer made the council very worried about the following the apostles were gaining, and so they forbid them from speaking about or healing in Jesus' name again. Once released, Peter and John returned to the others. All of them prayed together for strength from the Holy Spirit to continue their work.

The apostles continued to preach and wonderful healing miracles were performed. Crowds of people flocked to Jerusalem to join their numbers. Again they came to the attention of the authorities and again they were arrested. After being interrogated the apostles were whipped and ordered to stop their preaching. But once again the power of the Holy Spirit gave them the courage to continue their work.

St Stephen – a brave disciple

One of the disciples was a man called Stephen. He was blessed by God and spread the good news and even performed miracles. In time Stephen came to the attention of the elders and teachers of the law and was brought before them. False witnesses came and told lies about him, but Stephen remained calm. In reply, he made a long speech in which he accused the elders of being foolish and stubborn. He told them they were deaf to God's message.

At this the elders were furious and Stephen was run out of the city and stoned to death. Throughout the stoning Stephen called out to Jesus saying, 'Lord Jesus, receive my spirit! Do not remember this sin against them!'. In his bravery, Stephen had been willing to die for his faith. He became one of the first Christian martyrs. We celebrate this feast on 26th December.

St Stephen preaching outside Jerusalem by Vittore Carpaccio

Up for Discussion

Do you think the disciples were brave? Where did they get this bravery from?

The story of St Paul

One of the men at the centre of the persecution of the first Christian communities was a man called Saul. He dragged believers from their homes and threw them in jail. As a result, the community of Christians began to leave Jerusalem and were scattered throughout the different provinces.

One day Saul set out for a city called Damascus to look for followers of Jesus. His plan was to find and bring them back to Jerusalem to face prison. As he was coming near the city of Damascus a light from the sky suddenly flashed all around him and he fell to the ground. He heard a voice saying, 'Saul! Why do you persecute me?' The voice belonged to Jesus.

Saul got up but realised that he could not see. He was blind. His companions took him by the hand and led him into Damascus. For three days he remained blind. Then a man named Ananias came to him and placed his hands on him. He told Saul that he had been sent by Jesus, who wanted Saul to do his work. Immediately Saul got his sight back. After that he was baptized by Ananias and became known as Paul.

Paul went straight to the synagogues and began to preach that Jesus was the Son of God. He then travelled around to all the different Christian communities, helping them and making them united and strong.

As well as visiting, Paul also wrote letters to communities in places such as Corinth, Rome and Ephesus. In the letters he urged them to work together and for the members to take on different roles such as administration, teaching and leadership. Eventually, Paul became one of the greatest missionary people in the Christian Church.

People of God

The first Christians were a group who did not give up easily. They were seen as enemies by many Jews and were forced to suffer because of it. It was not just the Jews who they had to contend with, however. The Romans were becoming increasingly suspicious of them too. As time went by most of the apostles and hundreds of other Christians were killed because of their faith in Jesus. But the Christians remained strong. With the help of people like Paul their communities survived.

Soon the Christians began to establish set patterns of worship. They would meet together to celebrate the Eucharist and would read sections of the Jewish scriptures as well as parts of the letters from people like Paul. Eventually, the two books became known as the Old Testament and the New Testament.

As the communities grew in number, the apostles appointed leaders known as bishops to carry on their work. Others took on roles to help the bishops. The bishops and their assistants served the community by preaching and celebrating the Eucharist with them. But everyone in the community was called to have their own role. They were to love each other and spread the good news of Jesus in word and deed.

Each little group of Christians in the different areas became known as churches. Together they were known as one church, which meant they were People of God. They continued to follow the example set by the first Christians and prayed for and helped each other in any way they could.

People of God – Those who believe in God and try to carry out his will.

Over to You

Imagine that you are a member of the first Christian communities. Write a letter to your friend in another country telling them what it's like to be a Christian.

Higher Level

What's in a Name?

Names are very important. They give people their identity. People are sometimes called a name for a certain reason. Others have more than one name. Nicknames can often tell us something of a person's personality.

Up for Discussion

Discuss with your classmates if they know the story of how they got their name. Was it for any particular reason? Do they know if their name has a meaning behind it?

Jesus is known by many different names and titles. This is probably because he was such an important person. To add to that, he was a complex person. The different names and titles help people to understand the different sides to him. Some of the titles used for Jesus have a meaning behind them, just as our own names may have too.

Son of Man

Son of Man – Jesus came in human form to serve man.

This title is one which appears many times in the Gospels. In fact, Jesus uses it himself. In the Gospel of Mark Jesus is teaching his disciples. He tells them, 'The Son of Man must suffer much and be rejected by the elders, the chief priests and the teachers of the law. He will be put to death, but three days later he will rise to life'. Jesus is clearly speaking about himself here, so we know that he sees the Son of Man as an appropriate title. He seems to be referring to the fact that he has come in human form to serve man. It is also linked to the fact that Jesus was the Messiah.

In the Old Testament a prophet called Daniel had a vision about the Messiah and he uses the phrase Son of Man. Jesus later quoted from the Book of Daniel saying, 'And you will all see the Son of Man seated on the right of the Almighty and coming with the clouds of heaven'.

So it is clear that when Jesus uses this title to describe himself, he is using it to show that he is the Messiah.

Son of God

Jesus often refers to God as his father, so it is easy to understand where this title comes from. Christians believe that Jesus was literally the son of God. The early Church used this title to show who they understood Jesus to be. They believed he had a special relationship with God and this title explains just what this relationship was.

But there is more to this title than just a literal meaning. In ancient times the phrase was used to describe very holy or good men. In his Sermon on the Mount, Jesus said, 'Happy are those who work for peace; God will call them his children'. This shows that the early Christians used the title to show that Jesus was one who was doing God's work and was favoured by him.

In the story of Jesus' baptism, Matthew tells us, 'Then a voice said from Heaven, "This is my own dear son, with whom I am pleased"'. So we see that Christians called Jesus the Son of God to show that Jesus was doing the work of God and that he had a special authority from God to do this. This title also tells us that Jesus was divine as well as human.

Son of God – Jesus was literally the son of God. It is also a phrase used to describe very holy or good men.

New Creation

We associate the word creation with the Book of Genesis. Here we find the story of how God created the world. Part of this creation was that of human beings. We know that this human creation disobeyed God and brought sin into the world. But Jesus seemed to be a New Creation.

The early Christians saw him as totally different to any other human, so in this way he was a new creation. Paul, who we learned about earlier in this chapter, used the title New Creation when talking about Jesus. This was because he wanted to show the amazing and unique being that God had given to us in Jesus.

New Creation – Jesus, who was totally different to any other human, was an amazing and unique being that God had given to us.

Christ/Messiah

Christ / Messiah – The anointed one, who is given his power by God.

The two titles of Christ and Messiah are linked. The word Messiah means 'anointed one' and comes from the Hebrew language, which is what the Jewish people spoke at the time of Jesus. When the Hebrew Scriptures were translated into Greek, the word became Christ. So when Christians refer to Jesus as Christ they are showing that they believe he was the anointed one.

We know the Jews were waiting for God to send them a messiah, so the early Christians used this title to show that they believed Jesus was the one they had been waiting for and they believed he was sent by God. He was their messiah. He had indeed saved them; saved them from sin and from death.

Therefore, this title is much more than just a name. It is a statement of what the early Christians believed Jesus to be. In ancient times kings were anointed with holy oil to show that they had been given their power by God. Calling Jesus the anointed one is saying that he had a special authority from God.

Over to You

1. Why does Jesus have many titles?
2. Which of the four titles mentioned do you think suits him best? Why?
3. If you had to think up a new title for Jesus, what would it be and why?

Section B – Key Definitions

Ancient Judaism: The history of the Jewish people, including politics, culture and religion.

Conflict with authority: The tension between Jesus and those in power, such as the Pharisees.

Discipleship: Following the call of Jesus in thought, word and deed.

Eucharist: A thanksgiving meal, which is celebrated by Christians. It is one of the sacraments in the Catholic Church.

Evangelist: One of the four Gospel writers: Matthew, Mark, Luke and John. They were people of faith.

Evidence from oral to written tradition: How information about Jesus went from the spoken to the written word.

Gospel: Stories of Jesus' life that are found in the New Testament. The word means good news.

Kingdom of God: A way of living based on Jesus' message of truth, justice, peace and love.

Martyrdom: Being willing to suffer and die for your religious beliefs.

Memorial: Something that is done to remember and honour the memory of someone or something.

Messianic expectation: The Jewish people were awaiting a messiah (a redeemer), who would free them from Roman rule and establish a new Jewish kingdom.

Miracle: An amazing event performed by Jesus that showed the power of God.

Missionary: Continuing the work of Jesus on earth.

Parable: A short story told by Jesus to teach the people about the Kingdom of God. The story is based on earth with a message about heaven.

Passover: The festival celebrated by Jews to remember the events that led them to freedom.

Pentecost: The event marking when the apostles were given the gift of the Holy Spirit.

Section B – Key Definitions

People of God:	Those who believe in God and try to carry out his will.
Presence:	Jesus' presence (existence) after the resurrection was an everlasting one.
Resurrection:	Jesus was restored to life three days after he had died.
Sacrifice:	Being willing to give up something for the sake of others.
Synoptic:	The Gospels of Matthew, Mark and Luke are called synoptic because they present or take the same point of view. They have great similarities.
Table fellowship:	Jesus chose to share his meals with all to show that God's kingdom was for everyone.
The Holy Land:	The region where Jesus lived, preached and died. At the time it was known as Palestine.
The Roman Empire:	All the lands that Rome ruled at the time of Jesus, including the Holy Land.
Transformation:	The change that occurred in Jesus after the resurrection, making him alive in a new way.
Vocation:	A calling to serve God.
Witness:	To see and give evidence about something.

SECTION C

MAJOR WORLD RELIGIONS

AIMS

- To explore the origin and teachings of Islam, Judaism, Buddhism and Hinduism

HIGHER LEVEL ONLY
- To explore the tradition, faith and practice today of Islam and Judaism.

In this chapter,
you will become
familiar with the following concepts:
- The cultural context
- The founder
- Sources of evidence
- Beliefs
- Practices and ritual events
- Place of worship
- Symbols
- Development and expansion
- Tradition, faith and practice today (HL)

Chapter 10:

Islam

Cultural context –
How people lived in a
particular place at a
particular time.

In order to understand Islam fully
we must first take a trip back in
time to look at the way things were
before this religion began. That
way we can gain an understanding
of the cultural context or situation
in which Islam was born. The
cultural context means how people
lived in that particular place at that
particular time.

Inside Mecca

Let's imagine that we are tourists in a place called Makkah/Mecca in the
year 570 CE. Our tour guide might say the following...

> Ladies and gentlemen here we are in the wonderful city of Mecca. If you
> look around at the hustle and bustle you can see that Mecca is a busy,
> commercial town. You will notice lots of trading going on and
> business people who come here to buy and sell goods. While many of the
> people here may not be able to read or write, that does not stop them
> from enjoying themselves. We can see groups of men having a drink or
> taking part in a favourite pastime, gambling.
>
> The people you see here are known as Arabs, which means nomad or
> traveller. While there are a few Jews and Christians, the majority of these
> Arabs are **polytheists**. This means that they believe in many different
> gods. Indeed Mecca is an important religious place too. You will find lots
> of **pilgrims** here. They are people who have made a special journey to
> come here for religious reasons.

If you look directly ahead, you will see the building known as the Kaaba. This is a holy shrine, which people believe was built by Abraham and his son Ishmael as the first house of prayer to God. But people worship all kinds of gods here now. In fact, there are over 300 idols worshipped inside, even though it was meant to be a place of worship to the one true God. All the different pilgrims and travellers have brought their own beliefs with them, so it's a bit mixed up at the moment!

But all these people who come to worship their different gods bring money with them and buy animals for sacrifice. So this helps to keep Mecca a rich and important place.

Unfortunately, Mecca is not the safest place to be. There are many powerful leaders and different tribes in the area and they have been known to fight among themselves. Money and power are very important to people in Mecca. So now you know the kind of place Mecca is. Any questions?

Pilgrims – People who have made a special journey for religious reasons.

Polytheists – People who believe in and worship many gods.

Over to You

1. How would you describe religious belief and practice in Mecca in the sixth century?
2. How did Mecca become a wealthy city?
3. Why was Mecca an unsafe place to be in?
4. Would you say Mecca was a nice place to live in at that time? Why/why not?

The Founder of Islam

A **founder** is a person who starts or sets up something from the very beginning. The founder of Islam was a man named **Muhammad**. When followers of Islam say the name Muhammad, they follow it with the phrase 'Peace be upon him' as a sign of respect. This is his story.

Founder – A person who starts or sets up something from the very beginning.

Muhammad

Muhammad was born in Mecca in the year 570 CE. His father died before he was born and his mother later died when he was aged six, leaving him an orphan. For two years his grandfather looked after him and when he died his uncle, a wealthy merchant, raised him. Like a lot of young men at the time, Muhammad was unable to read or write but earned a good living as a shepherd and later as a businessman. He was honest and trustworthy and people respected him.

Muhammad – The founder of Islam.

95

Revelation – A vision or dream through which God makes himself known to a person and reveals or presents information to them.

Prophet – A person called by God to receive an important message and preach it to the people.

Convert – A person who changes from one particular religion to another.

Allah – The name given to God in the Islamic faith.

Islam – The religion meaning peace by submission or obedience to the will of Allah.

Muslim – A convert to Islam, meaning someone who has accepted the message of Allah.

When he was 25 he married a wealthy widow named Khadijah, who was 15 years older than him. Together they had five children. During this time Muhammad became very unhappy with the way things were in his native city. He saw people leading very selfish lives and not following any particular religion. He began to go to a cave on Mount Hira to meditate and pray to see if he could find answers.

During the month known as Ramadan, he received a revelation from God. A revelation was a vision or dream through which God made himself known to a person and revealed or presented information to them. The Angel Gabriel appeared to Muhammad and said 'Iqraa', which means 'read'. But Muhammad was unable to read and said so. The angel repeated the command three times and Muhammad found himself reciting what the angel said.

At first Muhammad was very frightened by the experience and went home to tell his wife Khadijah about it. They later told her cousin Waraqah, an old saintly man, who told them that it was the same Angel Gabriel who had appeared to Moses. Furthermore, he told them that this meant Muhammad was a **prophet**. A prophet was a person called by God to receive an important message and preach it to the people. Khadijah became the first **convert** to Islam. A convert is a person who changes from one particular religion to another.

The angel continued to appear to Muhammad for 23 years, revealing verses in the Arabic language. The angel said **Allah** had sent him. This is the name given to God in the Islamic faith. One of the most important things that Allah told Muhammad was to tell people that they were to return to worshipping him, the one true God. Muhammad was to teach them the moral laws needed for them to live good lives. The religion became known as **Islam**, which means peace by submission or obedience to the will of Allah. The converts to Islam became known as **Muslims**, which means those who have accepted the message of Allah.

When Muhammad began to preach his message in public and invited people to join Islam, the rich powerful leaders of Mecca became angry. They did not like the way Muhammad told the people to stop worshipping idols and leading materialistic lives. In fact, the businessmen felt threatened by his preaching, as they did not want things to change. Even when they tried to bribe him to stop, Muhammad remained faithful to Allah.

Before long Muhammad and his followers began to be persecuted and tortured. In spite of this the Muslims continued to have faith. In particular, Allah asked Muhammad and the Muslims to be patient. Nevertheless, in 622 CE the local leaders decided to kill the prophet. The Angel Gabriel told Muhammad to leave Mecca and after three days he arrived in a place called Medina. This event is known as the **Hijra** (migration) and the Islamic calendar begins from this date. His

followers who lived in Mecca soon journeyed to be with him. For a long time the Muslims continued to be persecuted and many of them died in battles trying to defend themselves.

In 629 CE Muhammad and thousands of Muslims marched back into Mecca. They went peacefully to the Kabba and cleared it of all the idols. It was once again a place of worship to the one true God, Allah. Muhammad forgave all those who had persecuted the Muslims. And so the religion was established. In 632 CE Muhammad died in Medina, where he is buried. He had lived a simple and holy life.

Hijra – The event that took place in 622 CE where Muhammad and the Muslims left Mecca. The Islamic calendar begins from this date.

Over to You

1. Draw a timeline showing the major events in Muhammad's life.
2. What kind of childhood did Muhammad have?
3. Imagine you are Muhammad. Write your diary entry on the night of power.
4. Explain the following words: Muslim, Hijra, prophet.
5. You and your classmates might like to do a role play of the life of Muhammad.

Sources of Evidence

The Qur'an

The main source or place we can go to find information about Islam is the sacred text of the religion called the **Qur'an** (Koran). Muslims believe the Qur'an is the word of Allah, which was revealed to Muhammad by the Angel Gabriel. It contains all their beliefs and moral codes. It cannot be changed and has been preserved in its original form. It is a document of faith, as it contains information about what Muslims believe. It is not concerned with historical facts.

Qur'an – The sacred text of Islam, which Muslims believe is the word of Allah.

From oral to written tradition
Like many sacred texts the Qur'an began as an oral piece of work. In other words, Muhammad preached it through the spoken word. He memorised the revelations he received and preached them to the people word for word. His followers then recited the words daily in their prayers. Once a year Muhammad used to recite all the verses revealed to him by the angel to make sure it was accurate. This means that the Qur'an was the word of Allah not the word of Muhammad.

Meanwhile Muhammad instructed scribes, who were learned people, to write down the verses. This was done for two reasons:

1. To record correctly the teachings of Allah.
2. To ensure the teachings would not be lost or forgotten as time went on.

At first the verses would have been written in Arabic on palm leaves and bark. Years later they were gathered together and published in book form in many different languages.

Chapters of Qur'an

The Qur'an is made up of 114 chapters or surahs. The shortest chapter has just three verses while the longest has 286 verses. It is a book of huge importance for Muslims. Most of them learn parts of it off by heart and indeed many can recite it all. They also try to learn it as it was written, in Arabic, even if they do not speak this language.

Hafiz – A person who can recite the entire Qur'an.

A person who can recite the whole book by heart is called **Hafiz**. Muhammad himself said, 'I leave behind me two things, the Qur'an and the example of my life. If you follow these you will not fail.' As well as containing beliefs about Allah it also gives a very detailed account of how Muslims should live their lives. It even has rules about food, clothing and hygiene. An interesting fact is that Arabic is read from right to left so the Qur'an begins on what many people think is the last page, and so for English speakers it looks like it is read backwards.

Other records and sources of information

The Sunnah

The book known as the Sunnah is formed from the Hadith. The Hadith is the traditions of Muhammad. They contain his words, actions, and approvals provided by him during his life. While the Sunnah is not treated in the same way as the Qur'an, it is given great respect. Muslims look to it for guidance. They see it as a role model for how they should live their lives.

Islamic Beliefs

Every religion has core or central **beliefs**. These beliefs give the religion its identity and often affect the lives of the believers. The core beliefs of Islam can be compared to a house. As you can see the house has five pillars. These pillars give it structure and hold it together.

Beliefs – Core or central ideas of a religion, which give it its identity and often affect the lives of the believers.

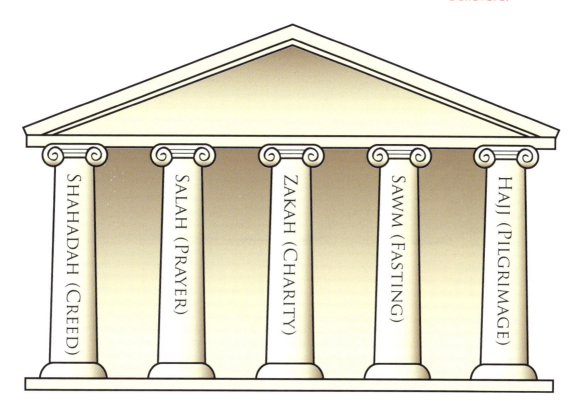

Five Pillars of Faith

1. Shahadah (Creed)
Like other major world religions Islam has a creed. Before they pray, Muslims must recite this creed. It says, 'There is only one God and Muhammad is his messenger'. In fact, devout Muslims will say the creed first thing in the morning and last thing at night. These words are part of the words whispered into the ear of newborn babies. The shahadah is very important for Muslims, as it is a declaration of their main belief. All their other beliefs and practices flow from it.

2. Salah (Prayer)
Prayer for Muslims is a way of life. Their prayer is what encourages them and supports them as they try to live the kind of life that Allah wants them to lead. Muslims are required to pray five times a day and it involves much preparation and planning. The different elements involved in prayer form a ritual.

Five Pillars of Faith –
1. Shahadah (creed)
2. Salah (prayer)
3. Zakah (charity)
4. Sawm (fasting)
5. Hajj (pilgrimage)

99

- **Wudu:** This is the washing that takes place before prayer. Muslims must ensure that they themselves are clean and also the area where they perform their prayers. Wudu consists of washing the hands, mouth and nostrils, face, arms up to the elbow, the head and neck and the feet and ankles. They remove their shoes too. As prayer involves kneeling on the ground, Muslims pray on a prayer mat, which can be brought anywhere with them.

- **Face Mecca:** Muslims must face the direction of Mecca in the southeast of Saudi Arabia when they pray. In the mosque, their place of worship, there is a niche in the wall that shows them which way to face. If they are praying at home, their prayer mat may have a compass on it so they can work out the right direction.

- **Adhan:** This is the call to prayer. When praying in the mosque or in a group this call is given when the time of prayer starts.

- **Ra'ka:** Each Muslim follows a set sequence of movements and says verses from the Qur'an to form a ra'ka, which is like a standard unit of prayer. After saying the words in the prayer the person does the following movements: fajr, zuhr, asr, magrib and isha.

Fajr

Zuhr

Asr

Magrib

Isha

The five daily prayers are:
1. **Fajr** – early morning between dawn and sunrise.
2. **Zuhr** – early afternoon when the sun is about halfway before setting.
3. **Asr** – late afternoon before sunset.
4. **Magrib** – immediately after sunset.
5. **Isha** – evening time after darkness has set in.

As we can see the movement of the sun and moon play a big part in prayer time. Because of this, the time for prayer will change slightly, depending on the time of year. For example in Ireland, the sun rises earlier in the summer months, so fajr will be earlier than in the winter.

3. Zakah (Charity)
The idea behind this pillar is to share the wealth that Allah has blessed you with. It also purifies whatever wealth you are lucky enough to have. The act of giving is a prayer in itself. Many Muslims pay the zakah during the month of **Ramadan**. They may give it to their local mosque who will distribute it amongst the poor and needy. Each Muslim gives 2½ per cent of their annual savings provided they reach a certain minimum. This means it is a fair system and people only give what they can afford.

4. Sawm (Fasting)
Fasting or abstaining from food and drink at particular times is a characteristic of many religions. In Islam this fasting takes place during the month of **Ramadan**. This event each year is a time for Muslims to concentrate on their faith. Every Muslim who is well and has reached puberty is expected to take part. It is not just about food, though. It is a time for Muslims to increase their efforts to live good lives. They pray more during this time and read the Qur'an.

Ramadan – The month of fasting in Islam.

Because Islam follows a lunar calendar the time of Ramadan moves forward by about 11 days every year. Muslims eat a light breakfast before dawn and then a light meal after sunset. If they miss a day of fasting for some reason, they are expected to make it up another day. Elderly or people with chronic diseases who cannot fast will instead provide a meal for a poor person.

101

Hajj – A pilgrimage to Mecca that every Muslim should make once in their lifetime, if they are able.

5. Hajj (Pilgrimage)

The **Hajj** is a pilgrimage to Mecca that every Muslim should try to make once in their lifetime, if they are able. Muslims come from all over the world to pray to Allah and to remember their prophet Muhammad. The Hajj takes place during the 12th month of the Islamic calendar. It is a time when all Muslims are truly united despite their differences – rich and poor, male and female, young and old – and are seen as equals. To show this equality all pilgrims wear a simple white dress called an **ihram.**

Fatima and Family Go on the Hajj

The following is an interview with a young Muslim girl called Fatima who went on pilgrimage with her family.

Q: Fatima, why was going on the Hajj so important for you?

A: Obviously, it is important because it is one of the pillars of my faith. I also wanted to meet other Muslims and show my great love for Allah.

Q: What happens when you get there?

A: Well, there is a series of different events that take place. We begin in Mecca at the Great Mosque. We walk around the Kaaba seven times and say prayers. Some lucky people get to touch it but we were too far away. Remember there are over two million pilgrims there, so it's quite crowded!

Q: So what happens next?

A: We then walk seven times between two hills called Safa and Marwa.

Q: Why do you do this?

A: We do this because Hagar, Abraham's second wife and mother of his son Ishmael, ran along the same path searching for water. The Angel Gabriel then appeared to her and led her to a spring of water. This is now called the well of Zam Zam. This part of the pilgrimage symbolises the search for that which gives true life.

Q: You must be tired after all that. Do you take a day of rest then?

A: No, we don't. We travel to Mina which is a village four miles east of Mecca. We camp here and pray together. The following day we go to the plain of Arafat. This faces the Mount of Mercy where Muhammad gave his last sermon. Here we spend the day of standing. We stand and pray from noon until sundown.

Q: That must have been very difficult?

A: It was hard but it was well worth it. Seeing all those people standing and praying together to Allah was an amazing sight. It made me feel part of something very special.

Q: It sounds amazing. I'd love to see it myself.

A: Unfortunately, I'm afraid you can't. You see, only Muslims are allowed into Mecca for the pilgrimage.

Q: I didn't know that. So what happens then?

A: That evening we begin the return journey to Mecca. We stop at a place called Muzdalifah, where we pray and collect pebbles for the next day.

Q: What do you need pebbles for?

A: We go to Mina the following day and use the pebbles to throw at the three pillars of Satan. The pillars represent the three times Abraham and his son were tempted to disobey God. Throwing the stones symbolises our own struggle against evil. While there, we also offer an animal sacrifice like a goat or a sheep. This represents the sacrifice Abraham was willing to make for God: his own son. We then give the meat to the poor, which I think is a nice gesture.

Q: Is this the end of the pilgrimage?

A: Not quite. We then travel 200 miles to Medina where we pray at Muhammad's burial place. Finally, we return to Mecca and circle the Kaaba one last time. All in all, our pilgrimage lasted about two weeks. It was a wonderful experience and it really helped to strengthen my faith.

Over to You
Crossword

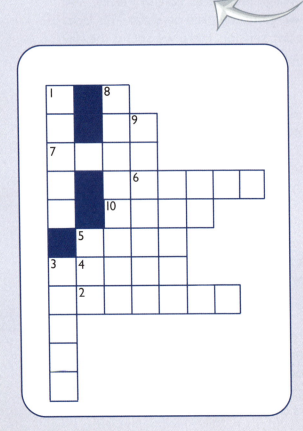

1 (down): The sacred text of Islam.
2 (across): A collection of Muhammad's words and actions.
3 (down): Muslims say this in the morning and the evening.
4 (across): Muslims must do this five times a day.
5 (across): The washing that takes place before praying.
6 (across): Where Muslims face when they pray.
7 (across): These words and actions make up a Muslim prayer.
8 (down): A Muslim pays this every year to charity.
9 (down): The month during which Muslims fast.
10 (across): The yearly pilgrimage.

Answers at end of chapter, on page 111.

1. Design a brochure for Muslim pilgrims going on the Hajj. Include a calendar of events and any information you think they might need. You might like to do this in groups.

Practices and Ritual Events

Rite of Passage – The events used to mark a persons journey through life

Rites of passage

1. Birth

When a Muslim baby is born the words of the Islamic creed, the Shahadah, are among the words whispered into the baby's ear. This is so that the first words the baby hears are those of Allah. Seven days later the naming ceremony takes place. An animal is sacrificed as a sign of thanks to Allah. Muslim boys are circumcised any time after the naming ceremony. Circumcision is when the foreskin of a boy's penis is removed.

2. Death

After Muslims die their bodies are washed. They are then dressed in white robes and buried as soon as possible. They are laid to rest on their right side facing Mecca. Special funeral prayers are said. Muslims believe that when they die they will go to either heaven or hell, depending on the kind of life they lived.

Festivals and celebration

A festival is a special time set aside by a religion to celebrate a certain aspect of the religion, in a particular way. Islam has two festivals. They relate to two aspects of Islam faith that we have already looked at: the Hajj and Ramadan.

Festival – A special time set aside by a religion to celebrate a certain aspect of the religion, in a particular way.

Eid al-Adha and Eid al-Fitr

The two festivals are called **Eid al-Adha** and **Eid al-Fitr**. The word Eid is Arabic and means 'a day which returns often'.

	Eid al-Adha	Eid al-Fitr
When	The day after Muslim pilgrims stop and pray on the plain of Arafat, during the 12th month of the Islamic calendar	The first day of the month of Shawal at the end of Ramadan
Why	It remembers Abraham's willingness to sacrifice his son for Allah. Allah accepted a lamb as a symbol of Abraham's devotion	It is used as an occasion to thank Allah for supporting muslims during Ramadan. It is a joyful festival celebrated by all
How	There are early morning communal prayers. The imam gives a sermon recalling the story of Abraham and his family. An animal is sacrificed as a symbol of the Muslims' obedience to Allah. The meat is shared between the family and the poor. The festival lasts for three days	There is early morning prayer in the mosque. Everyone attends wearing their best clothes. A small amount of money is paid by those who can afford it during Ramadan. This is given to the poor so they can join in the celebrations. Families and friends visit each other's homes. Children are given gifts and sweets. The festival lasts for three days

Imam – The leader of an Islamic community.

Islamic Place of Worship

Mosque – The Islamic place of worship.

The Islamic place of worship is called the **mosque**. Mosques come in all shapes and sizes but they all have certain characteristics in common.

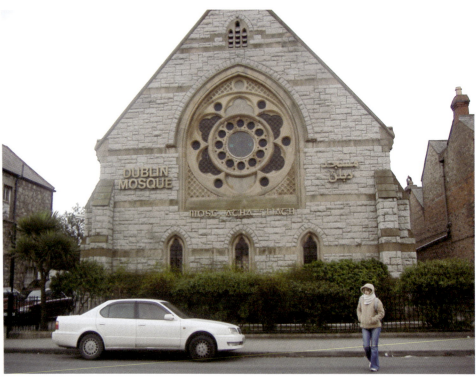

1. Mosques have no seats. This is because they need the space to perform their ra'kas. Instead the floor is covered with thick carpet or prayer mats. There may be bookshelves to hold copies of the Qur'an.

2. Everyone must remove their shoes before entering the mosque. This is to ensure that the place of prayer remains clean. It is also a sign of respect. Because of this, mosques have shoe racks just inside the door.

3. There are no pictures or statues in a mosque. This is because it is forbidden to worship anyone but Allah. As no one knows what Allah looks like, no images are allowed. Instead you will see beautiful geometric patterns and mosaics.

4. Each mosque has a niche in the wall called a **mihrab**. This indicates the direction of Mecca so people know which way to face when they pray.

5. There is a pulpit which is used by the imam to lead the prayers and give sermons.

6. A mosque has two separate areas. There is usually a gallery where the women pray. Men and women pray separately.

7. Mosques provide an area for wudu so Muslims can carry out the ritual washing before they pray.

8. Some mosques have a tower called a minaret from which the people are called to prayer.

Muslim men must attend the mosque on Friday as it is their holy day. They pray the noon prayers together and hear a sermon from the imam. However, if there is no mosque nearby, Muslims can perform their prayers anywhere.

Islamic Symbols

The history of Islam means that there are no symbols allowed. Remember that Muhammad cleared the Kaaba of symbols to idol Gods. This was to ensure that his followers were monotheistic, that is, they worshipped only one God. However, there is one symbol that can be seen on the top of mosques. This is the crescent moon. It symbolises the fact that Islam follows a lunar calendar. The five points of the star also represent the five pillars of Islam.

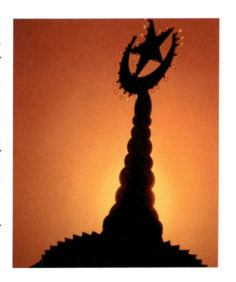

Development and Expansion of Islam

Caliph – The chief Muslim civil and religious leader. Also, the successor to Muhammad.

We have already looked at the story of Muhammad and how he established the Islamic religion. But how did the religion develop after this?

As we know the first followers of Islam suffered great persecution and hardship. They were forced to emigrate from Mecca to Abyssina, which is known as Ethiopia today. After Muhammad's death his close friend Abu Bakr took over the leadership and became the first **caliph.** He in turn handed leadership over to the second caliph called Omar. Omar was a great military leader and under his rule Islam began to spread to other countries.

By 650 CE Omar had led the Islamic army and conquered places such as Syria, Palestine and Egypt. In later years Islam also spread to places like Greece, France and Spain. Another reason for this was that Islamic travellers and merchants brought their new beliefs to the places they visited. People were impressed by what they heard about this new religion and Islam won many converts. That is why there are large Muslim communities in places all over the world today.

Schism

Schism – A split or a divide in a religion.

A **schism** means a split or a divide in a religion. Many world religions have experienced this in their history. The schism in Islam resulted in two main groups: the **Sunni** and the **Shi'a**. This split happened in 655 CE after Muhammad's death when a disagreement arose about leadership.

Shi'a – A group of Muslims who believe that anyone who takes over leadership after Muhammad must come from the same family as him.

The smaller of the two groups, the Shi'a Muslims, believe that anyone who takes over leadership after Muhammad must come from the same family as him. This leader can then interpret the Qur'an and its teachings in whatever way he sees fit.

Sunni – A group of Muslims who believe that the only true leadership comes from the Qur'an itself and how it has been interpreted by scholars.

The larger group, the Sunni, believe that the only true leadership comes from the Qur'an itself and how it has been interpreted by scholars.

Where in the world?

In the counties shown on the map the majority of the people living there are Muslims.

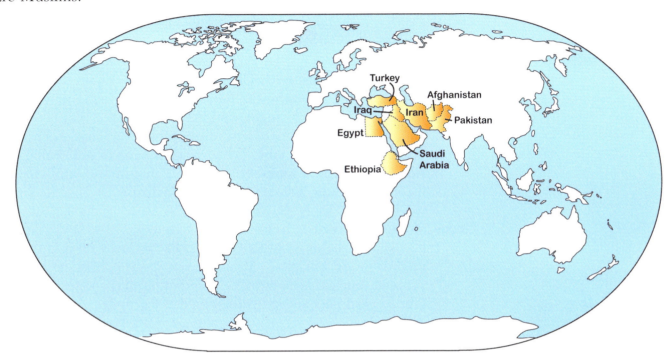

Muslims in Ireland

Ireland has seen a large increase in the number of Muslims living here in the last 10 years. This is due to many different reasons. Some Muslims have come from war-torn countries to seek refuge, while others are students who have come here to study. Some have come in order to seek jobs and are later joined by their families. While we do not know the exact number of Muslims living in Ireland today, it is thought to be over 10,000.

The Muslim population in Ireland has settled in well. They quickly set up a mosque on the South Circular Road in Dublin to cater for Muslims living here. As their numbers grew, a large mosque and cultural centre was built in the suburb of Clonskeagh. It is here that you will find the first Muslim primary school in Dublin.

Tradition, Faith and Practice of Islam Today

To compare two things means to look at what they have in common and also the differences between them. Islam has much in common with Christianity.

Some of the similarities with Christianity are:
1. They are both monotheistic faiths – they believe in one God.
2. They both believe in angels and life after death.
3. They have the same prophets, for example, Abraham and Moses.
4. Prayer, fasting and charity are important parts of both religions.
5. Both religions encourage love of neighbour and try to incorporate their beliefs into their daily lives.

Some of the differences between the two are:
1. Christianity believes Jesus Christ is the son of God and that he died for our salvation. Muslims see Jesus Christ as a great prophet, but see Muhammad as God's final and greatest prophet. Christians do not accept Muhammad as a prophet of God in their religion.
2. Islam does not accept the doctrine of the Trinity as part of its own faith, whereas it is one of the central beliefs of Christianity.

Haram – Things that are forbidden in Islam.

Halal – Meat that has been prepared in a certain way, so as to allow all the blood to drain out of the animal.

Lifestyle: food and clothes

The lifestyle of a Muslim is very much affected by their religious beliefs. We have seen already how their day is centred on their prayer rituals. This is different to other religions that do not have strict rules about praying. Muslims also follow strict rules concerning food and clothes.

In Islam certain things are considered **haram** which means they are forbidden. For example, a Muslim will not drink alcohol as it is haram. Certain foods are also haram such as pork. A Muslim must eat food which is **halal.** Halal meat is meat that has been slaughtered in a certain way so as to allow all the blood to drain out of the animal. A prayer must be said before an animal is slaughtered in order for it to be halal.

When it comes to clothes, men and women are expected to dress modestly and simply. So we can see that the lifestyle of a Muslim is very much influenced by their religion and is different in many ways to followers of other religions.

Over to You

Write a paragraph entitled 'A day in the life of a Muslim'.

Community structure

Islam is very different to Christianity in relation to community structure. In Christianity there are definite leaders in the community. For example, in Catholicism there is the Pope, cardinals, bishops and priests. These men are not allowed to marry and must take special vows. In Islam the leader of the community is called the **imam**.

Any Muslim man can become an imam as long as he leads a good Muslim life. They are usually very learned men, especially knowledgeable about the Qur'an. They are elected by the community and their main role is to lead the prayers in the community and help them understand their faith better. The imam of the mosque in South Circular Road is Yahya M Al-Hussein.

Yahya M Al-Hussein

Dialogue

The Islamic religion has much in common with the Christian religion as we have seen. Since coming to Ireland the two communities have worked hard at building a relationship based on respect and understanding. They have come together at times of importance such as 9/11 to pray to one God. They have sent leaders to visit each other's place of worship. They have also worked on educational programmes together. Both religions are eager to live in harmony through dialogue.

Over to You - Exam Style Question

Write an essay on Islam for your school magazine under the following headings: place of worship, prayer and sacred text.

Answers to the crossword on page 104.

1. Quran
2. Sunnah
3. Creed
4. Pray
5. Wudu

6. Mecca
7. Ra'ka
8. Zakah
9. Ramadan
10. Hajj.

Summary of Islam

Cultural context – How people lived in a particular place at a particular time.

Pilgrims – People who have made a special journey for religious reasons.

Polytheists – People who believe in and worship many gods.

Founder – A person who starts or sets up something from the very beginning.

Muhammad – The founder of Islam.

Revelation – A vision or dream through which God makes himself known to a person and reveals or presents information to them.

Prophet – A person called by God to receive an important message and preach it to the people.

Convert – A person who changes from one particular religion to another.

Allah – The name given to God in the Islamic faith.

Islam – The religion meaning peace by submission or obedience to the will of Allah.

Muslim – A convert to Islam, meaning someone who has accepted the message of Allah.

Hijra – The event that took place in 622 CE where Muhammad and the Muslims left Mecca. The Islamic calendar begins from this date.

Qur'an – The sacred text of Islam, which Muslims believe is the word of Allah.

Hafiz – A person who can recite the entire Qur'an.

Beliefs – Core or central ideas of a religion, which give it its identity and often affect the lives of the believers.

Five Pillars of Faith –
1. Shahadah (creed)
2. Salah (prayer)
3. Zakah (charity)
4. Sawm (fasting)
5. Hajj (pilgrimage)

Ramadan – The month of fasting in Islam.

Hajj – A pilgrimage to Mecca that every Muslim should make once in their lifetime, if they are able.

Rite of Passage – The events used to mark a person's journey through life.

Festival – A special time set aside by a religion to celebrate a certain aspect of the religion, in a particular way.

Imam – The leader of an Islamic community.

Mosque – The Islamic place of worship.

Caliph – The chief Muslim civil and religious leader. Also, the successor to Muhammad.

Schism - A split or a divide in a religion.

Shi'a – A group of Muslims who believe that anyone who takes over leadership after Muhammad must come from the same family as him.

Sunni – A group of Muslims who believe that the only true leadership comes from the Qur'an itself and how it has been interpreted by scholars.

Haram – Things that are forbidden in Islam.

Halal – Meat that has been prepared in a certain way, so as to allow all the blood to drain out of the animal.

Chapter 11:

Judaism

The Cultural Context

Monotheistic – A religion in which people believe and worship only one God.

Judaism is the oldest **monotheistic** world religion. It is known as the 'parent' religion of Christianity and Islam. The three religions have much in common but Judaism has many distinctive features of its own. The Jewish religion has a rich and interesting history which is very important to its followers. To understand the religion fully we must go back in time and delve into this history.

Polytheistic – A religion in which people believe and worship many Gods.

Hebrews – The name by which the Jewish people were known when they lived in Israel before the birth of Judaism.

Judaism began about 4,000 years ago in the land we now call Israel. At that time the Jewish people were known as **Hebrews**. They were a nomadic people, which meant that they travelled from place to place and made their living by farming and trading. The Hebrews were monotheistic but were influenced by **polytheistic** nations. The polytheistic nations worshipped many Gods. These Gods were often related to the natural world, so that the people worshipped a God of rain, sun, water, etc. There were many powerful nations, such as the Mesopotamians, the Babylonians and the Egyptians, who ruled in the Middle East at this time.

Founders of Judaism

Abram

Covenant – A special agreement between God and his people.

The story of Judaism begins with a man called **Abram**. Abram and his wife Sarah lived in a place called Haran. Though they had no children, they led a very comfortable and happy life. However, Abram believed that there was only one God and at the age of 75 this God spoke to him. The outcome was that God and Abram made a **covenant**. This was a special agreement between God and his people.

113

Promised Land – The place in Canaan chosen by God, which was to be the home of the Jewish people.

The first thing that God asked Abram to do was to leave his home and travel to a land called Canaan. This place was to be called the **Promised Land**. God said that if Abram and the Hebrews travelled to this land he would give Abram many descendants, in other words, children and grandchildren. This seemed very unlikely as Abram and Sarah were well past the age of starting a family!

However, God said: 'I will make a covenant with you. I will be your God. I will defend you and protect you. I will make your descendants as numerous as the stars in the sky. You, for your part, will be faithful to me. Your people will be obedient to my laws and follow my commands.'

Abram was faithful and obedient to God and set out on a difficult journey that would last many years. But God was true to his word and Abram and Sarah had a son called Isaac. When Isaac was a young boy, Abram believed that God wanted him to sacrifice his only son. To show his trust in God he was prepared to do it. But at the last minute God told him to stop and Abraham sacrificed a ram instead.

Patriarch – A founding father. Abraham was the first patriarch.

This act showed two things. First, that Abram was completely obedient and faithful to his God. Second, it tells us that God did not want human sacrifices but obedience and trust from his followers. After this Abram became known as Abraham, which means 'father of many nations'. Jewish people look to Abraham as the **patriarch**, which means 'founding father'. To show this covenant between God and his people, Jewish males are circumcised. This is where the foreskin of a boy's penis is removed. It is a small straight-forward procedure. The Jewish faith had begun.

Over to You

1. Judaism is the parent religion of _____ and _____.
2. When and where did Judaism begin?
3. What does nomadic mean?
4. What is a covenant?
5. Describe the covenant made between Abraham and God.
6. How did Abraham show that he trusted in God?
7. What does patriarch mean?

Development of the Jewish Tradition

All religions have key people in their story. These people help to shape the story of the religion. One of the most important stages in the Jewish story concerns a man named Moses.

Moses

Abraham's family continued to grow as God had promised. His grandson Jacob had 12 sons whose families became the Twelve Tribes of Israel. When the land was struck by famine Jacob took his family to the land of Egypt. After many years the fortunes of the Israelites changed and they became slaves to their Egyptian masters. Under the cruel leaders of Egypt called Pharaohs, they suffered great hardship.

Moses was a Jew who earned a living as a shepherd. One day he saw a bush that appeared to be on fire. As he got closer he realised that even though the bush was on fire it was not actually burning. Suddenly, he heard God's voice speaking to him. God told him that he was to go and help the Jewish people. At first Moses was frightened and unsure if he was able to do what God asked. However, he was a man of great faith, so he set off to see the Pharaoh.

Once in the presence of the Pharaoh, Moses asked him to let the Jewish people go so that they could return to the Promised Land given to them by God. Without hesitation, the Pharaoh refused.

Wanting to show the people that Moses was chosen by him to help them, God sent 10 plagues on Egypt. A plague was a terrible event indeed. They included swarms of locusts and hailstorms that ruined all the crops. Still the Pharaoh refused to free the Jews. Finally, God sent the last and the most terrible plague. An angel of death passed over each house in Egypt killing the firstborn son. The Jews were told to sacrifice a lamb and smear the blood on their doors so that the angel would know they were Jews and pass over their houses.

After this plague the Pharaoh agreed to let the Jews go. Led by Moses they set off but were soon chased by the Egyptian army. The Pharaoh had changed his mind. When they got to the Red Sea, God parted the waters allowing them to pass through. This event became known as the **Exodus** and is one of the most important moments in the history of the Jewish religion.

Exodus – When Moses led the Jewish slaves out of Egypt to Mount Sinai. This is one of the most important events in the history of Judaism.

After that Moses travelled on with the Jews to Mount Sinai. There he received the Torah. This gave details about how God wanted his people to live. The well-known Ten Commandments were part of the **Torah.** This was the second covenant that God had made with his chosen people, the Jews.

For the next 40 years the Jewish people struggled to keep their covenant with God. At times they doubted him but he was always present in their hour of need. In this way they learned to trust him and realised the importance of keeping their promises to him. Their great leader Moses died before they reached the Promised Land. He is still a great role model today for Jewish people.

Over to You

Imagine you are Moses. Write a series of diary entries describing the most important events of your life and how you felt at those times.

Kings of Israel: Saul, David and Solomon

The Israelites finally settled in their Promised Land. However, they constantly had to defend it from foreign invaders who wanted to take control of it. They realised that as long as they remained faithful to their covenant with God, then he would give them the power to defeat their enemies. In order to help them God sent them leaders called judges. In 1020 BCE they got their first king, Saul. It was King Saul who helped them unite all the different tribes of Israel.

David slays Goliath

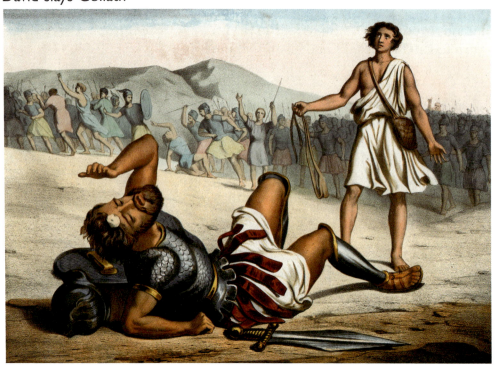

However, the greatest king of Israel was King David. He made Jerusalem the capital city and his son, King Solomon, built the first temple there, so that the people could worship their God. But this stability did not last and the kingdom eventually split in two with Israel in the north and Judah in the south. Gradually, the people began to forget their covenant with God. Soon they worshipped other Gods and failed to follow the Ten Commandments. But once again God sent them help.

The prophets

A **Prophet** is a person called by God to receive an important message and preach it to the people. They were like God's spokespeople. They reminded the Jews of their promise to God and warned that if they did not remain true to the covenant, then they would face disaster. Two of the most famous prophets were Jeremiah and Isaiah.

Over to You

Using a Bible, find the story of either the prophet Jeremiah or Isaiah. Write a report on your chosen prophet detailing how he became a prophet, what God asked him to do, and what message he preached to the people.

The exile

In 586 BCE the Babylonians conquered Jerusalem, the capital city of Judah. In the conflict, the temple was destroyed and many of the Israelites were taken into slavery. Once more they turned to their God for strength and support. As the temple was no longer there, they worshipped in their homes instead. The words of the prophets soon came back to them and they knew that they must return to the covenant.

Rabbi – A religious leader in the Jewish faith, also called a scribe.

After many years the people were allowed to return home from exile. They were overjoyed and built a new temple to thank and pray to their God. The law given to them in the Torah became the most important thing for them. To help them live how God wanted, they made new laws. Their religious leaders became known as scribes or **rabbis**.

In 63 BCE the Romans gained control of the Promised Land. The Jews were allowed to continue practising their own religion, but in 70 CE their temple was destroyed once more. This time the Jews began to disperse and set up new communities in the Middle East and Europe. Wherever they went they took their faith with them and tried to remain God's chosen people, the people of the covenant.

Over to You

Draw a timeline which shows the main events in the Jewish history.

Sources of Evidence

Every religion has important books or writings. These are known as sacred texts. They often tell the story of the religion or offer guidance on how the people of that religion should live their lives. They are described as documents of faith, as they are more concerned with meaning than with fact. The Jewish religion has several sacred texts that provide us with information about the religion.

The Tenakh

Tenakh – The name Jewish people give to the Hebrew Bible.

The Jewish Bible is known in Hebrew as the **Tenakh**. It contains three books:
1. The Torah (Pentateuch)
2. The Nevi'im (Prophets)
3. The Ketuvim (Holy Writings)

The Torah

The Torah is the most important sacred text for Jewish people. It consists of the first five books of the Old Testament, that is, the books of Moses (also called the Pentateuch). In them we find the history of the Jews from creation, God's covenant with Abraham, Moses and the Exodus from Egypt, etc. and their moral and legal codes.

The word Torah can also include the whole body of holy teachings that explain the Bible and guide Jews in their daily lives. These teachings are known as the **Oral Torah** or **Talmud.**

From oral to written tradition

Like most sacred texts the Jewish holy writings did not just appear overnight. They are the result of a long process, which begins with the spoken word. The history and beliefs of the Jewish people were first passed down from generation to generation through the spoken word. Eventually, people began to write it down so that it would not be lost or changed.

It is believed by some Jews that the Torah was written not just by one author but by many different people because it contains different styles of writing and some repetition.* The majority of the text is written in Hebrew. Today when any part of the Torah is being copied for use in worship, a trained scribe must write it in Hebrew. It is written on scrolls as shown in the picture.

* Orthodox Jews believe that the entire Torah is the word of God written by Moses.

The Torah is seen as being so sacred that it cannot be touched. It is held on scrolls and a special pointer stick used to read from it. The scrolls can be stored in a wooden case or are sometimes covered with beautifully embroidered cloth.

The Torah contains the 613 mitzvot or rules that were given to Moses on Mount Sinai. Included in these are the Ten Commandments, which we shall look at in more detail later.

Oral Torah

If the teachings of the Torah are difficult to understand, there are other sacred writings that help to explain them. After the written Torah appeared, people began to discuss what it meant and how it could be applied to their everyday lives. These discussions became known as the **Oral Torah** or Oral Law. They include the following sacred texts:

Oral Torah – Discussions on the written Torah that are contained in three texts: the Mishah, the Talmud and the Midrash.

1. **The Mishnah:** This is a written analysis of the Torah. It was written in 200 CE. In it there are instructions on how to deal with issues like marriage, divorce, legal matters and trade. It was put together by important scholars and rabbis of the time.
2. **The Talmud:** This is made up of ideas and stories from Jewish teachers and rabbis over a period of 800 years. They help the people to understand how to apply the old laws to new problems and are full of wise sayings.
3. **The Midrash:** These are writings which use examples from everyday life to help explain difficult parts of the Torah.

Up for Discussion

See if you can explain to your partner the different Jewish sacred writings. Make sure they tell you if you make a mistake!

Jewish Beliefs

Rites and rituals – Words or actions that are performed by Jews in a special way at a certain time.

Every religion has main or core beliefs which are at the centre of their faith. These beliefs are often expressed and remembered by the people through **rites and rituals**. These are words or actions that they perform in a special way at a certain time. The Jewish people's main beliefs can be summed up as following:

1. **Monotheism** – There is one, almighty, powerful God.
2. **Identity** – The Jews believe that they are God's chosen people.
3. **Covenant** – Jews must remain true to the covenants made with God through Abraham and Moses.

These beliefs affect the way in which Jewish people live their lives. Jews believe that they should remember God in everything they do and must always thank God for the good things in their life and accept the bad things.

Main beliefs of Judaism –
1. **Monotheism** – there is one, almighty, powerful God.
2. **Identity** – they are God's chosen people.
3. **Covenant** – they must remain true to the covenants made with God through Abraham and Moses.

Practices and Ritual Events

The best way to understand the rites and rituals of Judaism is to follow the life of a typical Jewish person from their birth up until their death.

Rites of passage

Rites of passage – Special ways of celebrating the important moments in life.

David was born into a Jewish family. People who are religious have special ways of celebrating the important moments in life. These celebrations are called **rites of passage**. For David's family his birth is a very special occasion. They want to thank God for his safe arrival.

Covenant of Circumcision

Eight days after he is born a special ceremony takes place called the **Covenant of Circumcision**. It is a sign that David is entering into the same covenant with God that Abraham did. It is a minor medical procedure carried out by a Jewish doctor. The foreskin at the tip of the boy's penis is removed.

David is brought to the synagogue, the Jewish place of worship, and his father says a special blessing over him after the operation takes place. He is then given a Hebrew name as well as an English one. His Hebrew name will be used at other religious occasions throughout his life. Afterwards there is a party. When David's sister Anne was born there was a special naming ceremony too.

Covenant of circumcision – This is a special ceremony that takes place when a newborn baby boy is circumcised as a sign that he is entering into the same covenant with God that Abraham did.

Bar Mitzvah

The next rite of passage that David will experience is his **Bar Mitzvah**. At 13 years old he is seen as an adult in his faith. The term Bar Mitzvah means 'son of the commandment'. David will have studied hard for this special day. He will wear the tallit, which is the prayer robe or shawl worn by Jews during morning prayer. He will also learn how to put on the tefillin. These are the two leather boxes containing biblical verses worn on the head and arm.

Bar Mitzvah – A ritual that occurs when a Jewish boy is seen as an adult in his faith. It means 'son of the commandment'.

David is called up in the synagogue to read from the Torah for the first time. He will have studied this beforehand as it is read in Hebrew! As he goes up to the bimah, David's father says a blessing. After the ceremony there is usually a big party for family and friends. He is now old enough to take part fully in all aspects of his faith. When David's sister Anne was 12 she celebrated her **Bat Mitzvah**. This means 'daughter of the commandment'. She learned about her special role as a woman in Jewish ceremonies.

Marriage: Kiddushin

At the age of 27 David has decided to get married. His wife-to-be Ruth is also Jewish. In Hebrew, marriage is called **kiddushin**, which means 'holy', as Jews believe marriage is holy. Before the wedding ceremony takes place, David signs a marriage contract called the **ketubah**. In it he promises to take care of Ruth.

Kiddushin – The Hebrew name for marriage.

The ceremony may take place in the synagogue but can also take place outside. It happens under a **huppah** or canopy. The canopy is a symbol of the couple's home but is open on all four sides to show how David and Ruth are connected to the rest of the community.

Seven blessings are said or sung. David and Ruth then take a sip of wine from the same glass. Next David places a ring on Ruth's finger and reads out the promises he has made in the ketubah. David then takes the wine glass and wraps it in a cloth. He places it on the floor and stamps on it. This symbolises the destruction of the temple in Jerusalem. It reminds everyone that life is fragile and there will be bad times as well as good. At this point all the guests shout, 'Mazal tov!' which means 'Good Luck!' After the ceremony there is a wedding reception. The main emphasis on marriage in Judaism is commitment.

Death: Shiva, Sheloshin and Yahrzeit

Death is a part of life that everyone must face. Our religion can help us to deal with this by marking it in a special way. The death of a Jewish person is surrounded by rituals and there are three stages of mourning.

When David dies, his funeral will take place within 24 hours of his death to allow the grieving to begin. Jewish people believe in expressing their feelings. When they hear of his death, David's family make small tears in their clothes as a sign of their grief. David's body is washed and wrapped in a plain linen shroud and in his tallit. The funeral ceremony is short. After a few prayers and a speech the burial takes place. The **Kaddish** is said, which is a special prayer of mourning.

For the next week David's family sit **shiva**, which means seven. Friends and family will come to David's house to pray and mourn with his family. His family sit on low stools that symbolise they are brought low by grief. Friends bring food and do anything else that needs to be done, so that the family can concentrate on mourning.

For the next month there is **sheloshim**, which means thirty. Male mourners visit the synagogue every day and recite the Kaddish. The third stage is **yahrzeit**, which means year time. The gravestone is erected. A special candle is lit and prayers are said for David. Whenever David's family visit the grave, they place small stones on it as Abraham did this for his wife Sarah.

Kaddish – A special prayer for mourning said by Jewish people.

Shiva, Sheloshim and Yahrzeit – The three stages of Jewish mourning. Shiva is the first seven days of mourning; sheloshim the first 30 days after the burial; and yahrzeit the first 12 months after the death.

Up for Discussion

1. What are the three main beliefs at the centre of Judaism?
2. What happens at the covenant of circumcision and why?
3. What ceremony takes place to mark a Jewish person's entry into adulthood?
4. Describe the different stages involved in a Jewish wedding.
5. Imagine you are a Jewish person. A family member has died. What happens?

Festivals and special times

Birthdays, bank holidays, weddings, graduations – these are all days that are different in some way to other days of the week. We usually mark them in some way. We may take a day off work or school, have a special meal or a party, or get together with friends and family.

Religions too have special times that are set apart as different or special. These are known as sacred times. This means they are holy. They are celebrated for different reasons and in different ways. Judaism has several sacred times and festivals. The chart below outlines three of the most important ones: Passover, Hanukkah and Yom Kippur.

	Passover	Hanukkah	Yom Kippur
When	One week in the spring	Eight days in December	One day in September
Why	To celebrate the Israelites' escape from slavery in Egypt at the time of Moses	To celebrate the victory over enemies who had made the temple unclean by bringing in idols. Temple lights were relit and the temple was fit again for worship	A time of repentance. The high priest prays to God to ask him to forgive the sins of the people
How	Families have a seder meal at which the story of the Exodus is read. Certain foods are eaten which represent parts of the story, e.g. bitter herbs recall the bitterness of slavery	One candle is lit each day until all eight are lighting together. Special foods are eaten and gifts are exchanged	For 10 days people think about what they have done wrong in the past year. Then they fast for 25 hours and go to the synagogue to pray for forgiveness

Prayer and practice

As we know already Jews believe that they should think of God in everything they do. So their religion affects their lives in many ways. Jews can pray anywhere and at any time. One of the most important times of prayer is at the weekend and it takes place in the family home and in the synagogue.

1. Shabbat (Jewish Sabbath)

This time of rest and prayer begins on a Friday evening at sunset and ends at the same time the following day. The importance of the family unit can be seen at this event. It is celebrated because in the Torah we are told that after God's work of creation he rested. His people were told to keep the Sabbath day holy and to use this day to rest and remember God. It is observed in the following way:

1. Before Shabbat begins the family clean the house and prepare all the food in advance. This is because no work of any kind is done once Shabbat begins, not even cooking.
2. The table will be set with the best tablecloth and dishes. The mother of the family lights two candles and says a special prayer to begin the Shabbat.
3. The father blesses the children and says the **kiddush** (blessing) over a cup of wine. The meal begins.

4. On the table are two plaited loaves of bread. These remind Jews of the manna or special bread that God provided them with while they were in the desert after escaping slavery in Egypt. Songs are sung between the different courses of the meal.

5. On Saturday morning there is a service in the synagogue when sections of the Torah are read.

6. When Shabbat is over on Saturday evening there is **havdalah**. This marks the separation of rest and work. It begins with the lighting of a plaited candle.

7. A box of sweet spices is passed around. This is a symbol of hope for good things to come during the week.

8. Everyone wishes each other 'Shavua Tov!', which means 'Have a good week!'

2. At the synagogue

Prayer also takes place in the synagogue and Jews are required to attend whenever possible. There are three services a day; in the morning, afternoon and evening. The services are short. The **Shema** is read – this is a prayer taken from the Book of Deuteronomy. It is the most important prayer in Judaism.

The Torah is also read. In order for there to be a public service in the synagogue there must be 10 adult males present. Any male over the age of 13 may lead the service so long as he can read Hebrew. Most Jews use a prayer book called a **siddur**. This has prayers that they can use at home or in the synagogue.

Shema – The most important prayer in Judaism.

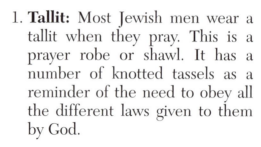

Other customs and practices

There are other elements to being a Jewish person. Like every religion there are certain customs or practices they follow.

1. **Tallit:** Most Jewish men wear a tallit when they pray. This is a prayer robe or shawl. It has a number of knotted tassels as a reminder of the need to obey all the different laws given to them by God.

2. **Kippah:** A kippah is a cap that Jews wear for prayer. They cover their heads as a sign of respect. Orthodox Jews wear the kippah at all times.

3. **Tefillin:** Tefillin are small leather boxes that contain tiny scrolls. The shema prayer and other passages of the Torah are written on the scrolls and they wear them on their head and arm, pointing to the head and heart. This is to remind them to serve God in heart and mind in all they do.

4. **Kosher food:** The word kosher means clean and pure. The rules about kosher food come from the Torah. Jews obey them as an act of obedience to God. Foods such as pork and shellfish are not kosher. For meat to be kosher it must be slaughtered in a certain way. Meat and dairy products are not eaten together either. In some places there are kosher food shops, which make it easier for Jews to follow their dietary rules.

Kosher food – Food that is clean and pure, and meat that is slaughtered in a certain way.

Over to You

1. Describe (a) how, (b) why and (c) when one Jewish festival is celebrated.
2. Imagine you are a Jewish mother or father. Write your diary entry for a weekend detailing what happens at Shabbat.
3. Draw a picture of a Jewish man ready for prayer. Label the different clothes he is wearing.

Place of Worship

Every religion has a place of worship and for Jews it is the **synagogue**. The word synagogue means a place of meeting. It is more than just a place for worship. It is also used for parties, meetings, office work and study.

Synagogue – A place of meeting. Jews use it as a place not only for worship but also office work, parties, study and meetings.

Synagogues come in all shapes and sizes, but they have several characteristics in common:

1. Every synagogue has a cupboard called the **ark**. In it you will find the scrolls of the Torah. The ark is behind a curtain on the wall of the synagogue that faces Jerusalem.

Ark – A special cupboard in the synagogue where the scrolls of the Torah are kept.

Ner Tamid – This is a light that always hangs above the ark in the synagogue. It is constantly lit and symbolises the everlasting covenant with God.

2. Above the ark is **Ner Tamid**. This is the perpetual light. Perpetual means it is always lit. This is a sign of the everlasting covenant with God. It is also to remember the menorah, the oil lamp, which was present in the Jerusalem Temple that was destroyed.

3. Above the ark you will also see two tablets or plaques. These represent the tablets of stone on which the Ten Commandments were given to Moses by God.

Bimah – This is the raised platform in the synagogue from where the Torah and prayers are read.

4. In the centre of the synagogue is a raised platform called the **bimah**. The Torah and prayers are read from here. There is also a lectern or reading desk where the scrolls are placed while being read.

Over to You

1. What is the Jewish place of worship called?
2. Describe three things you would see in it.

Other sacred places

Every religion has places that are sacred. Usually they are special because they are associated with a person involved in the religion or they may have been the scene of important events in the religion's history.

Another way of participating in worship is by going on pilgrimage to these places. A pilgrimage is a trip taken for religious reasons. It can help bring a person closer to their God and to other members of their faith community. The **Western** or **Wailing Wall** in Jerusalem is the most sacred place for Jews.

The Western or Wailing Wall – The most sacred place for Jews. It is the last remaining wall of the temple built for Jews in Jerusalem, which was destroyed by the Romans in 70 AD.

Welcome visitors to the most holy place in the Jewish religion. It is known as the Western or Wailing Wall. It is a site filled with history.

As you may know from your guidebooks, the Jewish people began to worship their God in the Temple in the time of King David. The Ark of the Covenant was kept there. This contained two tablets of stone bearing the Ten Commandments that God gave to Moses.

ARK OF THE COVENANT

The Temple was at the heart of the Jewish faith. Where is this great temple you might ask? Well, it was destroyed not once but twice. In 70 AD the Romans set fire to Jerusalem and the final Temple was lost. All that remained was the Western Wall. This is what you see before you today.

As you can see there are many Jews praying here. Many still hope that one day a new Temple will be built here. You will notice that men and women pray separately at the wall and men cover their heads as a sign of respect.

The wall is also known as the Wailing Wall as some Jewish people are overcome with grief when they come here, and remember all the persecution their people have suffered over the centuries. Any questions?

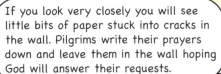

If you look very closely you will see little bits of paper stuck into cracks in the wall. Pilgrims write their prayers down and leave them in the wall hoping God will answer their requests.

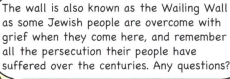

Jewish Symbols

A symbol is something that stands for something or someone else. It can be a picture or gesture that is used to explain the meaning of something when it is too difficult to put into words. Symbols are often used in religion. Three common Jewish symbols are:

1. **The Menorah:** Light is often used in religions as a symbol of hope and comfort. The menorah traditionally is a seven-branched candlestick holder. However the Hanukkah menorah usually has nine candles as seen here. It comes from the menorah that originally stood in the temple in Jerusalem.
2. **The Star of David:** This star became a symbol of Judaism in the middle ages. It remembers the great king of Israel, King David. It is found in synagogues and some Jewish people wear it as a sign of their pride in their faith. It is also to be found on the flag of Israel.
3. **The Mezuzah:** A mezuzah is a small case that holds a scroll on which the Shema is written. Most Jewish homes will have them attached to all the door frames in the house. The scrolls are handwritten and regularly checked to make sure the writing has not faded. Jews will often touch the mezuzah, then kiss their fingers as they pass it. This is a sign of love for what the writing means.

Persecution and Expansion of Judaism

Persecution – When a person is evicted from a place, hurt or even killed because of their religious beliefs and opinions.

Diaspora – The scattering of the Jews from Israel after it was taken over by the Romans in 70 CE.

The Jewish religion has had a very troubled history. We have read about their time in slavery in Egypt and being ruled by foreign invaders such as the Romans. Being persecuted means being evicted from a place, hurt or even killed because of your religious beliefs and opinions. Jews have suffered great **persecution** over the centuries and have paid a high price for their culture and beliefs.

1. After the Romans destroyed the Jerusalem Temple in 70 CE they forced the Jews to leave Israel. The Jews went to live in places such as North Africa and Europe. This event is called the **diaspora**, which means scattering.
2. In 1290 Jews were expelled from England and were only allowed to return in the 17th century.
3. Over a million Jews were forced to leave Russia in the 1880s because of persecution. A lot of them went to America to set up homes and businesses.
4. In the early 20th century many Jews began to move to Palestine. They set up communal farms on land they had bought from Arab people.

5. The worst period of persecution for the Jewish people occurred between 1933 and 1945 in Europe. This event became known as the **Holocaust**, which means burnt offering. When Adolf Hitler and his followers, the Nazis, came to power in Germany they began exterminating the Jewish population. They banned them from certain public places like theatres and parks. They destroyed their businesses and homes. By the time the Second World War started Hitler had set up concentration camps which were prison and death camps. The prisoners' only crime was for being Jewish. Millions died in gas chambers and crematoriums.

The Holocaust – The extermination of Jews by Adolf Hitler and Nazi Germany between 1933 and 1945.

Schism

It is not surprising that after such a troubled history the Jewish religion experienced some division. A split or separation in a religion is called a schism. Most religions have had schisms in their history. The schisms of the Jewish religion have led to many different branches of Judaism. Two of the largest Jewish groups are Orthodox and Reform Jews.

1. **Orthodox Jews:** Orthodox Jews are basically Jews that are very traditional. They follow the Torah very closely. Every aspect of their life is ruled by the Torah. Their services are held in Hebrew and men and women sit separately in the synagogue. The rabbi must be male.

Orthodox Jews – Jews that are very traditional and follow the Torah closely.

2. **Reform Judaism:** Reform Jews do not follow the same strict laws, such as the dietary ones, as do the Orthodox Jews. Their services are held in the vernacular language, that is, the native language spoken by everybody. Men and women sit together and they even have female rabbis. They believe many of the laws in the Torah really only applied to the first Jews who lived centuries ago. Reform Jews can now adapt these laws to suit life in modern times.

Reform Judaism – Jews that do not follow the same strict laws as do Orthodox Jews.

Where in the world?

There are thought to be approximately 14 million Jewish people in the world today. This is a much smaller number than the other world religions. One of the main reasons for this is that so many Jewish pople were killed during the holocaust. The largest groups are to be found in America, Israel and Russia.

Jews have been in Ireland since 1079. But after they were expelled from Portugal in 1496 many more arrived. They played a big part in Irish business and politics over the years. As recently as 1988 there was a Jewish Lord Mayor of Dublin, Ben Briscoe. In 2002 there were 1790 Jews in the Republic of Ireland.

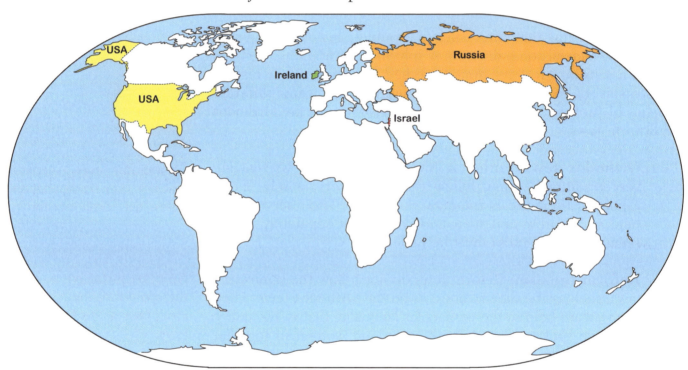

Over to You

1. Imagine you are a young Irish Jew on pilgrimage to the western wall with your family. Write a postcard home to your friend telling them why you're there and what you're doing.
2. Explain how Jewish people have been persecuted over the course of history.
3. What is a schism and what did it lead to in the Jewish religion?

■ (Higher Level)

Tradition, Faith and Practice of Judaism today

There are a lot of differences between the early Jewish community and the modern communities today. This is because of factors we have looked at already, such as persecution and schism. Practical changes mean there are fewer synagogues now in some countries because the population of Jews has been reduced. However, it is important to note that while certain Jewish practices have been adapted to suit life in the modern world, the core beliefs of Judaism have not changed.

Community structure and leadership

Every community has some sort of shape or structure to it. A structure holds the community together and helps it run smoothly. Jewish leaders are called **rabbis**. They are first and foremost teachers. They study the Torah closely and advise the people on how to apply it to their everyday lives. They also lead synagogue services and special ceremonies like funerals. A big part of their job is looking after the community, so they are involved in many community projects and visit families and those in need. A rabbi is highly respected by others in the community.

Yaakov Pearlman,
Chief Rabbi in Ireland

Education is very important to Jews, many children attend Jewish day schools where they receive an intensive Jewish education. Synagogues are places of learning as well as of worship. Children attend classes in the synagogue from a young age. The rabbi will give classes in Hebrew and also help the children study the sacred scriptures.

To compare and contrast two things means to look at the similarities and the differences between them. As Judaism is the parent religion of Christianity and Judaism they are bound to have lots in common. But there are also differences between them too. Let's take a look at Judaism and Christianity.

Similarities:
1. They both are monotheistic religions.
2. They both follow the Ten Commandments.
3. Love of neighbour is central to their moral rules.
4. Both use meals as part of their worship.

Differences:
1. Jews are still waiting for the Messiah to come, whereas Christians believe he has come already in Jesus Christ.
2. Christians celebrate their holy day on a Sunday, whereas the Jewish holy day starts on a Friday and continues until Saturday night.
3. Jews follow dietary rules.

Up for Discussion

Can you think of any other similarities or differences between Judaism and another world religion?

Dialogue

As we have learned, Judaism has had a strained relationship with other religions in the past. However, great steps have been taken to encourage peace and understanding between this historical religion and those faiths that have not shown it the respect it deserves in years gone by. Films like *Schindler's List* have highlighted the discrimination suffered by Jews in the past. People in today's world condemn times in history like the Holocaust.

Judaism and Catholicism have not always got along but after the Second Vatican Council Catholics were reminded of the need to embrace and respect other religions. This was highlighted in 1986 when Pope John Paul II visited a synagogue in Rome. This was the first time a pope had made such a visit. The Council of Jews and Christians was also set up to improve relations between the two religions.

Over to You - Exam Style Question

Write an article on Judaism under the following headings: Family / Relationships with other religions / Different types of Judaism.

Summary of Judaism

Monotheistic – A religion in which people believe and worship only one God.

Polytheistic – A religion in which people believe and worship many Gods.

Hebrews – The name by which the Jewish people were known when they lived in Israel before the birth of Judaism.

Covenant – A special agreement between God and his people.

Promised Land – The place in Canaan chosen by God, which was to be the home of the Jewish people.

Patriarch – A founding father. Abraham was the first patriarch.

Rabbi – A religious leader in the Jewish faith, also called a scribe.

Tenakh – The name Jewish people give to the Hebrew Bible.

The Western or Wailing Wall – The most sacred place for Jews. It is the last remaining wall of the temple built for Jews in Jerusalem, which was destroyed by the Romans in 70 AD.

Oral Torah – Discussions on the written Torah that are contained in three texts: the Mishah, the Talmud and the Midrash.

Rites and rituals – Words or actions that are performed by Jews in a special way at a certain time.

Main beliefs of Judaism –
1. **Monotheism** – there is one, almighty, powerful God.
2. **Identity** – they are God's chosen people.
3. **Covenant** – they must remain true to the covenants made with God through Abraham and Moses.

Rites of passage – Special ways of celebrating the important moments in life.

Covenant of circumcision – This is a special ceremony that takes place when a newborn baby boy is circumcised as a sign that he is entering into the same covenant with God that Abraham did.

Bar Mitzvah – A ritual that occurs when a Jewish boy is seen as an adult in his faith. It means 'son of the commandment'.

Kiddushin – The Hebrew name for marriage.

Kaddish – A special prayer for mourning said by Jewish people.

Shiva, Sheloshim and Yahrzeit – The three stages of Jewish mourning. Shiva is the first seven days of mourning; sheloshim the first 30 days after the burial; and yahrzeit the first 12 months after the death.

Shema – The most important prayer in Judaism.

Kosher food – Food that is clean and pure, and meat that is slaughtered in a certain way.

Synagogue – A place of meeting. Jews use it as a place not only for worship but also office work, parties, study and meetings.

Ark – A special cupboard in the synagogue where the scrolls of the Torah are kept.

Ner Tamid – This is a light that always hangs above the ark in the synagogue. It is constantly lit and symbolises the everlasting covenant with God.

Diaspora – The scattering of the Jews from Israel after it was taken over by the Romans in 70 CE.

Reform Judaism – Jews that do not follow the same strict laws as do Orthodox Jews.

Bimah – This is the raised platform in the synagogue from where the Torah and prayers are read.

The Holocaust – The extermination of Jews by Adolf Hitler and Nazi Germany between 1933 and 1945.

Persecution – When a person is evicted from a place, hurt or even killed because of their religious beliefs and opinions.

Orthodox Jews – Jews that are very traditional and follow the Torah closely.

Chapter 12:

Hinduism

The Cultural Context: Where it all began

Hinduism is one of the world's oldest religions reaching back 4,000 years to when it began in the Indus Valley in India. The name Hindu comes from the river Indus. Archaeologists have found clay statues of Gods and Goddesses similar to those that are now worshipped by Hindu people all over the world. There are approximately 900 million followers of the Hindu religion today. Hinduism is the predominant religion in India, Nepal and Bali.

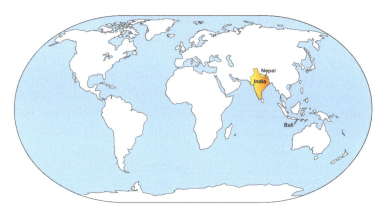

Founder and Beliefs

Hinduism has no founder. Although some believe it was founded by the rishis around 2000 BCE. The main emphasis of this religion is on a way of living rather than on a way of thought. The **creed** of a religion sums up what the followers of that religion believe in. What is important to Hindus is their belief in a supreme soul or spirit that has no shape or form. This is called **Brahman** and everything in the universe flows from this. There are many Hindu Gods and Goddesses (polytheism - belief in many gods) and they represent the many aspects of Brahman's power and character. Hindus are free to worship whatever God they like.

There are three important Hindu Gods:

1. **Brahma:** The one who created the world.
2. **Vishnu:** The one who protects people from all evil and wrongdoing. It is believed that he has visited the world nine times so far. On the tenth visit – his final visit – the world will come to an end.
3. **Shiva:** The one who destroys and then rebuilds. The universe goes through a process of birth, growth, destruction and rebirth. Shiva destroys the universe for it to be reborn.

Brahma   Vishnu   Shiva

Before they start to pray to a particular God, most Hindus have a statue or a picture beside them, as this helps them to focus. They believe that they must always do what is right and correct for themselves – this is called **dharma**. Hindus do what is right according to their social status or the stage they are at in life.

There are no set rules for being a Hindu but most Hindus share the same beliefs. They believe that when you die, your soul is reborn in another body as an animal or a person. This cycle of birth and rebirth is called **samsara**. Another word to describe rebirth is reincarnation. Whereas Christians believe you only live on earth once, Hindus believe that you are reborn over and over until you are perfect. Because of this belief, when you do good, good will come your way and if you do bad, bad will follow you. This is called **karma.**

Creed – A summing up of what the followers of a religion believe in.

Brahman – The supreme soul or spirit that Hindus believe in, and which has no form.

Hindu Gods –
1. Brahma, who created the world.
2. Vishnu, who protects people from evil and wrongdoing.
3. Shiva, who destroys and then rebuilds.

Dharma – The Hindu belief to always do what is right and correct.

Samsara – The cycle of birth and rebirth. It is also called reincarnation.

Karma – The belief that when you do good, good will come your way, and when you do bad, bad will follow you.

Over to You

1. What is the main emphasis of the Hindu religion? Explain it using your own words.
2. Do you think this is a good philosophy to have? Why/why not?
3. What does polytheism mean?
4. Explain the word Brahman.
5. What are the three important Hindu Gods? Find out the names of other Hindu Gods.
6. What is dharma?
7. What is samsara?
8. What is karma?

Sources of Evidence

Sanskrit – The language of Hindus.

Vedas – The oldest Hindu sacred texts consisting of four collections of prayers, hymns and magic spells.

Upanishads – An important Hindu sacred text that contains stories and parables, such as the Mahabharata and Ramayana.

Hindus have no one sacred text because they have many holy books. Their scriptures were passed by word of mouth (oral tradition) for many years before they were written down. The language of Hindus is the **Sanskrit** which is the language of ancient India but no longer spoken. The oldest Hindu sacred texts are from the four collections of prayers, hymns and magic spells called the **Vedas**. They were put together about 3,000 years ago and teach and guide Hindus on how they should live their lives.

Another important text is the **Upanishads**, which are teachings presented in the form of stories and parables told by teachers to their students. The two greatest stories are the Mahabharata and the Ramayana. They are both epic poems and teach the importance of honesty, loyalty and courage. The **Mahabharata** tells the story of a war between two royal families and the ups and downs of their everyday lives. The **Ramayana** was written about the 2nd century BCE. This tells the story about how the God Rama rescued his wife Sita from an evil demon king called Ravana. It teaches Hindus about love, courage and friendship.

Practices and Ritual Events

Rites of passage and Symbols

Rites of passage are different ceremonies that take place to mark important events. There are normally rituals that take place at these ceremonies. Let us now look at three different ceremonies in Hindu tradition.

Brahmin – A Hindu priest.

Baptism

Soon after a baby is born into a Hindu family a prayer is whispered into its ear by someone in the family. This is a prayer of thanksgiving for the safe arrival of the child. It also welcomes it into the world. When the family are gathered together the father dips his gold pen in honey and writes the word 'aum' on the baby's tongue. By doing this, they hope their child will speak the truth. The baby's hair is then cut at a later stage. This symbolises that any badness in a previous life will not affect this life. A symbol is then marked on their forehead.

Twelve days after the baby is born they are named at the naming ceremony. This is done in the presence of family members and the **Brahmin** priest. He makes a record of the baby's name for the family. The baby is then given a piece of gold. Red threads are tied to him symbolising protection.

Marriage

Arranged marriages are common to Hindu people. Arranged marriages are when parents plan for their son or daughter to marry someone that they choose to be suitable. The marriage service is held in the girl's home place or temple. This is a joyful and elaborate ceremony. The bride wears a red sari with beautiful jewellery. Her hands and feet are painted with a saffron dye. The groom also dresses well for the occasion.

Marriage is a sacred ritual in Hinduism. First the couple exchange garlands of flowers. The ceremony takes place around a fire, which symbolises the sun as the giver of all life. The priest leads the couple around the fire in seven steps. A prayer is said at each of these steps for food, wealth, strength, children, good luck, seasons and friendship. There is also an act of cleansing at the wedding, whereby the fire is taken around the room and the guests pass their hands through the flame and then touch their forehead.

Arranged marriage – When parents plan for their son or daughter to marry someone that they choose to be suitable.

Wedding celebrations may last two or three days with all the wedding gifts displayed. A banquet of food is also served.

Death

When a Hindu dies, the body is washed and then anointed with oil. The body is wrapped in a red cloth if female and a white cloth if male. They are laid on a stretcher and carried to the funeral pyre to be cremated. All Hindus are cremated not buried. By cremation the fire releases the soul from the person that has died.

A priest is often present to say prayers with the family. The closest male relative to the person who has died lights the cremation fire. The ashes are gathered and then scattered in a nearby river. If the family are planning a pilgrimage to the **River Ganges** they may decide to keep the ashes safe until that time. The waters of the River Ganges are believed to be sacred.

River Ganges – A river held sacred by Hindus. Many Hindus wish their ashes to be scattered in the Ganges when they die.

Hindus believe that the soul is a small part of the Brahman that has somehow fallen into our world of birth and death. The soul, or atma, is trapped in the human body and it must go through a series of lives and endure a long cycle of birth, death and at long last, rebirth. The whole process is called samsara and in every cycle the soul takes on a new body and in doing so is reincarnated.

Over to You

1. What is a rite of passage?
2. Describe each of the ceremonies.
3. What is a ritual? Are rituals evident in the rite of passage?

Religious festival – A special time usually remembered by fasting or celebration.

Hindu festivals – Three important Hindu festivals are Divali, Holi, and the Kumbh Mela.

Festivals and sacred times

A **religious festival** is a special time usually remembered by fasting or celebration. Festivals are times of music, dance, stories and food shared among friends. Gifts of sweets are exchanged. They are lively colourful occasions. The adventures of Rama and his wife Sita are important in many Hindu festivals. The most popular festivals are Holi and Divali, followed by the Khumbh Mela.

	Divali	Holi	Kumbh Mela
When	In late October or early November	At the beginning of spring in March or April	Four times every 12 years at four locations in India: Prayag, Haridwar, Ujjain and Nashik
Why	To mark the beginning of the Hindu New Year with a festival of lights. The festival marks the victory of good over evil	To mark the beginning of spring. It symbolises fertility	To make a pilgrimage to one of four places, where legends says during a battle between the Gods and demons that drops of the nectar of immortality fell from the skies
How	During this festival many lights are lit in homes, temples and workplaces, as light symbolises goodness. Hindus believe that the goddess of good fortune, Lakshmi, is present. She brings good fortune to the homes that have lights burning. These lights they believe attract her attention. There are many preparations made before this festival as homes are cleaned from top to bottom, new clothes are bought and flowers are displayed everywhere	People light bonfires as they are central to this celebration. They share the holy food around the bonfire with each other. Coloured water and powders are thrown at each other during this festival. This symbolises the playful nature of the God of Krishna	About 10 million Hindus gather together to bathe in the rivers, such as the Ganges. Rivers are very important symbols to Hindus as they mean a life without end

The Sacred Thread Ceremony

At this ceremony a boy seeks spiritual identity. He accepts a spiritual teacher as a father and the Vedas as mother. At this ceremony he receives a sacred thread, usually worn for his entire lifetime. The ceremony involves the boy shaving his head, bathing and wearing new clothes. The boy is given a spiritual name to symbolise his 'second birth'. After that the thread is wrapped around the thumb of his right hand and a prayer is chanted at dawn, noon and dusk. He takes a vow to study the Vedas and serve his teachers.

Over to You

1. What does the word festival mean?
2. How important is symbolism to these festivals?
3. Choose a festival that we celebrate in Ireland. Write about the festivities surrounding the event(s).

Arjuna was 13 when he made his first pilgrimage with his family. His family had not gone to Ujjain in 12 years, as this pilgrimage to celebrate Kumbh Mela only takes place every 12 years. This pilgrimage involves bathing in the place where the River Ganges meets the Jumma River. He was very excited to go on this sacred and holy journey. But there was much planning and conversation involved before his family left their village.

Pilgrimage: Let's Go!

We had a long way to travel as my family are from the western part of India. My dad told my brother and I that the River Ganges flowed in heaven before the God Shiva caught it in her hair and let it flow gently on to earth. I liked this story and begged him to tell us more but he said that he would tell us later on the journey. There were many people travelling towards the city of Varnasi where the river Ganges is.

When we arrived I could see the steps along the riverbank. There were pilgrims on the steps with flowers in their hands. My mom said that many gather there and bathe in the water to help cleanse themselves of any wrongdoing. I saw a man take water in his hands and then let it fall back into the water. I had learnt in school about this as a form of offering.

My dad had brought my uncle's ashes to the river to scatter them. I knew that my uncle would now find it easier to pass on to the next life.

My family stayed near the River Ganges for a couple of days. I enjoyed being with my family, especially my dad because he spent lots of time with us. At home he works very hard and we hardly see him at all. My mom was delighted that we all had such a lovely time. Maybe in 12 years' time I might have a wife to bring to this special place.

Over to You

1. What is meant by the word pilgrimage?
2. Why was this pilgrimage important to Arjuna and his family?
3. What happens at the River Ganges?
4. Find out about another place of pilgrimage for Hindus in India.

Place of Worship

Puja – The Hindu word for worship.

To worship something is to show it adoration and respect. Hindus worship and pray to their Gods in a temple or mandir. The Hindu word for worship is **puja.** Hindus are not required to gather in the temple at any particular time, so many of them worship in their homes. Worship is congregational at festival times, which means a large group attends.

Worship at home

In the home there is always a shrine to their favourite God. Its centrepiece is a statue or image of that God. Some shrines can be decorated elaborately or kept small and simple. In the morning a small lamp is lit, a bell is rung, incense is burned and fruit or flowers are offered while a daily prayer is said. The use of incense is believed to please the gods.

The sacred word 'aum' is chanted over and over just like at baptism when it is whispered into the ear of the newborn infant. Every aspect of the person is involved as the shrine contains many things that appeal to the five senses of sight, hearing, taste, smell and touch.

Hindus are vegetarians because of their belief in reincarnation. They believe it is wrong to kill a creature, as it is no different to themselves. They respect all animals but cows have a very special place. Its milk gives nourishment and its excrement (dung) is used as fuel for the fire. The cow cares and looks after human beings through its food and dung. It is a gentle animal and Hindus believe we should treat all people this way.

Worship at the temple

Garbagriha – The shrine room where the statue of the God or Goddess is kept.

Inside a temple there is a large hall with pillars along both sides. A carpet covers the floor from wall to wall and there are no seats. The shrine room where the statue of the God or Goddess is kept is called the **garbagriha.** A canopy covers the garbagriha. The priest looks after this area by dressing the statue in colourful robes and garlands before puja.

As people arrive at the temple they take their shoes off as a sign of respect for this sacred place. Women cover their heads with a sari, which is a long garment made of silk or cotton. Families sit together with their legs crossed as they face the shrine.

Fruit and sweets are offered to the Gods with love. The priest then says prayers over these offerings. The food is later served to those

gathered in the temple. Together people chant verses from the sacred texts. A sacred flame burns brightly throughout, before being waved towards the statues and then passed among those present as a blessing to them.

Five daily duties

Many Hindus believe there are five daily duties:

1. To perform puja or worship.
2. To say aloud parts of the scriptures.
3. To respect their parents and older people.
4. To give food and shelter to those that are lost.
5. To feed and care for their animals, especially the cow. In India the cow is regarded as a sacred animal. It is worshipped for its life-giving qualities. This gentle animal provides milk for food, leather to sell and droppings for fuel. Therefore, this animal is decorated with garlands of flowers and anointed with oil.

Over to You

1. What does puja mean?
2. Worship in the home is similar to worship in the temple. Describe both forms of worship.
3. Do you think symbolism is an important part of worship for Hindus? Why/why not?
4. Do you think the priest plays a significant role?
5. How important do you think are the five daily duties? Do you think one is more important than the other? Give a reason for your answer.

Hindu Prayer Life: Personal Prayer and Meditation

Prayer to many world religions is conversation with God. Hindu prayer is different as it involves repeating a name for the Brahman over and over. It is done using a mantra which is a phrase that Hindus use over and over during meditation. This helps them with concentration. This mantra is given to a Hindu for his or her lifetime by a spiritual **guru** or adviser.

Prayer is a personal thing to each Hindu as they worship a lot in their homes and only gather in the temple for holy days. Even while together in the temple, they pray alone. Their daily prayer is read from the Rig Veda, which is the 'mother of all Vedas'.

'Om. Let us think about God who made the world, may He guide our minds.' (Rig Veda 3, 62, 10)

Meditation is one way that Hindus pray. Designs like the **yantra** help people to concentrate when meditating too.

Guru – A spiritual adviser in Hinduism.

Yantra – A design that helps Hindus to pray.

Over to You

1. How is prayer different in the Hindu faith to other world religions?
2. Compare the way Hindus pray to another world religion?
3. What is meant by a mantra?

A Disciple of the Faith: Mahatma Gandhi (1869 – 1948)

Truth, purity, self-control, firmness, fearlessness, humility, unity, peace, and renunciation – these are the inherent qualities of a civil resister. Gandhi

Mohandas Gandhi was born on the northwest coast of India on 2 October 1869. His mother was a religious Hindu who regularly prayed to the Gods and fasted. His father took care of a part of India for the British who governed the country at the time. During Gandhi's youth he regularly ate meat and stole from family members to buy tobacco. This changed on the death of his father.

At the age of 14 Gandhi was married to a girl called Kasturbai, who was 13, and they remained together until her death in 1944. After they were married he wanted to go to London to study law. Once in London he remained loyal to his Hindu roots and began to read sacred writings. The Bhagavad-Gita, an important Hindu text, had a strong impact on him and led to him cutting down on his daily expenses, walking everywhere and eating less. In 1891 he returned to India as a qualified barrister. There was a surplus of barristers in India at the time so he decided to accept an offer from an Indian law firm in South Africa.

In South Africa, Gandhi experienced at first hand the life of Indians living there. Once he was thrown off a train, even though he had a valid ticket, because he was not sitting in the right carriage. He spent that night sitting in the cold railway platform. The turning point in his life came when he refused to give his seat to a white person on a stagecoach and was beaten up by the driver. From then on he committed himself to defend his dignity as an Indian and as a human being.

He encouraged the Indian population to challenge the conditions they were living under. Indians were required to get their fingerprints taken and carry a permit at all times. Any Indian who disobeyed this rule was fined, jailed or deported. After a

while he developed a method of direct social action called **Satyagraha**, which was based on the principles of courage, truth and non-violence. It was always his belief that the way people behave is more important than what they achieve.

In 1915 Gandhi returned to India. Using the same idea as he had used in South Africa, he led the campaign for India's independence from Great Britain. Many times he was arrested in South Africa and India. However, he believed it was an honourable thing to go to prison for a just cause. He used fasting on more than one occasion to impress on others the need to be non-violent.

Finally in 1947, India gained its independence from Britain. Gandhi had always hoped that India would be united, where Hindus and Muslims lived together in peace. However, there were many deep-rooted divisions between the two groups. The British responded to this by dividing ancient India into two independent countries; India with a Hindu majority and Pakistan with a Muslim majority. Gandhi rejected this as he still believed both could live together in harmony. Above all, he believed the partition of India was a tragedy. Religious riots soon broke out between the two groups. Gandhi once again began a fast to stop the bloodshed. After five days the riots stopped and Gandhi began to eat again.

At the beginning of 1948 Gandhi was walking to his evening prayer meeting. A young Hindu named Nathuram Godse approached him, pretending to seek Gandhi's blessing. He took a gun from his pocket and shot the Gandhi three times. The 'Father of a Nation' died saying the word 'Rama', the name of a Hindu God. On his death that night a light had gone out in the lives of the people.

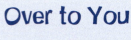

Over to You

1. What do you think the opening statement says about Gandhi?
2. How significant was the turning point in Gandhi's life?
3. What does Satyagraha mean? Would this work in today's world?
4. Why do you think Gandhi saw the partition of India as a tragedy?
5. Do you think his death was untimely? Why/why not?
6. Find out about other people who follow or followed the Hindu beliefs of non-violence, truth, honesty, etc.

Satyagraha – A method of direct social action developed by Gandhi that is based on the principles of courage, truth and non-violence.

145

Symbols

Many Hindu symbols include the whole notion of inner purity

- One of the main symbols of Hinduism is 'Aum' or 'Om. It is an important mantra and chanted at the beginning of prayers and rituals.

- Bindi is one of the most recognisable symbols of Hinduism. This is a coloured dot traditionally worn on the forehead of Hindu women. It is usually red and symbolises the energy of women.

- Many Hindu symbols include the whole notion of inner purity.

- The cow represents life for Hindus as Mahatma Gandhi said that the cow is the 'mother to millions of Indian People'.

Development and Expansion

Hinduism can be compared to many faiths including Christianity. All faiths have the belief that we must look to other faiths with respect and treat all people equally.

- In the Hindu faith we must do nothing to others that if done to you could cause you pain.
- In the Buddhist faith we are told to act towards others exactly as we would act towards ourselves.
- In the Christian faith we are encouraged to treat others as we would like to be treated ourselves.
- In the Islamic faith we are told that none of us truly believe until we wish for others what we wish for ourselves.
- In the Jewish faith we are told that what is harmful to us we must not do to others.

The above statements can have an effect on our behaviour towards members of all world religions today. Actions that are carried out by any person can have good and bad consequences (Karma).

Summary of Hinduism

Creed – A summing up of what the followers of a religion believe in.

Brahman – The supreme soul or spirit that Hindus believe in, and which has no form.

Hindu Gods –
1. Brahma, who created the world.
2. Vishnu, who protects people from evil and wrongdoing.
3. Shiva, who destroys and then rebuilds.

Dharma – The Hindu belief to always do what is right and correct.

Samsara – The cycle of birth and rebirth. It is also called reincarnation.

Karma – The belief that when you do good, good will come your way, and when you do bad, bad will follow you.

Sanskrit – The language of Hindus.

Vedas – The oldest Hindu sacred texts consisting of four collections of prayers, hymns and magic spells.

Upanishads – An important Hindu sacred text that contains stories and parables, such as the Mahabharata and Ramayana.

Arranged marriage – When parents plan for their son or daughter to marry someone that they choose to be suitable.

River Ganges – A river held sacred by Hindus. Many Hindus wish their ashes to be scattered in the Ganges when they die.

Religious festival – A special time usually remembered by fasting or celebration.

Hindu festivals – Three important Hindu festivals are Divali, Holi, and the Kumbh Mela.

Puja – The Hindu word for worship.

Garbagriha – The shrine room where the statue of the God or Goddess is kept.

Guru – A spiritual adviser in Hinduism.

Yantra – A design that helps Hindus to pray.

Satyagraha – A method of direct social action developed by Gandhi that is based on the principles of courage, truth and non-violence.

Chapter 13:

Buddhism

The Cultural Context: where it all began

Siddharta Gautama – The man who founded the religion called Buddhism.

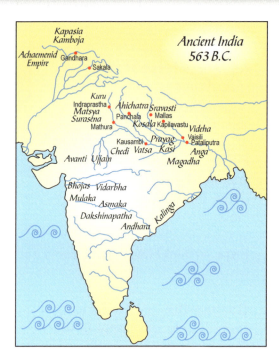

Ancient India 563 B.C.

The Buddhist religion is an offshoot of Hinduism. It began in the north of India around the fifth century BCE. At that time many people started to question what was happening around them. However, they were unable to find answers to questions about their religion. Many people therefore set out on a spiritual journey to find answers to the many questions they had about life. They left all their possessions and homes behind them. One such man was **Siddhartha Gautama**, who eventually founded a new religion called Buddhism.

Founder and Vision

Siddhartha Gautama: The Buddha

Siddhartha Gautama was the son of a rich king and queen in the border area between India and Nepal. Born around 563 BCE, he grew up in great luxury, shielded from all the wrongdoings of society. So protected was he that he was not even allowed to leave the palace grounds. At his birth a wise man prophesied that he would become a great ruler or a homeless wanderer one day. At the age of 16, Siddhartha married a beautiful princess and they had a son. Even so, Siddhartha was not happy behind the walls of the palace.

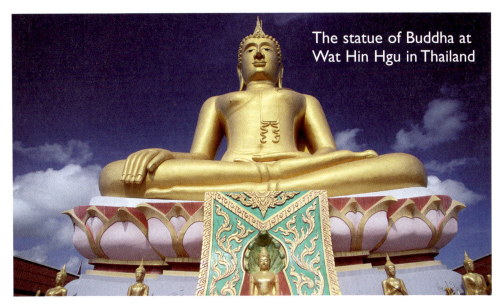

The statue of Buddha at Wat Hin Hgu in Thailand

One day he decided to escape outside to see what the world was really like. This journey was to affect him deeply and change his life. Outside the palace walls he first saw an old man, then a sick man and then a man who was dead. Even though he had no previous experience of suffering, Siddhartha began to see that life was full of it. After that he met a monk who had no possessions but was still very content with life. From that day on Siddhartha vowed that his life would be like the monk's, and so he left the palace and his wife and son behind.

For Siddhartha a life of prayer and fasting with some monks began. After spending some years with this group, he found that there were no real answers to the questions he had sought, so he moved on still searching. Also, he was quite sick from fasting. Many years passed and no answers came.

One day as he sat under a tree in Bodh Gaya in India, he closed his eyes and began to meditate. During the meditation he felt something inside. When he opened his eyes, he knew he had found the truth and a way out from the sufferings around him. His enlightenment showed him that people suffered because they were never happy with what they had, and always strived for more things in life.

After that, he believed that people needed to learn ways of thinking and behaving. He founded the theory **'Middle Way'**, which is a life lived between hardship and luxury. In his first sermon he set out his basic teachings. At the centre of this sermon was the Four Noble Truths, which states that life is full of suffering and the cause of suffering is greed. The only way to end suffering is the 'middle path', which is finding happiness between extreme luxury and extreme hardship.

Without delay, he went back to the monks to tell them about what he had discovered. They were impressed by his ideas and soon became his first followers. They named him **Buddha**, which means the 'Enlightened One.'

Middle Way – The theory founded by Siddhartha Gautama which states that people could find happiness in a life lived between extreme luxury and extreme hardship.

Buddha – A name that means 'Enlightened One' and which was given to Siddhartha Gautama by his followers.

Over to You

1. What do you think of the life that Siddhartha had before he escaped the palace?
2. On seeing the three people outside he was shocked. Why?
3. What do you think of the 'middle way' theory?
4. Do you think he deserved the title 'Enlightened One'?
5. Do you think people today are greedy? If so, in what way?
6. Outline how the life of Siddhartha was influenced by his belief in something good.

Sources of Evidence

Tripitaka – The sacred writings of Buddhism, which mean 'Three Baskets'.

There are many sacred writings that belong to the Buddhist faith. The Buddha was a great teacher but he never wrote anything down. After his death his teachings were passed on by word of mouth (oral tradition).

Around the time of Jesus Christ, Siddhartha's followers began to write down his teachings. They were written in Pali, an ancient north Indian language which probably was spoken by the Buddha himself. It was at this point that Buddhism began to split. Disputes arose over interpretations of rules and discipline. The Pali Canon (Canon meaning an agreed set of readings) consists of 45 volumes. Theravada Buddhism for example is found mainly in southern Asia and accepts the teachings called **Tripitaka,** which means 'Three Baskets'.

Tripitaka (Three Baskets)

In each of the three baskets there is an important teaching:

1. **The Vinaya:** Discipline involving rules for monks and nuns on how to live like the Buddha.
2. **The Abhidhamma:** The main teachings of the Four Noble Truths and Middle Way.
3. **The Sutra:** An explanation of the Buddha's teaching and ways of looking at life.

Discipline   Teachings   Explanations

Over to You

1. What is meant by a sacred text?
2. Do you think that all Siddhartha's ideas were passed down correctly by word of mouth?
3. What teachings are found in the Three Baskets?

Buddhist Beliefs

A creed is a religious belief that sums up what the followers believe in and live by. Following the Buddha's enlightenment he preached his first sermon revealing the 'Four Noble Truths'. He taught his followers to achieve a state of **nirvana**, which is a state of perfect happiness and peace. This is the opposite of suffering which most people experience every day. It was possible to achieve nirvana, he believed, by the following:

* The Four Noble Truths
* The Eightfold Path
* The Five Precepts.

Nirvana – A state of perfect happiness and peace or enlightenment. It is seen as ultimate salvation.

The Four Noble Truths

The most important Buddhism beliefs or truths are found in the sacred text called the Four Noble Truths.

1. **Duktha:** This truth means that life is full of suffering and to live is to suffer. There is no such thing as permanent happiness, as even the happiest moments in life come to an end.
2. **Samudaya:** This truth means that the main cause of our suffering is desire and greed. But it can end by following the Eightfold Path.
3. **Nirvana:** This truth means that we can find true happiness and peace by not being greedy and selfish towards others. Suffering can therefore be brought to an end.
4. **Magga:** This truth means that the Middle Way is the path to true happiness. There are eight steps on this journey and it is the solution to suffering.

The Four Noble Truths – These truths are Duktha, Samudaya, Magga and Nirvana.

It is only by believing that other people suffer that we can come to terms with our own daily struggles and difficulties. This is what is taught through the Duktha and Samudaya. It is developed further in the Magga (path), which has eight parts to it.

The Eightfold Path

The Middle Way is the Buddhist way of life. Each of the eight steps must be followed.

1. Right understanding (people should think about what they are doing with their lives)
2. Right thought (daydreaming is time wasting)
3. Right speech (when we speak, we should only speak good things)
4. Right action (people should not be selfish)
5. Right livelihood (in work, we should not harm any living creature)
6. Right effort (we should try our best at all times)
7. Right mindfulness (we should pay full attention to what we are doing)
8. Right concentration (we should try to concentrate all the time)

The Eightfold Path can be divided into three sections: wisdom, morality and meditation.

- **Wisdom** involves right understanding and right thought. This means having the correct view on life and following the Four Noble Truths.
- **Morality** involves right speech, right action, right livelihood and right effort. This means that you should live your life correctly and justly by not spreading rumours or gossip about another. You should think positively about life and keep the mind healthy.
- **Meditation** involves right mindfulness and right concentration. This means that you should free the mind from all distractions and focus the mind on enlightenment or nirvana (ultimate salvation).

The Eightfold Path –
The Buddhist way of life. It contains eight steps:
1. Right understanding
2. Right thought
3. Right speech
4. Right action
5. Right livelihood
6. Right effort
7. Right mindfulness
8. Right concentration.

152

The Five Precepts

The Five Precepts are like the Ten Commandments. They help Buddhists to stay true to their faith. The emphasis on Buddhist morality is on intention and the purpose of the intention. They clearly emphasise respect for life.

The Five Precepts –
These are rules that help Buddhists stay true to their faith.

1. One should not kill another living creature.
2. One should not steal from another.
3. One should not misuse the physical senses.
4. One should not tell lies to others.
5. One should not take drink or drugs.

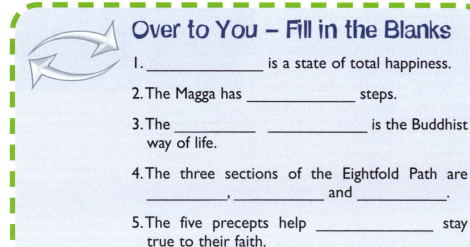

Over to You – Fill in the Blanks

1. _____ is a state of total happiness.

2. The Magga has _____ steps.

3. The _____ _____ is the Buddhist way of life.

4. The three sections of the Eightfold Path are _____, _____ and _____.

5. The five precepts help _____ stay true to their faith.

Over to You

1. Write about the Four Noble Truths in your own words.
2. Why do you think the Eightfold Path is important to Buddhists?
3. Compare the Five Precepts to the Ten Commandments. What is similar?
4. Describe two ways that Siddhartha followed the Eightfold Path.

Place of Worship

Temple – A holy place where Buddhists go to pray.

Relic – An object that belonged to a holy person, which is kept and treated as holy after their death.

Stupa or **pagoda** – A monument in a temple which holds the relics of the Buddha of the temple.

Buddhists worship in **temples** which are holy places. Many Buddhists go there to pray and make offerings. Buddhists do not worship in a community environment. They don't need other people to help them worship. In homes and Buddhist temples, images of the Buddha are to be found.

There is also a **stupa** or **pagoda** (monument) that preserves and enshrines the **relic** of the Buddha in the temple. The Stupa is a dome shape and symbolises the sacredness of the Buddha. A relic is an object that belonged to a holy person, which is kept and treated as holy after their death. It could be a piece of cloth. At the stupa Buddhists walk around it three times before kneeling or standing in front of it to worship. The actual Buddha statue or image is not worshipped. Buddhists only honour what the statue represents.

Practices and Ritual Events

Siddhartha Gautama was a holy man who achieved enlightenment and nirvana. He taught people what true happiness and peace was like. Buddhists today yearn to reach this stage like their founder. There is no weekly ceremony or holy day for Buddhists. There is also no set time for daily prayer. Buddhists worship in their homes as well as in the temple. They chant and meditate in silence while worshiping.

Meditation – A communal type of prayer that can be done on its own or in a group led by a leader. For Buddhists meditation is not a conversation with God, but a way to control their mind and help them make the right choices in life.

Meditation

Meditation is a communal type of prayer. It helps free the mind. It can be done by oneself but is best done as part of a group under the guidance of a leader. During meditation some Buddhists sit on the floor in a position similar to the Buddha during his meditation under the Bodhi tree. Other Buddhists say a mantra (repeating chant) that helps them concentrate. Others use prayer beads while they chant. Again all these things help Buddhists in their prayer life.

Buddhists do not see prayer as a conversation with God. For them it is an attempt to control their mind and help them make the right choices in life. Most Buddhists meditate each day. They recite the Three Refuges or Three Jewels of Buddhism. Which are:
1. I take refuge in Buddha
2. I take refuge in the four noble truths
3. I take refuge in the monastery.

The Buddha is not God; he is the most enlightened of human beings.

Buddhists so admire the Buddha that they walk clockwise around the stupa and then either kneel or stand to show respect and then pray.

Meditation helps a person to relax and therefore free the mind of all distractions and outside influences.

All Buddhists seek to achieve nirvana. Through meditation they can understand the teachings of the Buddha more, which helps them on the road to enlightenment.

Over to You

How important is meditation to Buddhists? Have you ever meditated in class? What was the experience like?

Rites of passage

There are a number of ritual events in Buddhism that involve ceremonies. A ceremony is a formal religious or public occasion celebrating an event. Let us now look at three Buddhist ceremonies:

Birth
When a baby enters the world in some Buddhist countries they are brought to the temple for the naming ceremony. The baby is blessed and water is sprinkled over them by a monk. A candle is lit and the wax is let drip into a water bowl. Through this, air, fire and water are all used, symbolising the importance of the elements. By bringing all three symbols together the child will have harmony in their lifetime.

Marriage

Buddhists have no wedding or marriage ceremony. It is not a religious event but when the marriage is registered, a lot of Buddhist couples go to the temple to receive a blessing. The following traditional blessings are used.

The bridegroom says: 'Towards my wife, I undertake to love and respect her, be kind and considerate, be faithful, delegate domestic management, provide gifts to please her'.

The bride says: 'Towards my husband, I undertake to perform my household duties efficiently, be hospitable to my in-laws and friends of my husband, be faithful, protect and invest our earnings, discharge my responsibilities lovingly and conscientiously'.
Families gather together to celebrate the event.

Death

Buddhists do not fear death. When a person dies their body is washed and laid in a coffin surrounded by flowers. Family and friends carry their dead to the temple. Death is a celebratory time for Buddhists as it releases one from suffering. A meal is shared among family and friends as a mark of celebration. The body can be cremated or buried. If a person is cremated their ashes are scattered in the nearby river or lake.

Over to You

Describe a ceremony that you have attended as part of your faith. Is it similar or different to that of Buddhism? Was it a public or private ceremony?

Buddhist festivals

There are many holy days held throughout the year for Buddhists. A festival is a time of celebration for all involved. Religious festivals often have fasting as part of the celebrations. Two important festivals celebrated by Buddhists are Vesak/Wesak and Vassa. Buddha recommended to his followers that if they were to get on they should 'meet together regularly in large numbers'. Festivals are important to the Buddhist community. They show devotion and gratitude to the Buddha and his teachings.

A Buddhist lights an oil lamp on Vesak day

	Vesak	Vassa
When	In the month of May, except in a leap year when it is in June	In the months of July to September (often known as the rainy season retreat)
Why	To celebrate the birth, enlightenment and death of the Buddha. It is called Vesak as it is the name of the month in the Indian calender	To try to be a better follower of the Buddha during this time
How	It involves a flower festival. A flower shrine is erected in front of the main temple shrine, since the Buddha was born around the month of May when many flowers were in bloom	It is a sacred time for monks and lay people. Time is set aside for meditation, and help is given to those who need it. At the end of the festival, offerings are brought to the monasteries for the monks

Over to You

1. Which Buddhist festival did you prefer reading about? Why?
2. Do you think it is important to take time out from school or work to spend with your family and friends? Why/why not?
3. Write about a religious festival that you know about when people take time off to spend with their family.

Sacred places

A pilgrimage is journeying to a holy place to pray and honour someone. In Ireland people make pilgrimages to Lough Derg and Croagh Patrick every year. Buddhists also go on pilgrimages to honour their founder and important stages in his life: his birth, his enlightenment, his first sermon to the monks, and his death. Many Buddhists make a pilgrimage to Bodh Gaya in India where Siddhartha achieved enlightenment.

Many Buddhists bring offerings with them to Bodh Gaya and sit quietly and pray. A temple was erected there as in other sacred places. Making a journey to such a holy place can deepen and strengthen the faith of the Buddhist. In some ways by making this journey they feel closer to their founder and it therefore helps them live the life he wanted for all his followers.

The Mahabodhi Temple in Bodh Gaya, India.

Over to You

1. What does it mean to worship?
2. How important is the temple to Buddhists?
3. What is honoured by Buddhists?
4. What is a pilgrimage?
5. Is pilgrimage important to Buddhists?
6. Find out more information on the pilgrimage to Bodh Gaya from the library or internet.

Symbols

The Lotus plant is an important symbol to Buddhists. Its flowers turn towards the heat of the sun just as the followers of the Buddha turn towards knowledge.

Development and Expansion

After Siddhartha gave his first ceremony to the monks he continued to preach for the next 40 years. He travelled all over India spreading his words of wisdom. At the age of 80 he died and passed into a stage of nirvana. In his last message he restated the hope of salvation for all Buddhists. Most Buddhists admire him deeply and look to his life and enlightenment as a model for themselves. His teachings rather than he himself play a large role in defining the religious life of Buddhism.

Sangha – A community of monks and nuns founded by the Buddha.

The Buddha founded a group called the **Sangha**, which is a community of monks and nuns. (This is very like what we call a monastery.) His son was said to be among the earliest groups of Buddhists. These men and women came from all walks of life. Everyone was treated with the same respect, which was an unusual thing at the time.

Time has not changed this group. They continue to pray, read the sacred texts and meditate as one. Together they follow the teachings of the Buddha closely. They do not believe in wealth and live their lives very simply with few possessions other than their robes and a wooden begging bowl. As a sign of obedience to the Buddha they shave their heads. Their robes are orange in colour.

The Sangha are treated with great respect in their countries and to place food in their begging bowl is regarded as a blessing. During the rainy season the monks spend this time together on retreat. For the remaining nine months they travel the countryside teaching. To this day being a **Buddhist** means to 'take refuge' in the Buddha, in his teachings and in the Sangha.

They are very important to the Buddhist community as they help to reach the way to Nirvana and therefore live the life encouraged by the Buddha himself.

The spread of Buddhism

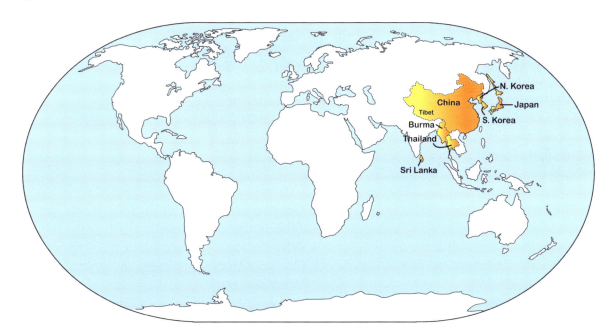

As Buddhism spread from India into other countries it adapted itself to the needs of individual cultures. Buddhism has experienced a huge revival in the last thirty-five years. Many people are interested in the religions and philosophies of the East. The whole idea of togetherness and inter-connection is strong. Against the materialistic society that we live in, the calm, peaceful way of life and moral standards of Buddhism is admirable. It is a religion that is true to itself. Buddhism has been divided into separate groups since the first century.

Buddhist – Someone who takes refuge in the Buddha, in his teachings and in the Sangha.

- **Theravada Buddhism:** This is the form of Buddhism in Sri Lanka, Burma and Thailand. Theravada means the tradition of the elders and was taught by senior monks. It is regarded as the Orthodox form of Buddhism.

Different forms of Buddhism –
• Theravada
• Mahayana
• Vajrayana

• **Mahayana Buddhism:** This is the form in China, Korea and Japan. Everyone is encouraged to practise Buddhism not just monks and nuns. They believe anyone can gain enlightenment. It is a more liberal form of Buddhism and is the largest division within the Buddhist faith.

• **Vajrayana Buddhism:** This is often called Tibetan Buddhism. It draws its ideas from Theravada and Mahayana Buddhism yet it is completely independent of both. The famous Dali Lama lives and preaches this type of Buddhism. These Buddhists believe that he is the reincarnation of the Buddha. Buddhists are peaceful people but they still encounter problems. In 1950 when Tibet was taken over by China, Buddhists were not allowed practise their religion. The Dali Lama was forced to leave Tibet and he moved to India.

In the West all three types of Buddhism are practised. Today there are about 350 million Buddhists worldwide. There are about 400 Buddhists living in Ireland now. Many of them practise a form of Buddhism called Nichiren Buddhism.

Over to You

1. The three groups of Buddhists are:
   A _____
   B _____
   C _____

2. Do you admire Buddhism? Why/why not?
3. Who is the Dali Lama?
4. Why do you think meditation is important today?
5. Do you think this religion is important today? Why/why not?

Nichiren Buddhism in Ireland

Read the following account of a young Buddhist living in Ireland today. She practices Nichiren Daishonin one of the many forms practiced throughout the world.

Nichiren Daishonin was a man who lived in 13th-century Japan. When he became a monk he studied vast amounts of scripture and realised the essence of all Buddhist teachings was chanting Nam-Myoho-Renge-Kyo. Anyone can practise this type of Buddhism today, regardless of race, creed, age or class. In Ireland people practise Nichiren Buddhism with the Soka Gakkai International (SGI), a lay Buddhist organisation. SGI members strive to live life every day developing the ability to live with confidence and create value in their own lives and in society.

I practise this Buddhism because it brings me great happiness. I cherish the friends that I have made here. When I chant Nam-Myoho-Renge-Kyo, I am able to transform any problem I may have into an opportunity for growth and happiness. We chant this phrase to be happy and for others around us to be happy. Also by chanting this phrase a person begins to see positive changes in his or her life. And as a person studies and learns more, the phrase begins to develop a deeper meaning. We chant sitting up straight and comfortably, while facing the **Gohonzon**. (This is a scroll of paper with Sanskrit and Chinese characters on it. It means an object of devotion for observing the mind.)

Once a month there are discussion meetings in one of our homes. These meetings are informal. I find the support and encouragement at these meetings invaluable.

When babies are born into this Buddhist practice there are no special ceremonies carried out. This is because Buddhists see birth as a part of the cycle of life. When Buddhists marry they follow the traditions of the culture. Wedding ceremonies are usually held at a place the couple chooses, like a hotel or rented hall.

In the end, Nichiren Buddhists believe that how we see the world around us depends on how we feel inside. We believe in a connection between ourselves and the world around us, and by becoming truly happy people we can make a positive influence in society.

This is the Butsudan, the Gohonzon is kept inside.

Over to You

1. Who was Nichiren Daishonin?
2. Why does the Buddhist practise this type of Buddhism?
3. What is the Gohonzon?
4. Why do you think the meetings held once a month are important?
5. What does she mean when she says that 'how we see the world depends on how we feel inside'?

Summary of Buddhism

Siddharta Gautama – The man who founded the religion called Buddhism.

Middle Way – The theory founded by Siddhartha Gautama which states that people could find happiness in a life lived between extreme luxury and extreme hardship.

Buddha – A name that means 'Enlightened One' and which was given to Siddhartha Gautama by his followers.

Tripitaka – The sacred writings of Buddhism, which mean 'Three Baskets'.

Nirvana – A state of perfect happiness and peace or enlightenment. It is seen as ultimate salvation.

The Four Noble Truths – These truths are Duktha, Samudaya, Magga and Nirvana.

The Eightfold Path – The Buddhist way of life. It contains eight steps:
1. Right understanding
2. Right thought
3. Right speech
4. Right action
5. Right livelihood
6. Right effort
7. Right mindfulness
8. Right concentration.

Relic – An object that belonged to a holy person, which is kept and treated as holy after their death.

Stupa or **pagoda** – A monument in a temple which holds the relics of the Buddha of the temple.

Meditation – A communal type of prayer that can be done on its own or in a group led by a leader. For Buddhists meditation is not a conversation with God, but a way to control their mind and help them make the right choices in life.

Sangha – A community of monks and nuns founded by the Buddha.

Buddhist – Someone who takes refuge in the Buddha, in his teachings and in the Sangha.

Different forms of Buddhism –
• Theravada
• Mahayana
• Vajrayana

SECTION D

THE QUESTION OF FAITH

AIMS

- To explore the situation of faith today.

- To identify the beginning of faith in the asking of questions and the search for answers.

- To recognise expressions of human questioning in modern culture.

- To identify the characteristics of religious faith.

HIGHER LEVEL ONLY
- To examine challenges to religious faith today.

- To offer opportunities for the exploration of, and reflection on, personal faith positions.

Chapter 14:
The Situation of Faith Today

Religious Belief and Practice

Religious Belief –
Religious belief means
the things that we
believe to be true about
God and the faith we
belong to.

Religious Practice –
Religious practice is how
we show these religious
beliefs. It means that we
put into practice in our
lives all that we believe.

Religious belief means the things that we believe to be true about God and the faith that we belong to.

Religious practice is how we show these religious beliefs. It means putting what we believe about God and our faith into practice in our lives.

In this chapter we will look at how religious belief and practice have changed over the last century in Ireland. Just like there have been changes in music, fashion and films, there have also been changes in religion. Some of these changes came about because of changes in society, historical events and religious events.

A personal account
When asked 'What are the greatest changes that have taken place in religious belief and practice in your lifetime?', 68-year-old Reena McDermott gave the following answer:

I remember…

When I was young it was very obvious when you walked into our house that we were a Catholic family. The Sacred Heart picture held pride of place and there were statues of Our Lady and St Joseph. Religion was a part of our daily lives as it was for most people at the time. Every morning and evening our parents listened while we said our prayers and there were holy pictures above our beds. Every evening after dinner the whole family would kneel in the front room while we said the rosary. Everyone had his or her own set of rosary beads. We prayed for many different things. I can remember praying for the conversion of Russia and for poor people all over the world.

Our weekly routine revolved around Church events. There was no meat for dinner on Fridays and every Saturday we went to confession. On Sunday morning you didn't eat until after you had been to Mass and received Holy Communion. Another memory I have is that when Daddy came home from Mass he would kiss the younger members of the family who were too small to receive communion and he would say, 'God Bless'. It was like he was sharing the experience of Holy Communion with them. At four o'clock we all went back to the church for Benediction. This was when the Blessed Sacrament was exposed and we said the rosary and sang hymns. The church was packed every week.

As well as attending Mass on Sunday the whole family went to the church on a Monday evening for miraculous medal devotion and Benediction. During the year there were many other religious festivals that we celebrated. Corpus Christi was in June and every house on our road would be decorated with bunting. The whole community made a procession through the parish and we had Benediction outside.

School also revolved around prayer. The day began and ended with prayer and we all stood at twelve o'clock and said the Angelus. Every day our teacher tested us on the catechism, which we had to learn off by heart. As we grew older we went to Sodality meetings once a month. These were gatherings where people came together to pray and listen to lectures on religious topics. There was one for men and one for women.

The biggest change in religious belief and practice came about in the 1960s. This was due to the decisions made at the Second Vatican Council, or Vatican II, as we called it. A very practical change was that the Mass was no longer to be said in Latin but in the vernacular, in other words, the language of the people who were celebrating the Mass. In the past the priest had said the Mass with his back to the people but now he faced them. There were other changes too like only having to fast for an hour before receiving communion instead of from the night before.

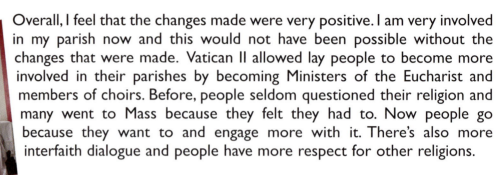

Overall, I feel that the changes made were very positive. I am very involved in my parish now and this would not have been possible without the changes that were made. Vatican II allowed lay people to become more involved in their parishes by becoming Ministers of the Eucharist and members of choirs. Before, people seldom questioned their religion and many went to Mass because they felt they had to. Now people go because they want to and engage more with it. There's also more interfaith dialogue and people have more respect for other religions.

One of the most important changes for me was a return to scripture. People had forgotten the richness and support that the Bible can bring to their faith. Vatican II encouraged Catholics to return to their sacred text. Some of the changes were difficult, especially for older members of the Church, but I feel that we now have a more vibrant church which is more relevant to our modern world.

Over to You

1. How would you know Reena came from a Catholic family if you walked into her home?
2. What part did religion play in school life when Reena was a child?
3. Explain three changes that came about because of Vatican II.
4. Did Reena think the changes made by Vatican II were positive ones? Why did she think this?
5. 'Some of the changes were difficult especially for older members of the church...' Why do you think this was the case?
6. Interview an elderly person you know or invite an elderly person to your class. Ask them about the changes that have taken place in their religious beliefs and practices over the years and what their opinion of Vatican II is.

Changes and Differences

There have been many changes in religious belief and practice over the last century in Ireland and throughout Europe. Some of these changes have been positive ones while others have had a negative effect. We will now look at the reasons for some of these changes, and also look at the differences between religious practice in Ireland and elsewhere.

1. The Schism

In 1054 a **schism** or **split** occurred in the Christian Church. Two traditions had developed in the Christian Church; one in the east of the Roman Empire with its headquarters in Constantinople and the other in the west, which was based in Rome. Their beliefs were basically the same but disagreements arose over things like leadership. Eventually in

1054 they went their separate ways and divided into the Catholic Church in the West and the Orthodox Church in the East. For a long time the two churches were in dispute but great progress has been made in recent decades. In 1965 the leaders of the two churches met and made peace.

Fill in the blanks ...

1. A schism is a _____.

2. In _____ they went their seperate ways and divided into _____ _____ in the west and the _____ Church in the east.

3. In _____ the leaders met and made peace.

The Orthodox Church

The main Orthodox Churches can be found in Greece, Russia, America and Ethiopia. Each branch of the Church is ruled over by a patriarch and the most senior of these is the Patriarch of Constantinople. Patriarch means founding father. Their beliefs are very similar to those of the Catholic Church, although there are some differences in terms of worship. While they also celebrate seven sacraments, their celebration of the Mass is slightly different. They place great emphasis on icons, and these are explored in more detail in Chapter 21.

An Orthodox church is quite different to a Catholic church. There are very few seats and these are mainly used by the elderly. The biggest difference is a feature called the **iconostasis**. This is a screen that separates the people from the area where the priests perform the mysteries or celebrations. Only members of the clergy are allowed behind these screens.

Candles are also a big feature in an Orthodox church and form an important part of the liturgy. The Orthodox Church does not believe in the doctrine of the Immaculate Conception and their creed is also different. Many of the feasts and holy days are the same as the Catholic Church, but an Orthodox person also celebrates their name day. This occurs on the feast day of the saint they were named after. Another big difference is that Orthodox priests can marry before they are ordained, if they wish.

Over to You

1. Where can the main Orthodox churches be found?
2. What does the word patriarch mean?
3. What are the differences in terms of worship and place of worship between the Catholic and Orthodox churches?

2. Politics

Two historical events show us how politics influenced and affected people's religious faith in Europe in the 20th century.

After the horrors of the Second World War many people's faith became stronger as they turned to their God to try and make sense of what had happened. The faith of the Jewish people changed forever after their experiences at the hands of Hitler in Nazi Germany. The Jewish population was greatly reduced and many lost their homes and livelihoods. However, they continued to remain a strong and faithful people.

In the years after the war some parts of Europe fell under communist rule, which made it difficult for some to practise their faith. America and Russia soon emerged as superpowers. There was fighting amongst these two countries as Russia wanted to spread communism while America wanted to limit it. The fall of the Berlin Wall in 1989 saw an end to this and people began to explore and express their religious faith more freely. The events of 1989 changed Europe forever.

3. Second Vatican Council (Vatican II)

The Second Vatican Council was a meeting of Catholic leaders that took place in Rome between 1962 and 1965. The Pope at the time was Pope John XXIII (23rd) and many saw him as a visionary man who helped bring the Church into the modern world. The Council wanted to reform many of the Church's practices, to work for unity among Christians and to encourage its members to work for justice and peace in the world. It was one of the most significant events in the history of the Catholic Church.

Jewish concentration camps during WWII

The Fall of the Berlin Wall in 1989

The meeting of the Second Vatican Council

Up for Discussion

1. What does the word technology mean?
2. What technology do you use in your home?
3. How do you think the media exposes us to different cultures and belief systems?

4. Modernity

The world we live in has changed in so many ways over the last century. Advances in technology and a higher standard of living for many are just some of the reasons why people's religious beliefs and practices have changed. People travel more and the media too exposes us to different cultures and belief systems. While the Catholic Church remains the largest religion in the world, Mass attendance and vocations are two areas that have seen a big decline in some countries.

Mass attendance

Years ago attending Mass on a Sunday was the norm for most Catholics in Ireland. Indeed many went during the week too. Churches were full and for most it was a family occasion. In recent years there has been a dramatic decline in the numbers of Catholics going to Mass. A survey done by the European Values Surveys (EVS) in 1981 showed that 83 per cent of Catholics attended Mass once a week or more, but by 1999 another survey saw that figure drop to 59 per cent. However, the number of people who said they believed in God actually rose by 1 per cent; from 95 to 96 per cent.

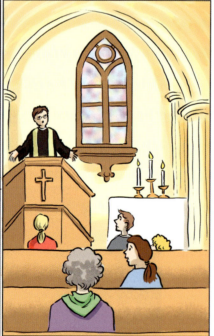

So if people still believe in God, why are they not practising their faith as much as before? Some possible reasons may be:

1. **Lifestyle:** Nowadays people live their lives at a much faster pace than before. Sunday was traditionally a day of rest. People seem to work longer hours and if they're not working they have many more opportunities for leisure time than they did before. Shops weren't always open on Sundays, believe it or not! In today's busy world many people feel they do not have the time or energy to practise their faith.

2. **Freedom:** Have you ever heard the old saying 'children should be seen and not heard'? Years ago going to Mass was a part of family life and children were expected to go along with their parents' wishes. Nowadays young people have much more freedom. A lot of young people still attend Mass with their families, but others are sometimes given the option of choosing for themselves whether to go or not. In general we live in a more liberal society.

3. **Church influence:** For numerous years the Church held a place of high importance in many people's lives. They looked to the Church for guidance and priests were well-respected members of the community. People today are much more independent and do not look to the Church as much for guidance. They are more inclined to look at their peer group and the media to give them direction.

4. **Media:** One way that the media influenced people in Ireland was through television. The chat show, *The Late Late Show*, appeared on Irish television in the 1960s. It was the first time that issues like contraception and divorce were discussed on national television. It opened up people to new ideas and opinions and they became less afraid to say how they felt.

Up for Discussion

Do you agree with the reasons for the drop in Mass attendance given above? Can you think of any others?

Over to You

1. What was Vatican II?
2. What did Vatican II hope to achieve?
3. Explain two historical events that changed religious belief and practice in Europe in the last century?
4. Give two reasons why some people are not practicing their religion as much as before?

Vocations

Becoming a priest or a nun is a very important life-changing decision. It requires huge commitment and faith. Statistics show that less people are making this commitment now than they did in the past. In 1980, there were 137 ordinations to the priesthood, but by 1999 that number had dropped to 49. In 2005, no priest was ordained in the Archdiocese of Dublin, the first time this had ever happened.

Because of this decline the average age of priests has risen too. This means that their workload has increased and in some parishes there are fewer Masses on Sundays because there are not enough priests to celebrate them.

So what are the reasons behind this drop in vocations?

1. **Education and employment:** Young people today have many opportunities when it comes to education and employment. Third-level education is not only free but offers a wide variety of courses at all levels. Unemployment is at an all-time low. This was not always the case, however. People in the past did not have as many opportunities.

One advantage of joining a religious order was that it allowed people to continue their education and it was a well-respected lifestyle.

2. **Materialism:** We live in a very money-driven world. Many people see success as having lots of possessions. New cars, bigger houses and exotic holidays have become all-important. People seek jobs with high salaries to give them a certain kind of lifestyle. Being ordained, on the other hand, is more about giving than receiving and is not about how much money you make.

3. **Public opinion:** In the past families felt it was an honour to have a son or daughter become a priest or nun. In fact, most families experienced a member of their extended family having a vocation. Because of the changes in our society already mentioned, such as materialism, this is not always the case today. Some people feel under pressure to get a certain type of job and might think that becoming a priest or nun is not what people would expect or want from them.

Up for Discussion

Has your parish been affected in any way by the drop in vocations? Maybe invite your local priest into your class to help you with this.

The Bigger Picture

Some of the issues we have looked at may lead us to think that religious belief and practice have changed in a negative way in recent years. We must remember, though, that there are two sides to every story.

While our Mass attendance numbers have dropped, we still have one of the highest Mass attendance rates in Europe. The fact that so many people still believe in God shows us that religion is still very important to people. In fact, in a survey in 1999, 70 per cent of Irish people said they pray once a week. This tells us that even though people may not go to Mass they have not forgotten about God.

The funeral of Pope John Paul II in the Vatican.

They also see religion as playing an essential part of life experiences such as birth, marriage and death. People have shown how important religion is to them in other ways too. At tragic or sad times, like 9/11 and the death of Pope John Paul II, people turned to prayer and to their faith for strength and support.

Faith and practice in the life of the adolescent

Adolescence refers to teenagers or young people. Just as certain things influence how we dress or what music we listen to as teenagers, our religious belief and practice can be influenced by outside factors. If we imagine our religious faith to be like a suitcase, we can unpack it and see what's inside or the different elements that make it up.

1. Family: Our family are our most important teachers and have the biggest influence on our lives. Even though we may not always agree with their opinions, we still look to them for direction and guidance. They are the people who first introduce us to our faith. They can give us a very strong religious foundation. They may encourage us to participate in religious events and lead us by example.

2. Friends: In our teenage years our friends are probably the most important people in our lives after our family. We value their opinions and want their approval. In terms of our religious faith and practice, they can have a positive or negative effect depending on their own faith. Seeing them practise their faith may encourage us to do the same. On the other hand, we may feel embarrassed to express our faith if our friends are not religious. However, faith is a personal thing and our real friends will respect our beliefs and values.

3. Media: The media is something we cannot escape from. It is everywhere we look and comes in many different forms; radio, television, internet and advertising. In general teenagers are the group that are most affected by it. They look to the media to see what is fashionable and what other people are doing.

If the media is negative about religious faith or practice, then young people can be influenced by this. However, the media can also be a good influence. It makes us aware of what's going on in the world and can draw our attention to important issues. For example, Mass is broadcast on a Sunday morning on national television, and in 2005 the newspapers wrote many articles concerning the election of a new pope.

Up for Discussion

What have been the biggest influences on your religious faith and practice?

Over to You

Exam Style Question

Write an article for your local newspaper entitled 'Changes in religious belief and practice in Ireland – for better or worse?'

In this chapter,

you will become familiar with the following concepts:

■ Life's questions and the questioner
■ Search
■ Meaning and meaninglessness
■ Reflection
■ Awe and wonder
■ Humanism

Chapter 15:

The Beginnings of Faith

Life's Questions

One day in class Pat was busy writing notes to his friend when there was a knock at the door. It was Mr Cleary, the school principal. The teacher was called outside for a moment, which gave Pat even more time to write to his friend John about the previous night. He laughed to himself as he scribbled the note. He had not a care in the world.

After a few minutes, his teacher came back into the room and told Pat that Mr Cleary needed to see him for a few minutes and to bring his school bag with him. Suddenly, Pat began to panic because the only time you were called to the principal's office was when you were in trouble.

When he went outside, the principal asked him to walk with him to the office. Pat felt absolutely sick. What would his parents say when he was sent home early from school and told not to come back for a few days? He knew they would be furious.

When he arrived at the office, his older sister Fiona was there. She looked as if she had been crying. Now he really began to panic! Mr Cleary told him to sit down, but Pat couldn't, as he knew something very serious had happened. Fiona began to tell her brother that their dad had gone to work that morning but had a massive heart attack and had died instantly.

Immediately, Pat started to shout 'no' at her. It was only just a few hours earlier that he had got out of his dad's car when he had dropped him to school. This couldn't be happening. His whole world seemed to turn upside down in those few minutes.

When Pat and Fiona arrived back at the house, their relations were beginning to arrive. After seeing his mother Pat went upstairs to his bedroom. For a while he just sat on his bed with his hands over his face. He began to ask how this could have happened. How could a 45-year-old man die without any warning signs? What would he do without his dad on a Saturday, as they always went to football matches together? How would his family look after his mother?

After a while there was a knock on the door. It was his Uncle Tim. Pat couldn't hold in the tears and the two of them sat together for a few minutes holding each other tightly in their grief.

Over to You

1. How did the day start off for Pat?
2. Do you think it was a good idea for Pat's sister to come to the school?
3. What do you think was said between Pat and Fiona on their journey home?
4. Do you think the questions Pat asked in his own mind in his bedroom were normal questions a teenager would ask in this situation?

The Questioner

You might have had an experience similar to that of Pat. You may have asked similar questions to the ones that Pat asked. What makes human beings different is our ability to ask questions. As human beings we ask many questions each day. In that way, we learn a lot from the questions that we ask.

Over to You

Think of the past few hours in your own life. Think about the questions you have asked or the ones you have thought about asking. Write them down and ask yourself which of these questions is most important.

A time to reflect

Question / questioner –
Asking questions means that
we are interested to learn
more about a particular
topic. The questioner is the
one who looks for this
information.

Over time people have always asked questions. Times in history like the Renaissance and Reformation were all periods of great questioning. The Renaissance was a time of rebirth in art, architecture, sculpture, and so on. The Reformation was a time to question what was happening in the Catholic Church at the time.

The Mona Lisa by Leonardo da Vinci is an example of Renaissance art.

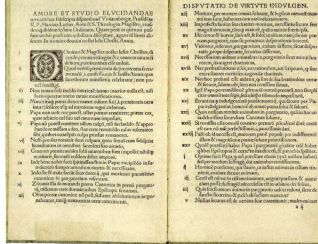

The 95 Theses. A symbol of the reformation.

Over to You

Imagine for a moment that you lived during one of these exciting times in history. What questions would you like to ask?

A sign of maturity

When we ask questions it is a sign that we are growing in maturity. We begin to look at life at a deeper level to how we looked at it as children. The questions we asked at four years of age are very different to the ones we now ask.

Our Search for Meaning

By questioning what is happening around us we are looking for meaning. Meaning refers to a sense of purpose. It helps us make sense of the various situations we find ourselves in. If we do not have a sense of purpose, life can seem meaningless for us.

People find meaning through their family, friends, music, money and religion.

The family

Many teenagers look to their family as a source of meaning. The family gives the adolescent a sense of belonging and purpose. Being part of a family unit is therefore very important. Families can be made up of one parent or two, but it is the strong link between each family member that is important. For many children they learn the basic values of love, honesty, trust and respect from the family. They develop a sense of respect and dignity for each family member.

Not everything in life runs smoothly and families are no different. It is often in the most difficult times of our lives that we grow and mature into better people. Family members may have arguments but this often clears the air, as each member wants only what is best for the other. For example, parents sometimes tell their adolescent son or daughter to be home at a specific time, which can lead to upset and anger, especially if their friends are allowed out later. Parents only want the best for their son or daughter.

The role of the family always plays a big part in the various soap operas on TV. It is clear from these programmes that families have differences of opinion, but at the end of the day their love for each other is evident.

Search – To search for something is to look at what is around us.

Question / questioner – Questioning what is happening around us we are looking for meaning. Meaning refers to a sense of purpose. It is something that has importance and significance for us.

Over to You

1. How important do you think the family is as a source of meaning in our lives?
2. Describe the family unit you belong to.
3. Describe your favourite family on TV at the moment. Why did you choose this family over another?

Friends

It is a good time to return to the story at the beginning of this chapter.

After the funeral Pat needed the support of his friends, especially at this very difficult time in his life. More than anything he needed his friends to call to the house to let him know what was happening in their lives. He didn't want them not to call. Even though he knew they wouldn't know what to say, he just wanted them around him all the same.

However his friends felt awkward because they didn't know the right words to say to make it better for Pat. One day after the funeral was over, Pat rang his best friend John. After a while John apologised for not ringing during the previous few days. He admitted that he just didn't know what to say to him. Understanding the situation, Pat said that he would have felt the same if he was in his position. This conversation cleared the air between them and within an hour they met up.

Sharing good times and bad times

Friendship is a very important aspect of our lives. It is important to share the good times as well as the bad times. Just like in the story, it is often difficult to know what is the best thing to do. It is only by talking these moments through that friends can come to a better understanding of themselves and others. Friendship adds meaning to our lives. Without friends we would be very lonely and isolated. It is therefore good to be able to discuss things with friends.

Over to You

1. What do you think are the main qualities in a friend?
2. Do you think Pat's friends were good friends? Why/why not?
3. How important do you think friendship is?

Music

The last few years have seen an increase in the number of people auditioning for talent programmes like *The X Factor*, *You're a Star* and *Pop Idol*. Queues of young people stand in the pouring rain or sunshine with many dreaming of success. When interviewed, they speak of music as their great love. It also brings passion to their lives. When they sing they feel completely free.

Music can bring meaning to our lives as it helps us express what we feel inside. From a song we can often tell how the singer feels. In the song 'I still haven't found what I'm looking for' by the band U2, it speaks about a search for meaning. In fact, life is a continuous journey searching for the unknown.

Up for Discussion

1. What is your favourite song? Why?
2. Have you ever written a song or a piece of music?
3. Who is your favourite musician/singer? Why? Do you think they express what they feel through song?

Money

Most of us at some stage or other have stated that we would like to win the National Lottery. Many of us have had dreams of how we would spend the Lotto money and have visualised ourselves in a big house with a big car and a big bank balance.

Then for a moment we stop and think and ask ourselves would this make us happy. For many of us money might help out a little, but it would not make us happy. In the long term we get our happiness from other sources. In the story of 'The Prodigal Son', which you will read about in Chapter 26, money did not bring happiness to the son. What made him happy was being able to return to his family.

Over to You

1. Have you ever dreamt of winning the Lotto? If so, what did you dream you would do with the money?
2. Do you think that money brings long-lasting happiness? Why/why not?

Religion

Aftermath of the South East Asian tsunami.

The tsunami in South-East Asia on St Stephen's Day, 2004 was a major challenge to our understanding of God. Hundreds of thousands of people died and whole villages were wiped out. We came to realise that the mystery of God is far beyond our understanding. However, it is valid to question if God had a part to play in the disaster. Was he the one that caused it to happen? To think this is to believe that God was punishing us for the evils of the world.

The question is do we want to believe in a God like this? The New Testament tells us about a God that 'holds each of us in the palm of his hand' and wants only what is best for us. His love for us is faithful and never-ending. It is therefore important to ask questions about life events. But religion does not give us all the answers. It would be impossible to do this, but it does try to help us understand what is happening in our lives. Jesus himself gave meaning to life. For him, each person was valued and loved for their uniqueness.

Awe and wonder – Admiration and respect for something or somebody, perhaps after a great event.

Awe and wonder

What we need to take from the tsunami was the response of the world to this terrible act of nature. It filled many people with awe and wonder. Many of us were in awe at the generosity of many people worldwide. There was a tremendous outbreak of love, generosity and care for the victims of the tragedy. Through this response, people lived out the message of Jesus Christ to give generously and to walk humbly with God.

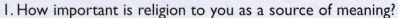

Over to You

1. How important is religion to you as a source of meaning?
2. How do you feel about a revengeful God causing the tsunami?
3. Give an example of when you felt God was holding you in the palm of his hand.
4. Can you remember anything that was done in your school or locality for the victims of the tsunami? Write a few lines describing the event.

Humanism

Christians, Jews and Muslims believe in an all-powerful God. They look to the Bible, the Torah and the Koran for guidance on their God. On the other hand, some people have no religious beliefs. They do not look to a religious code to show them how to treat others. Their faith is not in God but in humanity instead. Religion is not a source of meaning in their lives, as they find meaning in the way they respect and value life. These people are called **humanists**.

Humanists believe that there is no God or gods and that the greatest power is the human being. They also believe that we can make sense of life itself through our own experiences. An example of an Irish humanist is the former politician, vet and broadcaster, Justin Keating.

Humanism / humanist – A humanist's faith is not in God, it is in man. Humanists believe there is no God or Gods. They find meaning in how they respect and value life.

Justin Keating,
Irish humanist

Over to You

1. Where do humanists find meaning?
2. Find out about a famous humanist and write about them.

181

In this chapter,

you will become familiar with the following concepts:

- Trust
- Faith
- Personal faith
- Childhood faith
- Mature faith
- Stages of faith

Chapter 16:

The Growth of Faith

Forming an Image

An image is a picture we get in our mind when we imagine something. Some things are easy to imagine while others can be more difficult.

Over to You

Imagine each of the following. As you do, draw or write about what you see in your mind's eye: (a) a flower (b) a beach (c) Santa Claus.

These things are easy to imagine, as they are things that you are familiar with. You may have seen them yourself or seen pictures of them in books. If you compare them with your classmates' images, you may find that there are a lot of similarities.

Images of God

Think for a moment about your image of God. What does God look like? What kind of person is God?

Over to You

Draw your image of God. Write about your image of God. You can use some of the words listed below or think of more yourself.

kind … old … angry … powerful … father … magic … caring … reliable … wise … punishing … friendly … loving … generous … selfish

The source of images

Read the following story about where we can get our images from.

Aunt Nuala

Lucy was very excited. She and her Mum were off to the airport to collect her Aunt Nuala, who was her Mum's younger sister. Lucy had never met her before because she lived in Australia and the last time she came home for a visit Lucy was only a baby. Over the years Lucy had heard lots of stories about when her Mum and Nuala were young girls. And they used to get up to all sorts of mischief!

In her head Lucy had a picture of Aunt Nuala as being a very smiley person with a twinkle in her eye! Every year, Nuala always sent Lucy a birthday present and they always seemed to be just what she wanted. Last year, she had sent a box full of make-up and nail varnish! Mum wasn't too pleased but Lucy was allowed to wear them because Aunt Nuala had sent them all the way from Australia. As a result, Lucy thought that Nuala must be very cool to send something like that.

Whenever Nuala rang, she always asked about Lucy's friends and what she was up to in school. Because Nuala seemed to be interested in her niece, Lucy thought she was a good friend to have. When the day finally arrived when she would get to meet Aunt Nuala in person, Lucy just couldn't believe it. More than anything, Lucy hoped that Nuala would live up to the image she had of her in her head.

Up for Discussion

In this story Lucy had built up an image in her head about the type of person her aunt was. Did you ever build up an image of someone you hadn't met before?

Our image of God is like this. Lucy's image of Nuala came from stories she had heard from other people and things she had done for Lucy, like sending birthday presents. Having an image of God can be difficult because we have never seen God. Our image of God may come from stories we have heard from our parents or teachers, or from pictures we have seen, or even songs we have listened to.

Over to You

Write about where your image of God comes from. Share it with your classmates and see if your answers are similar.

Images from scripture

Scripture can help us to form an image of God. Read the following psalm and answer the questions that follow it.

Psalm 46

God is our shelter and strength,
Always ready to help in times of trouble.
So we will not be afraid, even if the earth is shaken
And mountains fall into the ocean depths;
Even if the seas roar and rage,
And the hills are shaken by the violence.

Come and see what the Lord has done.
See what amazing things he has done on earth.
He stops wars all over the world;
He breaks bows and destroys spears, and sets shields on fire.
'Stop fighting,' he says,
'and know that I am God,
supreme among the nations.
Supreme over the world.'

The Lord Almighty is with us;
The God of Jacob is our refuge.

Over to You

1. How is God described in the first verse of the psalm?
2. What is the image of God presented in the second verse?
3. Which image of God do you prefer? Why?
4. The psalms are often compared to poetry. Try writing your own poem about your image of God.

Personal Faith

Look at the following extracts taken from a series of letters that ordinary people wrote to God.

Dear Holy God,
I went to see you at Mass yesterday. I did not make any noise in the church. Next week is my birthday. I really want a doll's house. I know you will get one for me. You can do anything. I have been a very good girl. I learned a new prayer in school. I do not know what it means. But it sounds nice. We are going to say it every day.
Emily (aged 6)

Personal Faith –

A persons own religious belief

Dear God,
I can't believe my Junior Cert is starting next week. I know I haven't gone to Mass a lot lately, but if you help me with my exams I promise I'll go every week. To be honest I was a bit angry with you because I asked you to help my dog Tiger get better but you didn't. Why not, God? Why do you only help sometimes? At times, I'm not even sure if you're there.
James (aged 15)

Dear God,
Things have been hectic at work lately but I'm glad I took the time to go to that concert in the church last night. It was lovely to see everyone in the parish and the music helped to remind me that Christmas is about more than just shopping!

I've been praying a lot lately for my friend Eve who is sick. I know you're with her giving her strength and that you'll be with us all no matter what happens. Please keep her in your loving care.
Thank you.
Sheila (aged 36)

Up for Discussion

How would you describe the faith of Emily, James and Sheila? How different are their faiths?

Stages of Faith

Stages of faith – The growth and development of faith from childhood, through adolescence to maturity.

Like most things in life our faith changes and grows as we get older.

Childhood faith

Childhood faith – A simple trusting faith which is influenced by those around us.

At this stage our faith could be described as very simple and trusting. Our faith is very much influenced by those around us who teach and care for us. We can tend to see God as a type of magician. We think he rewards our good behaviour and punishes our bad behaviour. We don't really understand our faith but practise it as we see others doing it. So we do it too without asking any questions.

Adolescent faith – A challenging stage of our faith development when we ask many questions.

Adolescent faith

This can be a difficult stage of our faith journey. We are seeking answers to lots of questions and we may challenge God to give us answers. We may feel God does not understand us and that we do not understand him. We are influenced by things like our friends and the media. We

186

can see God as an authority figure that watches us and waits to see if we do right or wrong. As a result, we may not give time to our faith.

Mature faith

At this stage our faith journey has led us to a place where we are comfortable with our faith. We do not have all the answers to our questions, but we know that that is okay and that we are not afraid to keep searching. We have a very real and meaningful relationship with God and he is someone we turn to in good times and bad. We work at this relationship and it is an important part of who we are.

It is important to remember that different people reach the different stages at different times. There is no particular age when we should be at the next level. Also, some people may never reach the mature stage of faith.

Mature faith – The final stage of our faith development when we have reached a meaningful and comfortable stage with God.

Over to You

Write a paragraph entitled 'The stages of faith'.

Exam Style Question

A. Choose **one** of the sketches opposite.
  a. Name the image of God the artist had in mind when drawing this picture.
  b. What does this image tell us about the artist's understanding of God?

B. Read this 'letter to God' written by a six-year-old child.
  Dear God,
  Thank you for the lego the new baby gave me. I prayed for a baby sister but got a brother. It's okay though. He's quiet and sleeps alot. The lego is great.
  Love, Alex.

  a. Describe **one** thing about this letter that is typical of a child's faith.
  b. Suggest **one** way in which Alex's faith may change in adolescence and explain why this might be so.

Image of God (*Number 1*)

American Bible Society

Image of God (*Number 2*)

YOU'VE GOT TO FOLLOW MY PLAN

Redemptorist Publications

In this chapter,

you will become familiar with the following concepts:

■ Prayer
■ Worship
■ Monotheism
■ Polytheism

Chapter 17:
The Expression of Faith

Prayer

Prayer – A conversation with God whether in a formal or informal setting.

Prayer is a way of sharing our lives with God. When we pray we welcome God into our lives. We ask him to bless us and keep us safe. When we pray we grow closer to God. We do not have to show our best side to God as he knows us completely. Each one of us is held in the palm of his hand. This gives us the confidence that we are loved by God, even when we fail to do good.

We do not have to pray aloud using words because prayer can be a simple thought, a sign or an action. Prayer can be **formal**, for example saying the Our Father, or **informal**, where we use our own words to express to God how we feel. We can also pray in any place where we feel comfortable.

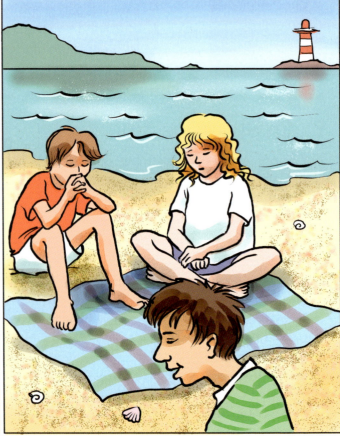

Up for Discussion

Choose from the following list of ways that help you to pray. Discuss with the person beside you your particular preferences.

- Walking along a beach listening to the waves crashing against the shore
- Playing your favourite sport
- Playing your favourite CD
- Going out on a date
- Reading a book
- Chatting with friends over coffee
- A prayer meeting
- Being present at a concert
- Visiting relations
- Visiting a holy place
- Relaxing by the fireside
- Being present at a wedding or funeral
- Going on a holiday
- Walking through a forest on a cold frosty morning
- Getting ready for a special occasion
- Doing an exam

A time to pray

Prayer is an integral part of our being. Prayer gives us support and comfort in times of trouble. It also gives us the opportunity to ask God for guidance and help in the way we live out our lives. It is often in times of difficulty that we turn to God to seek his help and love.

Bridge over Troubled Water

When you're weary, feeling small,
When tears are in your eyes,
I will dry them all;
I'm on your side. When times get rough
And friends just can't be found,
Like a bridge over troubled water
I will lay me down.
Like a bridge over troubled water
I will lay me down.

When you're down and out,
When you're on the street,
When evening falls so hard
I will comfort you.
I'll take your part.
When darkness comes
And pain is all around,
Like a bridge over troubled water
I will lay me down.
Like a bridge over troubled water
I will lay me down.

Sail on silvergirl,
Sail on by.
Your time has come to shine.
All your dreams are on their way.
See how they shine
If you need a friend
I'm sailing right behind.

Like a bridge over troubled water
I will ease your mind.
Like a bridge over troubled water
I will ease your mind.

Lyrics by Paul Simon

Over to You

1. What do you think of the title of the song?
2. Do you think the song is a good example of prayer?
3. What do you think is the main message coming from the song?
4. What emotions/feelings are discussed in the song?

Prayer and friendship

Read the following prayer about the importance of friendship. Think about the friends that you have now. While reading the prayer, keep in mind the gift that God has given to each of us: the gift of friendship.

For My Friends

God, we give you thanks as the day comes to an end,
For those who mean so much to us,
And without whom life could never be the same.
We thank You for those to whom we can go
At any time and never feel a nuisance.
We thank You for those to whom we can go
When we are tired, knowing that they have,
For the weary, the gift of rest.
We thank You for those with whom we can talk,
And keep nothing back, knowing that
They will not laugh at our dreams or mock our failures.
We thank You for those in whose presence
It is easier to be good.
Amen.

Prayer and music

Liam Lawton comes from the parish of Edenderry, Co Offaly. He was ordained a priest in 1984 and worked for a while in the Carlow Cathedral parish and Knockbeg College. He was then granted time to pursue his ministry in music full-time. His firm belief is that when you sing you pray twice.

When Liam Lawton sings it is like the voice of Christ awakening in each of us. He is a humble and gracious man with no ego. His vocation is to write sacred music for the Church in today's society. Through his music he wishes to reach out to people in their darkest hour. His performance in New York after the 9/11 tragedy is proof of this. So too is the song he wrote for the many victims of the tsunami in South-East Asia on St Stephen's Day, 2004.

By means of his music he hopes to bring young people back to an ever-changing church. He believes that Christians today have a lot to learn from the early Celtic Church in Ireland. This is because the Celts experienced God everywhere and they had a true concern for creation. These themes are evident in the music that Fr Lawton composes.

Over to You

1. What do you think is the key to Fr Lawton's successful ministry?
2. How important do you think music is to prayer?
3. How important was his music to the world events named?

Worship

Worship – Worship means giving God respect, honour and praise.

To worship means giving God the respect, honour and praise that he truly deserves as creator and father of us all. Prayer is a form of worship. Through the sacraments we worship God publicly. Every sacrament is an opportunity to praise and thank God for the gifts which we have received from him. When we celebrate the Eucharist, we thank God for creating each and every one of us and for sending his only son to live and die amongst us.

God's Presence

I am a little stone.
I can be your best friend.
I can teach you to pray.

Put me under your pillow.
Then at night when you lie down
You will feel me and remember
To thank God for the day.

Put me down on the floor
Beside your bed.
Then in the morning when
You stub your toe against me
You will remember to thank God
For the new beginning.

Put me in your pocket
Then throughout the day
You will feel me when looking for money
And you will remember to pray
For those who have nothing.

Hold me in your hand
When you pray.
I will remind you that
God is a secure rock you can trust.
Feel my unique shape
And know there is no God like our God.

Over to You

1. How can we show worship to God?
2. In the poem, how is God's presence felt every day?
3. What do you think that the line 'God is a secure rock you can trust' means?
4. Pick out a line from the poem that shows a sense of worship. Why did you choose that line?

Two people of religious faith

People can express their faith in many ways. Here are the stories of two people, Frances Margaret Taylor and Edmund Rice, who had a deep religious faith.

Frances Margaret Taylor

Frances Margaret Taylor was an exceptional and extraordinary woman. She was born into an English Anglican family in 1832. She was a person with a great heart and had a love for everything that was good. Alongside Florence Nightingale she nursed soldiers during the Crimean war. The conditions they worked in were appalling but they rarely complained, as there was a lot of suffering around. Some of these soldiers were Irish Catholics. She was so touched by their faith that she herself became a Catholic. She believed that if she were to die, she would want to be in the faith of those she nursed. Her continued faith was an act of love. She made a plea that 'someone will rise up to plead the cause of the poor and to help them, not by doling out alms of this world's goods, but by those words and acts which make them feel we have alike one hope, one end, one master.' In a nutshell these words sum up the dreams and hopes of a great-hearted Victorian woman, Frances Taylor.

When Frances was young she enjoyed the countryside and the simple joys of outdoor life. She was always sympathetic towards the poor and downtrodden of society. At the age of 10, her father, a clergyman, died. It was because of this that her family moved to the city of London.

In 1853 when Frances was 21 years old she went to an Anglican Sisterhood to help with the terrible outbreak of cholera in the west of England. Her sister Charlotte stayed with her for a few months but felt this was not her true calling. Their nursing experience was a huge advantage to both girls especially as the Crimean War had broken out and there were a lot of wounded soldiers to be treated. There can be no question that Frances enjoyed nursing the cholera stricken people. She risked her own life in doing this. Frances was a most human character, full of fun and mischief. She was an intensely passionate person with a big heart.

France believed poverty could be material, moral or spiritual. She founded The Order of the Poor Servants of the Mother of God in 1869. This new order of

sisters was free to work with and for the poor. Their spirit was one of reverence for every person. Their aim was to restore the dignity of the children of God especially to the destitute and demoralised poor of the great cities. In 1872, she made her final vows of poverty, chastity and obedience and became known as Mother Magdalen. Her great love for the poorest of Gods children came from her conviction that they shared the poverty of Jesus in a special way. She saw herself and her sisters as servants, as by serving they imitated Christ on earth. She also saw a vision of Christ growing within each person in wisdom, understanding and love.

In the book, *Penny Apples*, by Bill Cullen, Portland Row retirement home is mentioned which was a nursing home for the elderly founded by The Poor Servants. It has now been transferred to St Gabriel's in Edenmore, Dublin. The last convent Frances founded was the workhouse in Loughlinstown and later the sisters served in Rathdrum and Youghal. The sisters, work in the poorest parts of Africa and South America and the spirit of Margaret Taylor is still alive in schools in Carriagtwohill, Raheny and Castledermot.

Over to You

1. What was Frances Taylor's mission?
2. What kind of childhood did she have?
3. Why did Frances decide to become a Catholic?
4. What was the vision behind her work?
5. Why do you think she is seen as a person of great faith today?

Edmund Rice

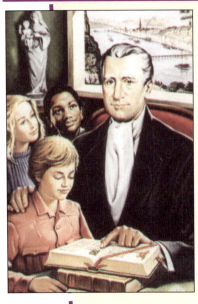

Edmund Ignatius Rice was born on 1 June 1762 in Callan, Co Kilkenny. He received a good education before going to work in his uncle's business. In 1775 he married Mary Elliott, but she died after giving birth to a baby girl that was disabled. After his wife's death, Edmund's life was never the same again.

Edmund was a wealthy man but became more and more disturbed by the poverty that Catholics lived in. His prayer life deepened and his reading of the scriptures also grew. Instead of shutting himself away in a monastery, he decided to do something significant for the children of Waterford. He set a school up for boys. But his real desire was to found a religious order of men that would educate these children and give them the dignity and self-respect they deserved.

In 1808, seven men took their vows and became the Presentation Brothers. This was the first congregation of men to be founded in Ireland. The Brothers not only educated boys but fed and clothed them too. In

1820, the order became known as the Christian Brothers, but a small group of the brothers kept the name Presentation Brothers. By 1825, there were 30 Christian Brothers working in 12 towns and cities, educating 5,500 boys free of charge.

Edmund's spirituality was practical, for he believed there was a great need 'to give to the poor in handfuls'. Many boys were given a better life because of him. The poor saw him as 'a man raised up by God'. The motto of the Christian Brothers comes from the Book of Job 1:21: 'The Lord has given, and the Lord has taken away; blessed be the name of the Lord forever.'

This clever businessman, loving and devoted husband and father, grieving widower, modern educator and brave founder of the Christian Brothers was declared to be Blessed Edmund Rice by Pope John Paul II in Rome on 6 October 1996. His feast day is May 5th.

Over to You

1. What sort of life did Edmund have?
2. How significant do you think was the death of his wife?
3. What was his philosophy on life?
4. How important do you think was the founding of the Presentation Brothers? Explain your answer.
5. What does the motto of the Christian Brothers mean?
6. What does blessed before his name mean?

Monotheism and polytheism

The meaning of *mono* is one and *theos* means God, so monotheism is belief in one God. Examples of monotheistic faiths are Judaism, Christianity and Islam.

The word *poly* means more than one and *theos* means God, so polytheism is a belief in more than one God. Each element of nature is controlled by a different God. So you could have a God of sun or a God of rain. An example of this kind of faith is Hinduism or the ancient Egyptian Gods.

The Egyptian God Horus, the falcon-headed sky God and the Goddess Hathor.

Monotheism – Mono means one and theos means God, so monotheism is the belief in one God.

Polytheism – Poly means more than one and theos means God, so polytheism is a belief in more than one God.

Chapter 18:

Challenges to Faith

■ (Higher Level)

The World around Us

World view –
Our world view is how we see the world around us.

An earthquake in Pakistan, 2005.

Have you ever thought about the importance of each of us in the world? Have you ever thought why we were born in a particular place at a particular time? Have you ever thought about how you should live in this world?

These questions are asked by millions of people around the world. Our **world view** helps us think about what is happening around us and helps us to live our lives. Our world view comes from everything we know from religion, philosophy and science.

Some ways of understanding the world around us are based on a religious belief. Other ways of understanding our world are unrelated to religion. Many people today see the world from a very strong non-religious point of view.

Many of us at times question the existence of God, especially when something bad happens to us or to the world around us. Many questioned the existence of God when an earthquake hit Pakistan in October 2005.

Over to You

Can you think of other examples when God's presence was called into question? Write about them.

Reflection

It is important to **reflect** on the existence of God. There are different responses to the existence of God.

Theism

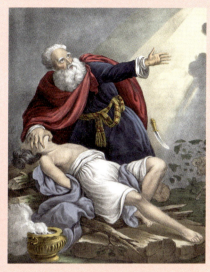

The word **theism** means to believe in God. Christians and other monotheistic faiths believe in one God – a God that created each and everyone one of us in his likeness. They also believe he created the world for us. God is there as a guide and a friend leading us to the Promised Land. Christians believe that God revealed himself through his son Jesus Christ. The Jewish community believe that God revealed himself through the prophet Abraham and then Moses. Muslims believe that God revealed himself through the words of the prophet Muhammad.

Theism – To believe in God.

Atheism – To deny the existence of God.

Agnosticism – The belief that the human mind is not capable of knowing whether God exists or not.

Atheism

Atheism denies the existence of God. The absence of their belief in God can be a deliberate choice. Or it can be as a result of their inability to believe in religious teaching. For atheists God is not real.

Agnosticism

Agnosticism is the belief that the human mind is not capable of knowing if God exists. If God cannot be explained by reason or science he does not exist. The human mind cannot know anything that is beyond it. If we cannot say for certain, then God does not exist. Therefore, we can only know what is happening in the present world and not the afterlife.

GOD DOES NOT EXIST!

Secularism

Secularism – This practice opposes the influence that religion has on our society.

Secularism is the way we make our choices in life that excludes God. A secularist opposes the influence religion has on our society. Some secularists do not want public figures to make reference to God. For example, during her first term as President of Ireland, Mary McAleese often used the words 'God willing' or 'with God's help' in her public statements. Before she was inaugurated for a second term of office, secularists asked her to stop making references to God in her public statements.

Does this mean that God should not have a place in the Ireland of the Celtic Tiger? The President was simply using language that she had used throughout her life. She was not expressing a particular theological point of view.

For some time in Ireland there have been calls to stop the Angelus being broadcast on RTÉ television and radio. It is believed by some people that the Angelus has no place on the schedules of the State broadcaster. However, the Angelus is only a few minutes of quiet reflection. It gives an opportunity for people of all religions to take some time out and think about what is happening around us.

Materialism: A belief that the only real things in life are material things, e.g. money or possessions.

Materialism

Materialism is the belief that the only real things in life are material things. This belief that there is no 'higher' power like God is held firmly by materialists. A materialistic life is about having money, lots of material possessions and living life to the full. Materialists live life in this way because they believe there is nothing else in store at the end of time. Also, materialists consider that the scientific way of looking at things is the only way, as scientific truth is the only truth.

Over to You

1. Do you think it is important to reflect upon the existence of God? Why/why not?
2. Explain the following terms in your own words: theism, atheism, agnosticism, secularism and materialism. What evidence do you have?
3. Do you know of anyone who follows these values?
4. Do you think these values bring people true happiness in life? Why/why not?
5. Do you think the experience of God in one's life is more important than material goods? If so, state why.
6. Do you think the everyday words issued from President McAleese were offensive? Who do you think would be offended by them?

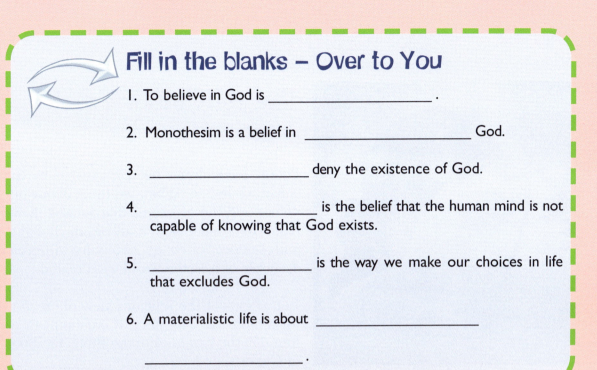

Fill in the blanks – Over to You

1. To believe in God is _____ .

2. Monothesim is a belief in _____ God.

3. _____ deny the existence of God.

4. _____ is the belief that the human mind is not capable of knowing that God exists.

5. _____ is the way we make our choices in life that excludes God.

6. A materialistic life is about _____

_____ .

Religion and Science

The worlds of religion and science have had a difficult relationship in the past. For years people believed that you could not believe in both religion and science – you had to choose between them. There were arguments and disagreements between people who studied religion (theologians) and those who studied science (scientists). This was because they had very different viewpoints.

The world of science is based on facts and concrete evidence, whereas the world of religion comes from faith and placing trust in things that cannot be proven or measured in a scientific way. One area in particular that caused a clash between the two was the question of creation.

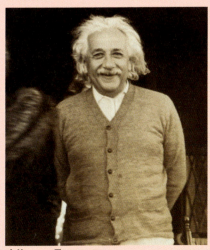

Albert Einstein.

Pope Benedict XVI.

Creation

*God creating the Animals
by Jacopo Tinloretto*

The religious view of creation

People have always been fascinated by the world we live in. When we think about our planet and the creatures that inhabit it, we begin to wonder how it all began. Religion and science offer us two very different accounts of how the world was created.

Let us look at the religious view of creation for a moment. The story of creation can be found in the first book of the Bible: the Book of Genesis.

In the beginning God created heaven and earth. The earth was a formless void. God said, 'Let there be light', and there was light. God saw that light was good and divided light from darkness. God called light 'day' and darkness 'night'. Evening came and morning came: the first day.

God said, 'Let there be a vault through the middle of the waters'. And so it was. It divided the waters under the vault from the waters above the vault. God called the vault 'heaven'. Evening came and morning came: the second day.

God said, 'Let the waters under heaven come together into a single mass, and let dry land appear'. And so it was. God called the dry land 'earth' and the mass of waters 'seas'. God saw that it was good.

Creation – The story of how the world began.

God said, 'Let the earth produce vegetation: seed-bearing plants, and fruit trees on earth, bearing fruit with their seed inside, each corresponding to its own species'. And so it was. God saw that it was good. Evening came and morning came: the third day.

God said, 'Let there be lights in the vault of heaven to divide day from night, and let them indicate festivals, days and years. Let there be lights in the vault of heaven to shine on the earth'. And so it was. God made the two great lights: the greater light to govern the day, the smaller light to govern the night, and the stars. God saw that it was good. Evening came and morning came: the fourth day.

God said, 'Let the waters be alive with a swarm of living creatures, and let birds wing their way above the earth.' And so it was. God created great sea-monsters and all the creatures that glide and teem in the waters in their own species, and winged birds in their own species. God saw that it was good. God blessed them, saying, 'Be fruitful, multiply, and fill the waters of the seas; and let the birds multiply on land'. Evening came and morning came: the fifth day.

God said, 'Let the earth produce every kind of living creature in its own species: cattle, creeping things and wild animals of all kinds'. And so it was. God

saw that it was good.

God said, 'Let us make man in our own image, in the likeness of ourselves, and let them be masters of the fish of the sea, the birds of heaven, the cattle, all the wild animals and all the creatures that creep along the ground.' God created man in the image of himself, in the image of God he created him, male and female he created them.

God blessed them, saying to them, 'Be fruitful, multiply, fill the earth and subdue it'. God also said, 'Look, to you I give all the seed-bearing plants everywhere on the surface of the earth, and all the trees with seed-bearing fruit; this will be your food'. And so it was. God saw all that he had made, and indeed it was very good. Evening came and morning came: the sixth day.

Thus heaven and earth were completed with their entire array. On the seventh day God had completed the work he had been doing. He rested on the seventh day. God blessed the seventh day and made it holy.

Such was the story of heaven and earth as they were created.

Fundamentalism

For hundreds of years people accepted the religious view of creation. They took it to be literally true. To believe in something literally – or take it word for word – is called fundamentalism. Religion seemed to provide all the answers to the questions people had about the world. However, as time went on new advances and discoveries in science seemed to contradict the religious view of creation.

> ## Over to You
>
> 1. Why do you think there was a difficult relationship between religion and science?
> 2. What was created on each day of the week?
> 3. What do you think was the most important thing created and why?
> 4. Why not draw a picture or chart of the story of creation? This may help you to remember what happened on each day.

Fundamentalism – A literal interpretation of sacred scripture.

The scientific view of creation

Galileo

Galileo was an Italian astronomer from the 17th century. Using a telescope, he discovered that planet Earth orbits the sun. Up until then people had believed that the Earth was at the centre of the universe and that the sun and other planets moved around it. At the time it seemed the most obvious theory to believe. This is because, while standing on the Earth, it does look like the sun and moon are the ones moving, while we stay still.

The Church became very concerned at the discoveries of Galileo. For years they had taught that the Earth was at the centre of the universe. Obviously, they did not want people to think that they had been teaching the wrong facts. It might make people wonder if they had been incorrect in their other teachings too. So because of this fear they banned Galileo from teaching that his theory was fact.

However, Galileo believed strongly in his work and in 1632 he published his findings. As a result, he was put on trial by the Catholic Church and found guilty of heresy. Heresy is an opinion or belief that contradicts religious teaching. To avoid being sent to prison, Galileo recanted or publicly took back what he had said.

Charles Darwin.

Darwin

Galileo was not the only man of science who ran into difficulty with the Church. Charles Darwin, a British scientist, became famous for his theory of evolution. He offered an explanation in 1859 as to how different species came into being. According to Darwin, all life forms, that is, plant, animal and human, evolved or developed. A process called natural selection meant that plants and animals changed or adapted to suit the environment they were in, in order to survive. They had all originally come from one living organism and had developed over millions of years. This theory totally contradicted the account of creation found in the Book of Genesis. The Catholic Church rejected Darwin's theory as they had done with Galileo.

The Big Bang

Many scientists now believe that the universe was created between 10 billion and 20 billion years ago from a cosmic explosion that hurled matter in all directions. This theory became known as the Big Bang theory.

Working together

The work of the scientists mentioned above caused a division between religion and science that was to remain for many years. Eventually, the Church apologised to Galileo and accepted his teachings. They also saw merit in Darwin's ideas but the damage had been done.

Today there is a much healthier relationship between the two worlds of religion and science. This is due to the fact that people began to see that there was no need to choose between the two. Both contain great lessons. The difference is that they are teaching us two different things. Science is concerned with how the world came about, whereas religion is concerned with why. They are seeking answers to different questions.

In fact, many believe that the only way to get a full and true meaning of the world is to appreciate what both have to say. As Albert Einstein once said, 'Science without religion is lame, religion without science is blind.'

Fundamentalists would not agree with this view. They believe that we should take the account of creation found in Genesis as the only explanation of how the world was created. More liberal thinkers would say that we must remember that the writers of Genesis were concerned with teaching a message about God and not science. Their account wanted to show God as a powerful, loving creator. They were also writing at a very different time when people and the world were nowhere near advanced as they are today.

Today many people who hold a religious faith accept the Big Bang theory as the answer to how the world was created. At the same time they believe that there is also value in the Genesis account of creation. This is because it teaches us important truths about God and why the world was created.

Over to You

1. What kind of relationship did Galileo have with the Church and why?
2. Explain Darwin's theory of evolution.
3. Do you think science and religion should work together? Why/why not?

Exam Style Question (From 2003 paper)

A. Describe in detail a religious world view of creation.

B. Identify **one** similarity between the scientific and religious views of creation and explain how they are similar.

C. Identify **one** difference between the scientific and religious views of creation and explain how they are different.

D. Identified below are some world views that could challenge a person's faith. Tick ✓ **one** only and explain how it could be a challenge to a person's faith.

Agnosticism ❏   Atheism ❏   Secularism ❏

'A WORLD-VIEW IS A SET OF ASSUMPTIONS WHICH WE HOLD ABOUT THE BASIC MAKE-UP OF OUR WORLD.'

created?
meaningless?
accidental?
designed?

Ian Mitchell

Section D – Key Definitions

Adolescent faith:	A challenging stage of our faith development when we ask many questions.
Agnosticism:	The belief that the human mind is not capable of knowing whether God exists or not.
Atheism:	To deny the existence of God.
Awe and wonder:	To be filled with curiosity and have an admiration or respect for something or someone.
Creation:	The story of how the world began.
Fundamentalism:	A literal interpretation of sacred scripture.
Humanism / Humanist:	A humanist's faith is not in God, it is in humankind. Humanists believe there is no God or Gods. They find meaning in how they respect and value life.
Materialism:	A belief that the only real things in life are material things, e.g. money or possessions.
Mature faith:	The final stage of our faith development when we have reached a meaningful and comfortable stage with God.
Meaning / Meaninglessness:	Meaning is something that has importance or significance for us. Meaning gives us a sense of purpose in life. When things become meaningless they are not important to us any more.
Monotheism:	Mono means one and theos means God, so monotheism is the belief in one God.
Personal faith:	A person's own religious beliefs.
Prayer:	A conversation with God.
Polytheism:	Poly means more than one and theos means God, so polytheism is a belief in more than one God.
Question / Questioner:	Asking questions means that we are interested to learn more about a particular topic. The questioner is the one who looks for this information.
Religious belief:	Religious belief means the things that we believe to be true about God and the faith we belong to.
Religious practice:	Religious practice is how we show these religious beliefs. It means that we put into practice in our lives all that we believe.
Reflection:	When we reflect, we think about something that is happening in our lives and try to understand how we feel about it.
Search:	To seek answers or reasons for things around us.
Secularism:	This practice opposes the influence that religion has on our society.
Stages of faith:	The growth and development of faith from childhood, through adolescence to maturity.

SECTION E

THE CELEBRATION OF FAITH

AIMS

- To show how ritual and worship have always been part of the human response to life and to the mystery of God.

- To identify how communities of faith express their day-to-day concerns in various forms of ritual.

- To explore an experience of worship.

HIGHER LEVEL ONLY

- To explore the link between patterns of worship and mystery and that which is of ultimate concern to individuals and communities.

In this chapter,

you will become familiar with
the following concepts:

■ Places of significance
■ Actions of significance
■ Times of significance
■ Sacredness

Chapter 19:

The World of Ritual

Places of Significance

'For me, there's no place like my granny's house. I love the smell of baking from the kitchen and all the old photographs on the walls. She has a story to tell about each one. There's something really special about that old house.' *Ruth*

'Every year as a child we went to Blackwater in Wexford for our holidays. Even now as an adult, when I walk along that beach, I can remember the fun we had and the taste of the sandwiches my mother brought for the picnic.' *Peter*

'My favourite place has to be my bedroom. It's the one place I can go and have time and space to myself. It's full of all the things I love and I decorated it myself in the colours I especially like. It's my haven.' *Susan*

The people above described places that are important to them.

Over to You

1. Why are the places mentioned important to Ruth, Peter and Susan?
2. What's your favourite place? Why did you choose this place?

Places of special meaning or importance

Sometimes very ordinary everyday places can be important to people. When a place has a special meaning or importance, it can be described as a **place of significance**.

These places can be personal to people because of memories associated with them or the people who live there. There are also communal places of significance. This means that whole communities or even an entire population of people often see these places as special. They may be important for different reasons. They may be of historical importance or places of natural beauty.

Burren, Co Clare

Eiffel Tower

GPO, Dublin

Places of Religious Significance

Places can also become significant for religious reasons. Two such places are Croagh Patrick in Co Mayo and Lourdes in France. These are known as places of pilgrimage. People go on pilgrimages to such places because they are associated with religion in a special way. Over the years followers of each of the major world religions have gone on pilgrimage to sacred or holy places.

We will now look at two of these places to discover why people go on pilgrimage and what happens in these places of significance. These activities can be called **actions of religious significance**. This is when people perform special prayers or rituals, for example, while on pilgrimmage.

Place of religious significance – When a place is associated with religion in a special way.

Action of religious significance – When people perform special prayers or rituals, for example, on pilgrimage.

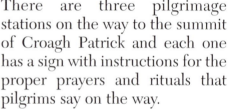

Croagh Patrick

Croagh Patrick is a mountain near the town of Westport in Co Mayo. It is known by many people simply as 'The Reek' and has been a sacred site since ancient times. However, it was the patron saint of Ireland, St Patrick, who made it a place of significance for Catholics. Christian tradition says that Patrick went up this mountain and spent 40 days praying, fasting and reflecting there. Pilgrims now come from all over the world to pray in this sacred place, and the last Sunday in July is particularly special. It is known as 'Reek Sunday' and each year at this time more than 25,000 pilgrims visit the mountain.

The first step on the pilgrimage path is a statue of St Patrick. Many people stop and pray here and it is special for those who cannot make the journey to the top of the mountain. The more able pilgrims continue on up the mountain and many even make the trip barefoot as a sign of devotion.

Pilgrims climbing Croagh Patrick.

There are three pilgrimage stations on the way to the summit of Croagh Patrick and each one has a sign with instructions for the proper prayers and rituals that pilgrims say on the way.

First Station

The first station is at the base of the mountain and here pilgrims walk around a mound of stones seven times, saying seven Our Fathers, seven Hail Marys and one Creed.

Second Station

The second station takes place on the summit and has four different stages. The pilgrims first kneel and say seven Our Fathers, seven Hail Marys and one Creed. They then pray near the chapel where Mass is said everyday for the Pope's intentions. Next they walk around the chapel 15 times while saying 15 Our Fathers and 15 Hail Marys. Finally, they walk around the area known as Patrick's Bed seven times, again saying seven Our Fathers, seven Hail Marys and one Creed.

Third Station

The third station takes place at Roilig Mhuire. Here the pilgrims walk seven times around each mound of stones, again repeating the sequence of seven Our Fathers, seven Hail Marys and one Creed. Finally, they walk around the whole enclosure of Roilig Mhuire praying.

Lourdes

Lourdes is a place of religious significance in France. It has been an important place of pilgrimage for Christians for many years. The story behind Lourdes is an amazing one. In 1858, a young girl named Bernadette Soubirous saw a vision of the Virgin Mary there. She was only 14 at the time and was an ordinary girl from a very poor family.

Bernadette Soubirous

While out collecting firewood one day she saw an apparition of Our Lady in a little grotto outside the town. The vision continued to appear to her for the next six months. At first people doubted her and her story caused a lot of arguments in her village. However, after much investigation the Church agreed that Bernadette's experience was in fact true. During one of her apparitions, Our Lady told Bernadette to dig a hole in a piece of barren land near the grotto. A spring of water appeared and soon people began to speak of being cured of illness by the water that flowed there.

A crowd of Roman Catholics visit the Basilica where the Virgin Mary is said to have appeared to Saint Bernadette.

Today millions of people travel to Lourdes to visit this sacred place and see for themselves where the visions took place. It is particularly significant for people who are ill or disabled. They go to pray at the grotto and ask for healing. Many also bathe in the water from the grotto and as a result there have been genuine cases of people being miraculously cured. However, even for those who are not cured, Lourdes is a special place of spiritual healing and prayer.

Over to You

1. In groups, research one of the following places of pilgrimage.

   - The Holy Land
   - Mecca
   - Knock
   - Lough Derg
   - Rome
   - The Ganges River
   - The Wailing Wall.

   Find out why it became a place of significance and what happens there. See if you can find photos of the place or perhaps talk to someone who has been on pilgrimage there.

2. Answer the following questions in relation to either Croagh Patrick or Lourdes:

   a. Why is this a place of religious significance?
   b. What actions of significance take place here?
   c. How does this place help to strengthen a person's religious faith?

Why places become significant

1. Places can be associated with an important person in a religion. The person may have been born there, lived there or visited the place during their lifetime.
2. There may have been visions or apparitions at the place.
3. The place may be an important part of the founding story of a religion.

Why people go on pilgrimage

1. To strengthen their relationship with God.
2. To learn more about their religion.
3. To show devotion to their God.
4. To ask for help or guidance from God.
5. To perhaps thank their God or ask for forgiveness.

Significant buildings

Buildings can become places of significance too. All the major world religions have buildings that are important to them. Usually this is because these buildings are where followers gather together and worship their God. Even though these buildings may be different in size or shape, they have certain common features or characteristics associated with their religion.

We will now look at a building of significance in the Catholic religion. You can find information on buildings of significance in other religions in chapters 10–13.

A Catholic church

This is a picture of St Mark's Church in Tallaght, Dublin. It is an example of a modern church. The cross on the top of the building helps us to identify it as a Catholic place of worship.

Catholic churches may vary in style, size or shape but they all contain the following features:

1. The altar
The altar is where the celebration of the Eucharist takes place. It is the main area of focus during the Mass.

2. The ambo
The ambo or lectern is where the priest or Ministers of the Word read the readings and gospels from.

3. The presider's chair
The priest is called the presider because he is the one who leads the congregation. The presider's chair is where he sits during the Mass.

5. The baptismal font
The baptismal font is where people are baptized into the Christian community.

7. Candles
Candles are sometimes found in front of holy statues. People light them as a symbol of the prayers they say.

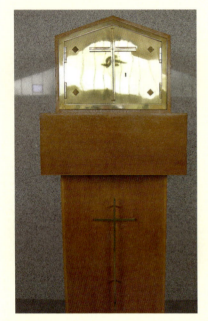

4. The tabernacle
The tabernacle is where the body of Christ is kept in between Masses.

6. Statue of Our Lady
Statues are often found in different areas of the church and may be of Our Lady or different saints.

8. Stations of the Cross
The Stations of the Cross consist of 14 separate images found around the walls of the church. They depict scenes from the Crucifixion and the last important moments of Jesus' life.

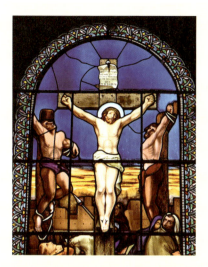

9. Stained glass window
Stained glass windows are colourful images which may show scenes from Bible passages.

10. Confessional box
The confessional box is where people receive the sacrament of reconciliation.

11. Crib
At Christmas, you will find a crib in the church. This is built to look like a barn or cave and depicts the story of Jesus' birth.

Sacredness

A place of worship like St Mark's Church is very special to people of that faith. Going there helps them to feel close to God and to focus on their spiritual life. People show great respect in these buildings of significance. They can be described as **sacred** or holy places.

Sacred spaces can also be found in other buildings besides official places of worship. Your school may have a sacred place such as a prayer room.

Sacredness – Places can be described as sacred or holy when they help people to feel close to God and help them focus on their spiritual lives.

Over to You

1. Describe your local place of worship.

2. How does being in a building of religious significance help to bring a person closer to God?

Times of Significance

Time is very important to humans, however people don't always value time especially in today's busy world. It is something we often take for granted as we go through our daily and weekly routines. However, like places and buildings, certain times have become significant.

Certain times of the year may be important for an individual. What might be an ordinary Monday for you may be a very special day for another person. There are also communal days of significance which may be celebrated by a whole group of people. If a time has significance for someone, they usually mark it by celebrating in a special way.

Spirit Week

The posters had been up for weeks now. Every noticeboard was packed with information of the events that would be taking place. There was an air of excitement round the whole school. Even the teachers were talking about it! Everywhere you looked there were preparations taking place.

Ciara knew the first years were organising a basketball match against the teachers and the money they raised would be going to charity. But she still wasn't sure of the point of Spirit Week. Eventually, she decided to ask her sister Emer about it. After all, Emer was in sixth year and so had lots more experience of the school.

'Spirit Week is all about the school community coming together and having fun!' Emer began. 'It takes a lot of hard work and co-operation but it's worth it.'

'But why do we have it in October?' Ciara wondered.

'Because that's when the school extension was opened 10 years ago,' explained Emer. 'It also helps first years like yourself to settle in and see what a great school we have.'

'Are you mad? How can you say school is great?' cried Ciara.

'You'll see,' laughed Emer, 'it's one of the best times of the year for our school and there's so much happening that we don't get any homework for the week.'

That news brought a smile to Ciara's face and she began to think maybe her new school wasn't such a bad place after all.

In this story we can see how times of significance are often times of great joy and also much preparation. They involve people in a special way and can bring whole communities together.

Over to You

1. What is being celebrated in each of the pictures?

2. Are they personal or communal times of significance?

3. Name another personal and communal time of significance that you experienced.

Times of Religious Significance

Time of religious significance – When important people or events that take place in the history of the religion are celebrated.

Just like places and buildings, certain times have become significant for religious communities. These times are usually significant because of an important event that took place in the history of the religion. Or they may be set aside to remember an important person in the religion.

Liturgical calendar

The Christian community has its own calendar, which separates the year into times of significance that are celebrated. This is called the **liturgical calendar**. Just like we have the different seasons of spring, summer, autumn and winter, the Church also has different seasons in its year. Throughout these seasons certain days have been given special significance and are celebrated in a particular way.

Advent

The liturgical year begins with the season of Advent, which means 'the coming'. The season of Advent lasts four weeks leading up to Christmas. Throughout Advent, Christians anticipate the coming of Jesus Christ. During this sacred time, Christians show their love to all through their generosity and tolerance of others.

Christmas

During this time Christians celebrate the birth of Jesus. The 25th December is a holy day of obligation. This means that Christians should go to mass on this day. The word Christmas means 'The Mass of Christ'. Often people go to mass on Christmas Eve, which is often called a vigil mass. We don't know when exactly Jesus was born. The date 25th December was set up by Pope Gregory I in 354 CE and we have celebrated Christmas on that date since then. The feast of the Epiphany or 'Little Christmas' as it is often called is celebrated on the 6th of January.

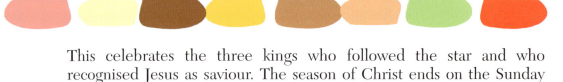

This celebrates the three kings who followed the star and who recognised Jesus as saviour. The season of Christ ends on the Sunday following the feast of the Epiphany.

Ordinary Time

Ordinary Time falls into two parts of the liturgical calendar.
1. The first is between Christmas and Lent.
2. The second is between Easter and Advent.

During this time we learn from the gospel about the miracles Jesus performed and the parables (stories with meaning) that he told. Ordinary time makes up most of the liturgical calendar.

Lent

Lent for Christians takes forty days. This does not include Sunday. This event recalls the time Jesus spent in the wilderness before embarking on his public ministry. Shrove Tuesday, or 'Pancake Tuesday' is the last day before Lent begins.

Lent is a time to prepare for Easter. Christians often give up something like sweets or fizzy drinks but this is only one aspect of it. Lent begins on Ash Wednesday. Ashes are placed on our forehead to show that although we are sinners, we can follow Christ to a new way of life. The week before Easter Sunday is called Holy Week. Each of these days has a special importance in the Christian calendar: Palm Sunday, Spy Wednesday, Holy Thursday, Good Friday and Holy Saturday.

Easter

Easter is the most important time in the liturgical year. This was the time when Jesus died on the cross and rose from the dead so that all people could have the chance to share eternal life with God. Easter is celebrated on a Sunday between March 22nd and April 25th. This decision was taken by the Council of Nicaea in 325 CE, that Easter must be celebrated on the first Sunday after the full moon after the Spring

Equinox. The celebration of Easter begins with a vigil mass on Easter Saturday night.

The feast of the Ascension is celebrated forty days after Easter Sunday. This marks the day when Jesus no longer appeared to the disciples and ascended into heaven. Ten days after this Christians celebrate the feast of Pentecost when the Holy Spirit came to the disciples and gave them the courage to continue with Jesus' message.

Over to You

1. What is meant by the liturgical year?
2. What is a holy day of obligation?
3. How is the liturgical calendar divided?
4. What is the most important part of the liturgical calendar? Why?
5. What is ordinary time? What do we learn during this time?

Moveable feasts

Some other very significant times are celebrated, but the days on which they are celebrated vary from year to year. The most significant time in the Christian liturgical calendar is Easter. As you know from your Easter school holidays, the actual dates for this important season change every year.

Like other times of significance in the Christian religion, Easter is important in three ways:

1. It remembers in a very special way the passion, death and resurrection of Jesus.
2. It helps us to renew our Christian faith and brings us closer to God.
3. It reminds us of the coming of the kingdom of God and our promise of eternal life. So this time has significance in our past, present and future.

Over to You

On your own or in groups, you may like to research a time of significance in your religion. Find out when, how and why this time is celebrated. There may be a time of significance coming up soon. Ask your teacher!

Experiencing Worship, Sign and Symbol

Experiencing Worship

Worship – When we express our deep love and affection for God.

In the previous chapter we looked at various sacred places that are important to Christians, such as Croagh Patrick and Lourdes. You learnt that many people make an annual pilgrimage to Croagh Patrick and celebrate the importance of this place. Many communicate with God in a special way on this mountainside. Through this communication we can keep in touch with our faith in God and it helps us to share our lives in a special way with others. This expression of deep love and affection that we have for God is called **worship**. To worship God takes time and effort but it comes with many rewards.

An ancient Egyptian Funeral Ceremony.

The ancient Greeks, Romans and Egyptians worshipped their gods, especially at the death of their loved ones. At the time of burial offerings of jewellery, food or coins were placed in their tombs. These people believed that their lives had a purpose even in death.

People can worship God in many ways whether they are together or alone. It can be done in an informal way where there are no words used or actions carried out. Or it can be in a formal way whereby actions and words play a large part. For Christians the greatest kind of formal and community worship is in the celebration of the Eucharist or Mass.

Elements of worship

At Mass people gather together in communal prayer and thanksgiving for the love that God shows to each of us in our daily lives. During the introduction to the Mass we make the sign of the cross together and ask for God's forgiveness through the penitential rite. As a community of believers we listen to the word of God through scripture readings from the Old and New Testament. We kneel and stand together for the Liturgy of the Eucharist where we receive Christ's body and blood. We are then dismissed into the wider community to love and serve God. When we live our lives as God intended us to do, we are showing love and gratitude to him.

Muslim's praying in a Mosque.

An Orthodox Jew praying at the Western/Wailing Wall, Jerusalem.

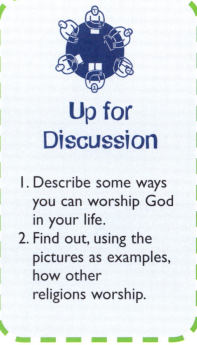

Up for Discussion

1. Describe some ways you can worship God in your life.
2. Find out, using the pictures as examples, how other religions worship.

Ritual

A **ritual** is a religious ceremony that involves a series of actions that are performed without any variation. They are symbolic actions that help us express our beliefs, values and deepest concerns. All rituals serve as a way of communicating what is important to us and what has meaning for us in our lives. Many Christians take part in rituals when they gather as a group to worship God. Catholics celebrate the Eucharist every Sunday. This is the most important ritual for Catholics. Other ways of celebrating their faith are done through pilgrimage and prayer.

Religious rituals have a special meaning to all involved as it helps them become closer to God. It allows them to celebrate the presence of God in their lives. They are important because they allow people to gather together to experience something that has meaning. When people want to talk to each other they can meet casually, but when they want to talk to God they do this by praying or taking part in a ritual. Rituals are not routines. Brushing your teeth every morning and evening is routinely done, but it is not a ritual because it is not a symbolic action. Rituals allow links to be made between the worshipper and God.

Ritual – A religious ceremony that involves a series of actions that are performed without any variation.

The Little Prince

In Antoine de Saint-Exupéry's story *The Little Prince* there is a passage where the fox describes the value of repeating rituals to the little prince. The fox explains that the repetition of a ritual does not necessarily make it routine.

'Please – tame me!' he said.

'I want to, very much,' the little prince replied. 'But I have not much time. I have friends to discover, and a great many things to understand.'

'One only understands the things that one tames,' said the fox. 'Men have no more time to understand anything. They buy things all ready made in shops. But there is no shop anywhere where one can buy friendship, and so men have no friends anymore. If you want a friend, tame me…'

'What must I do, to tame you?' asked the little prince.

'You must be very patient,' replied the fox. 'First you will sit down at a little distance from me – like that – in the grass. I shall look at you out of the corner of my eye, and you will say nothing. Words are the source of misunderstandings. But you will sit a little closer to me, every day…'

The next day the little prince came back.

'It would have been better to come back at the same hour,' said the fox. 'If, for example, you came at four o'clock in the afternoon, then at three o'clock I shall begin to be happy. I shall feel happier and happier as the hour advances. At four o'clock, I shall already be worrying and jumping about. I shall show you how happy I am! But if you come at just anytime, I shall never know at what hour my heart is too ready to greet you. One must observe the proper rites…'

'What is a rite?' asked the little prince.

'Those also are actions too often neglected,' said the fox. 'They are what makes one day different to the other days and one hour different to other hours. There is a rite, for example, among my hunters. Every Thursday they dance with the village girls. So Thursday is a wonderful day for me! I can take a walk as far as the vineyards. But if the hunters danced at just any time, every day would be like every other day, and I should never have any vacation at all.'

Over to You

1. What are the main points of the story?
2. Do you think the repetition of a ritual makes it routine?
3. Do you like this story. Why/why not?

The Mass

Many people on a Saturday evening or Sunday morning gather together at Mass. At the Last Supper, Jesus and his disciples celebrated the Jewish Passover meal with bread and wine. This was performed to celebrate the Jewish people's freedom from slavery in Egypt and reaching the Promised Land. In the Jewish Passover the blood of the lamb, which had been sacrificed and put on their doors, saved people. To **sacrifice** something is to give it up for the good of something that is more important.

When Jesus sacrificed himself on the cross, God began to have a better relationship with his people. At the Eucharist Jesus is present and his sacrifice on the cross is too, because they are one and the same thing. The bread and wine are changed into the body and blood of Christ and we too are changed when we are told to go forth and spread the good news and to love and serve God. By doing this, we too may have to make sacrifices. The Eucharist is the greatest act of worship for Catholics. The word Eucharist means **thanksgiving**. But what are we thankful to God for? We are thankful for him giving us life – for our creation. Jesus' death on the cross meant that each of us could be saved from sin.

Sacrifice – When something is given up for the good of something that is more important.

Eucharist – A word meaning thanksgiving.

Christmas in a Wheelchair

In 2002 Ciaran McCarthy was paralyzed in a freak rugby accident. In this story he tells us of the importance of life and his first Christmas at Mass in a wheelchair.

As he took his place in the church, Ciaran noticed that on the window ledges huge, white candles flickered slightly as a draught touched them, and then shone as brightly as before. Despite the solemnity of the Mass the incense smelt more beautiful than a springtime primrose. He recalled his Christmas childhoods and the Christmas Eves where he would stay awake all night to catch a glimpse of Santa's red cloak.

He arrived at this vigil Mass in plenty of time. He felt relaxed with the divine spirit within him and at one with his family. The meaning of Christmas had not changed just because he was now in a wheelchair. He still believed that to live through love would bring both peace and joy to his life.

At Mass the priest wore his best gold and white embroidered

vestments, and the pale wax candles on the altar gleamed amid the lilies. The pungent scent of greenery mingled with the waxy smell of burning candles. The final candle on the Advent wreath was lit ceremoniously. So many of our images of Christ are etched in light — the silver of frost and moonlight, the shining star of Bethlehem guarding the Magi, the radiance of the lighted candles.

Some old customs can momentarily transfigure our existence and let the eternal shine through. One such is the singing of the carols. They are simple ways of expressing those parts of Christianity that ordinary people find most interesting. They are memorable because they are tangible. They celebrate things that we can touch and see and warm to: a mother and baby, a stable, donkeys, shepherds, straw and hay.

Over to You

1. What words describe the character of Ciaran?
2. What did he experience at Mass?
3. Do you think Ciaran is deeply religious?
4. Have you ever experienced the wonder of God and his creation in a sacred place? Describe the experience.

The order of the Mass

There are four different parts to the Mass:

1. The Introduction
2. The Liturgy of the Word
3. The Liturgy of the Eucharist
4. The Conclusion.

Introduction

There are five parts to the introduction of the Mass:

1. **Entrance procession and priest's greeting**. At this point we make the sign of the cross as a community of believers.
2. **Penitential rite:** The word penitence means being sorry for sinning. We reflect on our wrongdoings and we ask for God's forgiveness.
3. **Kyrie:** Together the followers of Christ say 'Lord have Mercy, Christ have Mercy' after the priest.
4. **Gloria:** Through this prayer we praise God.
5. **Opening prayer:** The priest explains in the opening prayer what this Mass is about, e.g. graduation, class Mass, or other kinds of special occasions.

Liturgy of the Word

1. The Word of God is spoken from the Bible. The first reading is from the Old Testament, while the second reading is from the New Testament.

2. Between the two readings is the responsorial psalm and there are 150 to choose from in the Old Testament. Ministers of the word read all these readings. (These are lay people who volunteer to read in the church.)
3. After that the Gospel is read. It can be taken from Matthew, Mark, Luke or John. The priest reads the Gospel.
4. The priest normally says a few words after the Gospel, where he comments on the readings. This is called the homily.
5. When the priest is finished everyone stands for the Creed. The Creed explains what Catholics believe about the Church and God.
6. Members of the congregation read the prayers of the faithful. Here we pray for things like his holiness the Pope, peace, our families and community.

Liturgy of the Eucharist

1. Members of the congregation present the gifts of bread and wine at the altar. This is called the offertory.
2. The Eucharistic prayer follows. This is a prayer of praise and thanksgiving for Jesus Christ. The words of the Last Supper are spoken: 'This is my body …. This is my blood … do this in memory of me.' Jesus is now present under the appearance of the bread and wine, as we pray.
3. The Lord's Prayer is spoken as we stand together as a community of believers. 'Our Father who art in Heaven…'
4. The sign of peace is an important part of the ceremony as it is an invitation to offer peace to those around you.
5. We receive the body of Christ from the priest or minister of the Eucharist. Like food, the consecreated bread gives us nourishment and strength.

Conclusion

1. The priest in his final blessing tells us to 'go forth and spread the good news'.
2. We are then dismissed and we leave with the knowledge that we are safe in the hands of God.

Participation

To participate means to take part in or take on a role in something. There are many ways that we can become involved or **participate** in our local church. We are called through baptism to take our rightful place in the church. We are expected to sing and speak with full hearts and do everything with the grace and dignity it deserves.

As lay people we can actively participate in the readings, prayers of the faithful, offertory or give out communion. We can also become involved in the music of the Mass as 'when we sing we pray twice'. By fully participating in the Mass, we come to understand more clearly the message of Jesus Christ and therefore can go out into the world and spread the good news.

Participation – Being involved in the activities of your local church and doing everything with the grace and dignity it deserves.

Over to You

1. Name the four parts of the Mass.
2. Describe in detail each part.
3. Do you think any one part is more important than the other? Why?
4. Have you ever participated in Mass in your school or in your parish? If so, what part did you play? Did it help you to understand things more clearly?
5. Organise a class Mass, choosing your readings, your songs and your gifts. Describe the experience.

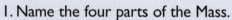

Sign and Symbol

Sign – An action, word or picture that gives a single message.

Think for a moment of things that are difficult to explain. There are many things that we find hard to put into plain words. Everyone knows the smell of warm scones cooking in the oven, but it is quite difficult to describe the smell to others.

Colours are even more difficult to explain, especially to someone who is visually impaired. A lot of colours have associations with various things: red symbolises danger, yellow symbolises brightness, etc. In describing yellow we might say that it is the colour of the sun, it gives warmth and energises us. This does not describe exactly what yellow is; it only gives us an idea of what it is. When we describe things like this we are using **sign** and **symbol**.

Sign

A sign is an action, word or picture that gives a message. It may be written using language or drawn with illustrations.

A sign is used to pass on information. Therefore, the information must be clearly stated for it to be understood. All over the world red and green symbolise the same thing at traffic lights. When the light is green we move forward and when the light is red we stop. We see lots of signs on our roads today. One example of this is roadworks ahead or a lane closing further on.

Up for Discussion

1. Describe the road sign for roadworks and lanes closing.
2. Describe any other road signs that you have seen in Ireland or abroad.

Symbols

Symbols are important means of communication but they are very different to signs. It is an action, word or picture that gives a message but is different to a sign. It can have many meanings and the power to affect people.

Symbol – An action, word or picture that gives a message but is different to a sign. It can have many meanings and the power to affect people.

Symbols can be used when we find it difficult to put into words what we want to say. They can also help with our emotions. Hitler's salute in Nazi Germany meant many things to people: fear, respect, honour, etc. When a person kisses you on the cheek it can also mean many things: hello, goodbye, I love you, I am sorry for your loss or trouble, encouragement, etc. Think about a rainbow. This also represents many things that are beautiful yet we only see it after a rain shower. It gives us new hope and new life after rain. Symbols can teach and affect us at a deeper level which signs cannot reach.

PRAYER
I look lovingly at your world, and I invite it to speak to me, to help me to see far beyond the surface of things. May I continue to keep an eye out for the many ways your love is revealed to me.
Amen.

Over to You

Describe some other examples of symbols and what they mean to you.

Signs and symbols are very different and should not be used interchangeably, i.e. as if they had the same meaning. Signs have one meaning while symbols have many meanings attached to them. A stop sign is very clear, while water has many meanings. Religious symbols like water evoke many thoughts for us.

Over to You

Think about water. What is it used for? Write a list of things with which you associate water.

Religious signs and symbols

Christians all over the world use signs and symbols every day to help them worship and pray to God. Every sacrament is a sign of the presence of God around us. A sacrament is a religious ceremony in which participants receive the grace of God such as at baptism, holy orders or last rites. The symbols that we use at these special times bring into our lives joy, peace, acceptance, forgiveness and love. We celebrate with God at these times.

When we make the sign of the cross we are reminded of the love that God has for each of us. It is a special prayer for us and is a powerful symbol. When we go to have confession heard, the priest makes a sign of the cross over us, symbolising that we are forgiven for any sin we have committed. When someone is dying the priest makes a sign of the cross on his or her forehead. Holy water, blessed candles, statues and rosary beads are all sacramental items. They help us pray to God and thank him for the wondrous gifts he has given to each of us.

Over to You – Exam Style Question

1. You have been asked to design a place of worship / reflection for an airport. People of all religious traditions and of none will use this place of worship / reflection. Choose two of the following to include in your design: Light, Water, Sound, Incense, Prayer Books, Seats, Tables, Kneelers, Prayer Mats. Explain why each of the two is suitable for this place of worship/reflection.

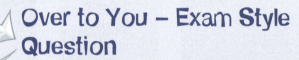

Icons

Icons – Sacred pictures that are painted on wood.

Icons are sacred pictures that are painted on wood. The word itself comes from the Greek word meaning 'image'. Icons help people to pray and concentrate on God. The pictures usually show Jesus, Holy Mary or the saints. They also tend to show a very calm and peaceful person depicting heaven as a similarly calm and peaceful place.

Eastern Orthodox Christians believe that icons can bring us closer to heaven because they remind us of the people that are there already who we know and love. Because of this many people light candles and pray in front of the icon.

Over to You

Junior Certificate 2003
Read the following article and answer the questions below.

Visiting the Russian Orthodox Church in Dublin

The Russian Orthodox Church has a community of 850 members in Dublin. Their church in Harold's Cross is the most westerly Russian Orthodox church in Europe. Every Sunday the congregation gathers for worship at the Church of Saint Peter and Saint Paul. As women enter the church they wear scarves on their heads. By the door there is a sign asking people to switch off phones. There is a small table at the entrance where parishioners write petitions on scraps of paper. In the centre of the church there is a lectern bearing an icon with two elaborate brass candleholders on either side. As people enter the church they take candles to light as offerings at the central lectern. They bow and kiss the icon. They touch their foreheads against the icon and some kneel before it and bow their heads to the floor.

Some parents lift their children so they too can touch the icon. Small icons sit in simple frames on the windowsills. As you go into the main body of the church you notice some people going from icon to icon, kissing each, then bowing and praying before them. There is also a long line of people waiting patiently to approach a priest hearing confessions in a corner, as there are no confession boxes in the church. The Sunday service is two hours long and mostly sung. The singing is led by the church Deacon who is described as 'the voice of the community'. A choir, singing in the balcony, assists him. The congregation stands throughout the ceremony. There are no seats in the church except for one or two pews around the walls. The priest celebrates the liturgy behind a large wooden screen on which are painted icons of Jesus, Mary, and the Angels. A central gate in the screen stands for the gateway to Paradise. The inner area beyond the screen, where the priest celebrates the liturgy, is a simple space with a small tabernacle, altar and table.

The Russian Orthodox community relies on help from donors and sponsors for the repair and upkeep of the church, which was in a state of disrepair when they took it over. They had to bring all the icons and equipment from Russia. Volunteers worked for several weeks, from six in the evening to midnight, so that it would be ready for the Easter celebrations. The congregation seems delighted to have their own church building now. As one man said: 'This is not just a place for us to practise our faith. It is a base for our community. It is important for our children to grow up in our traditional way, with our values and everything we take from our ancestors.' The people at worship in the Church of Saint Peter and Saint Paul clearly love the formality, the incense, and the music of the ceremonies and rituals.

From the *Irish Independent* and *The Irish Times*.

Over to You – Exam Style Questions

1. Pick two rituals mentioned in this article and explain what each expresses about a person's faith.
2. From your reading of this article describe two ways in which people show that icons are important to members of the Russian Orthodox Church.
3. Imagine you are a reporter sent to interview an icon painter. In the course of the interview you ask: 'Why are icons described as symbolic paintings?' Write the answer the painter gives to this question.
4. How does this article show what is meant by any two of the following words? Faith / Sacredness / Tradition / Identity.

Sacraments

Sacrament – A religious ceremony where participants receive the grace of God.

A **sacrament** is a religious ceremony in which participants receive the grace of God. God's love for us is communicated in a very special way through the sacraments. Catholics believe that during these special moments when the community is gathered together, God is present in a very special way.

There are seven sacraments in the Catholic Church and two in some Protestant faith traditions. The reason for this is simple and you may already have come across it in your history class when you studied the Reformation. Catholics believe that Jesus initiated seven sacraments, while the Protestant churches believe that there is only evidence of Jesus teaching two sacraments in the Gospels: baptism and the Eucharist (The Last Supper). However, they also celebrate and mark the other sacraments just not in the same way.

Protestant faith traditions, such as the Salvation Army, do not celebrate any sacraments. What is more important to them is what is in their hearts and not outward signs.

SACRAMENTS

Sacrament	Type	What it celebrates	Meaning	Primary words and symbols	Ongoing effect
Baptism	Initiation	Welcome and rebirth	Being born into new life in the community of Jesus	Water, white garment, lighted candle, signing of the cross, anointing with oil.	Membership in the church, call to witness
Confirmation	Initiation	Growth in the Spirit	Strengthening of new life	Laying on of hands, anointing and sealing with chrism	Completes baptismal grace, call to witness
Eucharist	Initiation	Jesus' saving death and risen presence in our midst	Remembering Jesus' death and experiencing his real presence	Bread, wine, words of consecration	Deeper relationship with Christ, spiritual nourishment
Reconciliation	Healing	Forgiveness	Repairing broken relationship with God, others, and church	Confession of sins, words of absolution, laying on of hands	Liberation from sin
Anointing of the Sick	Healing	God's healing love	Living the fullness of life in Christ, even in sickneess and death	Laying on of hands, anointing with oil, words of petition	Strength, peace, courage to endure
Marriage	Vocation	Covenant of love	Forming a bond of union, like that of Christ and the Church	Husband and wife, rings, vows	Permanent union of a man and a woman
Hold Orders	Vocation	Ministry in the Church	Taking responsibility for a particular leadership role	Laying on of hands, anointing with oil, prayer of priestly consecration	Sacred powers for service to the Church

Sacraments of initiation

Baptism, Confirmation and Eucharist are called the sacraments of initiation because in participating in them we become full members of Christ's body here on earth. The word initiation means to become a member of something. By participating in these sacraments, we are called to be members of the Christian community.

Baptism

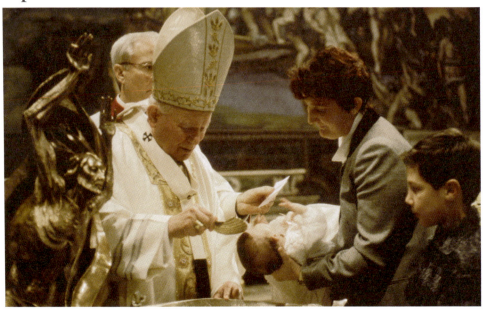

At baptism we are called to follow Jesus Christ and live as he had lived. Through the waters of baptism we become part of the Christian community.

Confirmation

At confirmation we receive the gifts of the Holy Spirit through the oil of chrism. There are seven gifts of the Holy Spirit: courage, wisdom, understanding, knowledge, reverence, awe and wonder at the presence of God, and right judgement.

Eucharist

On our communion day we celebrate receiving the body of Christ for the first time with the Christian community. By receiving Christ's body into ours we are able to live better lives as Christians. We become more united with each other, as we are one body on earth.

Sacraments of healing

There are many examples in the Bible where Jesus showed us the importance of healing. Healing as Jesus showed us is not just a physical thing. It is also a spiritual matter because he forgave the sinners for their wrongdoings. Through the sacraments of healing we are given much comfort and support in our lives.

Reconciliation
In this sacrament we have a special opportunity to meet the risen Christ and to celebrate with him our efforts to do good. When we receive God's forgiveness for our sins, we are filled with the strength to continue to live as Christ wants us to live. When we genuinely try to be reconciled, then the love of God can be seen around us.

Anointing of the sick
In this sacrament the risen Jesus is present to heal and strengthen the person who is ill. The special words and symbols used in this sacrament are all signs of God's presence and that people are not alone in their suffering.

Sacraments of vocation

In the sacrament of marriage and holy orders we are called to live out the message of Jesus Christ on earth. Through marriage two people share a special bond with each other. Through the sacrament of holy orders, a person is ordained into the priesthood or religious life to serve God's people. Serving God's people is also called public ministry.

Holy Orders
Sacraments of vocation are special ways that we are called to serve by God. Priests are ordained through the sacrament of Holy Orders and are called to serve as ministers on earth. They serve the people of God on earth by preaching the Gospels and giving the sacraments.

Marriage
Through the sacrament of marriage two people are called publicly to make a covenant or promise to love each other for the rest of their lives. The priest represents the Church and gives a special blessing to the couple. For the rest of their lives they are called to remain faithful and loyal to one other.

All sacraments are communal celebrations. The presence of Jesus in the community serves to strengthen all who are present and helps us to live as Jesus did on earth.

Over to You

1. What does the word sacrament mean?
2. List the seven sacraments of the Catholic Church.
3. Why do some Protestant faith traditions only have two sacraments?
4. What are the sacraments of initiation? Why do they fall under this title of initiation?
5. Describe a sacramental ceremony you attended.
6. How important do you think the sacraments of healing are?
7. The sacraments of holy orders help us live out the message of Jesus Christ on earth. How necessary is this in modern day Ireland? Discuss.

Sacrament of baptism

Identity – When a person is known and recognised as being part of a church community.

Baptism is a ceremony of welcoming. Today most people are baptized as infants in a public ceremony, but some parents opt not to get their baby baptized until a later stage when the child can understand the meaning of baptism. Through baptism we become part of the Christian community. It establishes the infant's identity as part of a church community. Identity is important as it gives ownership of something to all. It is when a person is known and recognised as being part of a church community.

Water is a very important symbol in baptism as it brings new life to all. All our sins are washed away and forgiven with water. It cleanses and purifies us of any wrongdoing. At baptism, the parents and godparents play an essential role in promising to encourage and nurture the infant's faith throughout their lives.

Water

For recreation and refreshment we use water. We can drink it, swim in it and ski on it when it freezes over. It cools us on a warm sunny day. It is vital for our human life as we cannot live or survive without it.

It also has a very special meaning for the Christian community. In the book of Genesis, God breathes on the water to bring a kind of order to the world. We also read about Moses leading the Israelites to freedom through water in the Book of Exodus. In the New Testament, water is also significant as Jesus himself is baptized in the River Jordan.

It is therefore not surprising that water is an important symbol in baptism. The pouring of water over a baby's head symbolises new life to the infant. The priest names the child at this time, which further establishes their identity. The water of baptism and one's identity symbolises a lifestyle that is rooted in Christian faith.

The oil

Oil has many healing qualities. In baptism, the anointing of oil on the infant's chest takes place before the water ritual. This is associated with

asking God for strength for the person. The anointing of the new Christian with chrism (consecrated oil) on the head takes place after the water ritual. It signifies being the chosen one and therefore sharing in the blessings of life.

The candle

Imagine for a brief moment being in the dark in a place that is unfamiliar to you. How does it feel? Then imagine a candle being lit to banish all darkness. Now how do you feel? Words like safe, secure and relief probably come to your mind. The burning of candles fascinates and excites us during our lives. Light removes the darkness and gives us a direction to move **towards**. Jesus once said, 'I am the light of the world'. At baptism the godparents hold this light over the infant. The flame is received from the paschal candle. The new infant receives the light of Christ into their lives. Through this they are encouraged to become 'a child of light'.

A white garment

When we buy something new we always feel good. We look forward to an occasion when we can show off our new outfit. In baptism the newly baptized baby is clothed in a white garment after the water ritual. This white shaul symbolises that he or she shares in the resurrection of Jesus Christ. This infant is now a 'new creation' of Christ, ready to set out on a new journey.

Over to You

1. Write a brief note on each of the symbols of baptism.
2. Why do you think a lighted candle is held over the infant at baptism?
3. Have you ever been at a baptism as a spectator or participant? Write a note on your experiences of baptism. If not, find out information from the library or internet on adult baptism.

Chapter 21:
Worship as a Response to Mystery

- (Higher Level)

Encountering Mystery

With a cup of tea and the latest book by his favourite author John Grisham, Fr Mike Flanagan settled down for the evening. He loved a good story packed with mystery that really made you think. By the time he was halfway through the book he still had no idea how it was going to end. Later as he went to get himself a biscuit from the kitchen, his eyes were drawn to a photo on the mantelpiece above the fire. The image of a new baby girl, his niece Jenny, brought a smile to his face.

Earlier that day he'd taken the photo when he visited his sister in the hospital. He still couldn't quite believe that his little sister Rose was a mother! Seeing her with Jenny had made him think back to their childhood togeth-er. Rose had always been such a tomboy it was hard to believe that she was now a doting mother. But he was proud as punch when she asked him to be Jenny's godfather. It amazed him to think that this little baby might grow up to be a tomboy too just like her mammy. Seeing her tiny fingers and toes that morning made him reflect on how wonderful the miracle of life was. It only seemed like yesterday that Rose had rung to tell him the good news that she was pregnant. And now there was a new little person in their family.

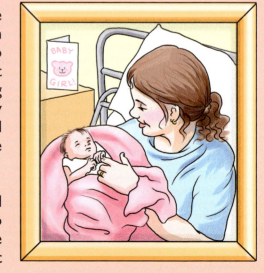

Having got his biscuit Fr Mike returned to his armchair. He picked up his book again and continued reading, looking forward to solving the mystery behind the story. At nine o'clock he put the book down and turned on the television news. The top story that hour was about an earthquake that had taken place in a South American country. As pictures of the disaster came on the screen he said a silent prayer for all the victims and their families. Most of the people affected seemed to be from a very poor area and he wondered why something so terrible could happen to these poor people who had so very little. It made him think about how unfair life could be at times. He decided to hold a special prayer service the next day in the church, so his community could pray for all those who had suffered from the earthquake. There was a good chance too that the parish would organise some events to help raise money for the victims.

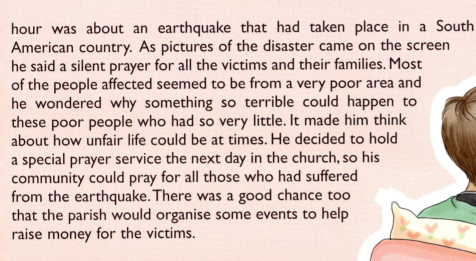

Later that night Fr Mike finished the last page of his book. Finally, the mystery had been solved. The ending had been such a surprise that he was still thinking about it as he settled down to sleep. After being asleep for what seemed like only a few minutes, the phone rang and he woke with a fright.
'Yes ... yes, I see. I'll be there in 10 minutes.'

One of his parishioners, old Mrs Kelly, had been very sick for the past fortnight. Her daughter had phoned to ask him to come over right away. It looked like Mrs Kelly didn't have long left and her family wanted him to give her the sacrament of the sick. As he quickly got ready to leave the house, the young priest hoped that he would make it in time and that he could give some comfort to the family. Without doubt Mrs Kelly was a lovely woman. It was hard to believe that the end of her life was so near. Only last month she had been busy arranging flowers for the church and singing in the choir. She was so full of life. Often Fr Mike had to deal with death in his job but it still didn't make it any easier to understand or explain. Without further delay he jumped in his car and made his way to Mrs Kelly's house.

As he drove home through the deserted early morning roads Fr Mike felt so tired. Mrs Kelly had passed away peacefully a few hours earlier. Afterwards he had stayed with her family and listened to their stories about the wonderful person she had been. They had asked Fr Mike to say the funeral Mass in a few days' time. More than anything they wanted it to be a Mass of thanks for the life she had led. As he drove along the road Fr Mike noticed the sun was coming up. The sky was a beautiful shade of red and purple.

Struck by the beauty of the dawn, he pulled the car over and got out to

breathe in the fresh morning air. The only sound he could hear was the early morning birdsong. The world was beginning to wake up to a new day. Just as his niece Jenny's life had begun, Mrs Kelly's had ended. But he believed that Mrs Kelly was beginning a new life with God. It was the same God that had somehow created this beautiful morning scene. He wondered how it all was possible. Just like the book he had read last night, life was one big mystery.

Over to You

Do you identify with anything Fr Mike said or experienced? Explain why.

Reflection and Wonder

Ultimate concerns in life – Important life-changing events make people reflect and wonder.

The above story is all about mystery. Some mysteries are easily solved like the one in the book that Fr Mike was reading. Others, like the mystery of life and death, are not so easily explained. These could be called **ultimate concerns in life**. They are important life-changing events. They often make people reflect and wonder. This means that they think deeply about the event and ask questions about the meaning of it.

Let's look more closely at the events of the story.

1. The birth of his niece made Fr Mike think about the miracle of life. A baby being born can often make people reflect on where we come from and why we are here.
2. The news report of the earthquake made Fr Mike think about life and wonder why bad things sometimes happen to good people.
3. The death of Mrs Kelly made Fr Mike wonder about life and death. The experience of death can make us reflect on the way we live our lives and make us wonder about what happens after we die.
4. The sunrise made Fr Mike stop and think about the mystery of creation. A beautiful nature scene can make us reflect on the world around us.

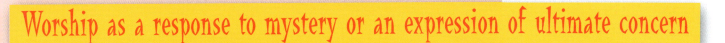

Worship as a response to mystery or an expression of ultimate concern

In the story Fr Mike encountered or met many examples of the mysteries of life. Because these mysteries are hard to explain or understand people respond to them in different ways. How did Fr Mike respond? In many cases he turned to God. People who believe in a religion often turn to God to express how they feel about these ultimate concerns in life. They believe that God is present through, or can help them understand, these experiences. They respond to these mysteries through worship.

People respond to mystery or ultimate concerns in life through worship.

- **Birth of a child** – sacrament of baptism.
- **Suffering from natural disaster** – praying to God.
- **Death of a loved one** – funeral Mass.
- **Nature scene** – prayer of thanks.

'We Care'

Mrs Murphy had spent the last 30 years of her life taking care of those around her. She was a devoted Catholic who attended Mass many times each week. To those who knew her she was a joyous, faithful person who had time for everyone around her.

Then she suddenly became sick and dependent on those that she had once taken care of. Now the roles were reversed. The once active lady was now confined to bed, as physical pain prevented her from getting up. Many of the things she had taken for granted became a daily concern for her now. Who would help her wash? Who would help her dress? Who would bring her food?

In her prayers Mrs Murphy always thanked God for the wonderful life she led, but now she found herself asking God to comfort her in her sickness. She needed to hear the healing words of God about compassion and forgiveness.

Many times she read the Parable of the Lost Sheep. In this parable

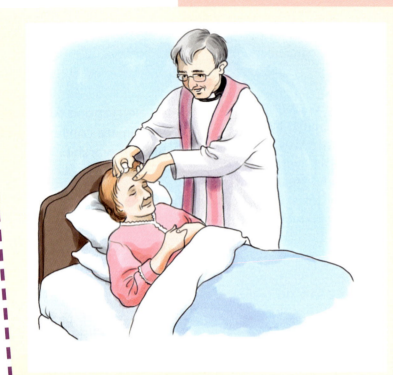

Jesus explains that no community is truly whole unless all its members are caring for each other. The whole community is affected by the well being of everyone.

It was after reading this parable that Mrs Murphy decided to ask the local priest to anoint her. Having experienced all the love and care from her family and her friends during her life, but especially now that she was ill, her need to be anointed came naturally. This sacrament helped her understand her illness. The anxieties that she felt soon began to ease. She felt like the lost sheep; she too had been found. Also, it reaffirmed her belief in Jesus who had suffered on the cross too.

Parable of the Lost Sheep (Luke 15:4-7)

Suppose one of you has a hundred sheep and loses one of them. Does he not leave the 99 in the open country and go after the lost sheep until he finds it? And when he finds it, he joyfully puts it on his shoulders and goes home. Then he calls his friends and neighbours together and says 'Rejoice with me; I have found my lost sheep.' I tell you that in the same way there is more rejoicing in heaven over one sinner who repents than over 99 righteous persons who do not need to repent.

Celebration

The fears and anxieties that Mrs Murphy felt because of her illness are common to those who are sick. When people are dying they often speak about a sense of loneliness or isolation in their lives. They often talk about their fears, frustrations and their helplessness too. Some turn to prayer, while others speak of God abandoning them.

The Catholic sacrament of anointing the sick is a statement that God's love for us is even stronger in times of sickness, and he does not leave us. He too carried a cross. In the midst of suffering we need to hear the word of God. It is therefore something to **celebrate**, as God is always close by looking out for each sheep in his flock.

Celebration – The sacrament of anointing is a celebration of God's love for us.

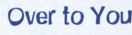

Over to You

1. How did Mrs Murphy's life change for her when she became sick?
2. There were many things she took for granted in life. How important is it to stop from time to time and reflect on our lives and the things we take for granted?
3. How important do you think the Parable of the Lost Sheep is to Christians?
4. Do you think the sacrament of anointing is something to be celebrated? Why/why not?

Encounter with God

When we are sick we feel miserable and lonely. We long for the day when we will be better again. Throughout the ages the Church has continued Jesus' mission towards the sick. When people are sick we say a prayer for them privately or together as a community of believers. We comfort the sick also and support them where possible. Through the sacrament of anointing, we **encounter the risen Jesus**. This means that Jesus himself is present to heal and strengthen the person that is sick.

The priest, community of believers, symbols and the special words used in the sacrament are all signs that Jesus is present with us. Through this sacrament we have an opportunity of meeting the risen Jesus. Our suffering is placed in the presence of Jesus who holds us tightly in the palm of his hand. Today a person can receive this sacrament more than once. It is a sacrament that is shared by the whole family of the person that is sick, which gives a great amount of comfort and peace.

Through the sacrament of anointing, we encounter the risen Jesus.

Footprints

One night a man had a dream.
He dreamed he was walking along the beach with the Lord.
Across the sky flashed scenes from his life.
For each scene, he noticed two sets of footprints in the sand:
One belonging to him, and the other to the Lord.

When the last scene of his life flashed before him,
he looked back at the footprints in the sand.
He noticed that many times along the path
of his life, there was only one set of footprints.
He also noticed that it happened at the very lowest
and saddest times in his life.

This really bothered him
And he questioned the Lord about it.
'Lord, you said that once I decided to follow you,
you'd walk with me all the way.
But I have noticed
that during the most troublesome times in my life,
there is only one set of footprints.
I don't understand why when I needed you the most,
you would leave me.'

The Lord replied,
'My precious, precious child, I love you
and I would never leave you.
During your times of trial and suffering,
when you see only one set of footprints,
it was then that I carried you.'

Communication through the Sacrament

Through the sacrament of anointing, the community is united as one as it prays together. The priest welcomes each person present but especially the sick. We are asked to pray together for their intention.

The priest then reads from the scriptures explaining the main points to those present. Together as a community of believers we watch as he lays his hands on the sick person's forehead, praying in silence. He then anoints the person with oil showing the love God has for each one of us. By doing this we are also freed from any sin or wrongdoing. Together we pray the Our Father before receiving Holy Communion. Finally, the priest blesses the sick person.

As well as the sick person, the family receives comfort and support as they pray together and share a special bond of love.

Communication through the sacrament – Through the sacrament of anointing the community are united as one as they pray together.

Over to You

1. How do you think we encounter the risen Jesus in this sacrament?
2. What do you think is the main message coming from the poem 'Footprints'?
3. Describe the importance of the sacrament to the family of the sick.
4. Is it a healing process for those around the sick person?

In this chapter,
you will become familiar with the following concepts:

- ■ Communication with God
- ■ Penitence
- ■ Praise and thanksgiving
- ■ Petition
- ■ Intercession
- ■ Personal prayer
- ■ Communal prayer
- ■ Meditation
- ■ Contemplation

Chapter 22:

Prayer

Communication with God

Prayer – A conversation between God and human beings.

Prayer is something that is a part of all religions. In this chapter we will look at what prayer is, different types of prayer, how we pray, how prayer can be difficult at times and the importance of prayer in the lives of spiritual people.

Prayer can mean different things for different people. But no matter what religion we have or how we choose to pray, we can say that prayer is a conversation between God and human beings.

Every relationship we have needs communication. Without it our relationships with others would fall apart. When we communicate, we talk or express to someone how we feel or what we are thinking. When we communicate with friends or loved ones, we are open and honest and we do it on a regular basis. By doing this we get to know each other better. Prayer is our way of doing this with God.

But what do we say when we pray? Imagine a typical phone conversation between friends...

Hi Sarah, it's Katie. How are you?

I'm fine too. I just wanted to say sorry for the fight we had yesterday. It was silly and I feel really bad about it...

By the way, thanks a million for the lovely birthday card. I got it this morning. You were so good to remember...

I have a favour to ask. I'm going to a party at the weekend and I was wondering could I borrow your pink top? I'd be really careful with it...

Thanks. In case I forget, Ruth has a really important hockey match tomorrow. I know she'd appreciate it if you gave her a call to wish her good luck...

Listen, I have to run, my mum is calling me. Thanks again for the card. Talk to you soon. Bye!

Types of prayer

Prayer of penitence

In this conversation Katie says a number of things. Can you see what they are? The first thing she does is to say sorry. If we hurt someone we love or do something wrong, we say sorry and ask for his or her forgiveness. At times we may hurt God by doing something he has asked us not to do. We can pray to him about it. This is a **prayer of penitence**.

Prayer of praise and thanksgiving

The next thing Katie did was to thank Sarah for the birthday card she sent her. It is important to thank others when they do something for us in order to show our appreciation. We may want to thank God for things he has given us like the birth of a new family member or for a safe journey somewhere. This is a **prayer of praise and thanksgiving**.

Prayer of petition

Katie then asked Sarah could she borrow a top to wear. When we need something for ourselves we often turn to God for help. It could be that we want to do well in an exam or we might be worried about something. This is a **prayer of petition**.

Prayer of intercession

After that Katie asked Sarah to phone their friend Ruth to wish her good luck in a match. We often turn to God to ask his help for other people. We may ask for a sick relative to get better or that God would watch over and protect our friends. This is a **prayer of intercession**.

Prayer of penitence – Saying sorry to God.

Prayer of praise and thanksgiving – Saying thank you.

Prayer of petition – When we ask God for something for ourselves.

Prayer of intercession – When we ask God to help others.

Up for Discussion

Have you used these types of prayer before? Which do we use most often?

Over to You

Write out your own phone conversation with God like the one above. In it use each of the different types of prayer: penitence, praise and thanksgiving, petition and intercession.

Formal and informal prayers

The types of prayer we have looked at so far are called informal prayer. This is when we ourselves make up the words to say to God. There is another type called formal prayers when we say a set pattern of words which are familiar to the community of faith. We often say these with others when we are in our place of prayer like a church or mosque. The two most common Christian formal prayers are the Our Father and the Hail Mary.

Up for Discussion

What other formal prayers do you know? Do your classmates know the same ones? Where did you learn them?

Ways of Praying

Now that we have examined different types of prayer we will look at different ways of praying.

Personal prayer

Personal prayer – When a person prays alone and has a private conversation with God.

This person is praying alone. She can use whatever words she wants and can do it wherever she chooses. When people pray in this way they can have a very personal and private conversation with God. This is **personal prayer**.

Communal prayer

Communal prayer – When people gather in a sacred place and share prayers with others.

In this picture a community of people are praying together. By gathering together and sharing our prayers with others, we are praying as God asked us to and we can share our faith with others. This is usually done in a sacred place such as a church, temple, mosque or synagogue. This is **communal prayer**.

246

Singing as prayer

Saying words is not the only way to pray. A man called St Augustine once said, 'to sing is to pray twice'. Lots of religions use songs as a way of praying. A song can create a good atmosphere and people can put great effort into making it sound good. Songs that are used in order to pray are called hymns. By singing or playing instruments when we pray, we are using the talents that God gave us to praise him.

Over to You

1. In groups, write down the names/words of your favourite hymns.
2. Are the hymns you listed of penitence, thanksgiving, petition or intercession?
3. Compare your group's hymns with the other groups.

Meditation

A type of prayer which is very common in Buddhism and Hinduism and also popular in Christianity is **meditation**. This is when we become quiet and focus our thoughts on God.

Meditation – When we become quiet and focus our thoughts on God.

Guided meditation

Here is an example of a guided meditation. This is when we are led through a meditation by listening to another person and using our imagination. As you will see relaxing is a very important part of meditation. Your class may like to do this meditation with your teacher as the guide.

- Close your eyes and begin to concentrate on your breathing.
- Take deep breaths and feel your whole body relax.
- Begin to clear your mind and allow your imagination to picture what you hear…
- Imagine you are walking on a deserted beach.

- Feel the breeze on your skin and hear the sound of the water gently breaking on the shore...
- Up ahead you see a man sitting on the sand. As you approach you realise that it is Jesus. Sit down with him and begin to talk...
- You feel very relaxed in his company. Tell him about something you are worried about...
- He tells you that he is with you and that God will help you...
- Thank him for something good which has happened in your life this week...
- Think back over the last week. Is there anything you need to say sorry for?
- Listen as Jesus tells you how much he loves you...
- The time has come for you to leave this place but Jesus tells you that he will always be here any time you need him...
- You say your goodbyes and continue walking down the beach...
- As you walk further away you turn and see Jesus still sitting there and you feel comfort in knowing that he will always be there for you...
- Begin to return from the beach back into the room where you are, and when you are ready open your eyes.

Over to You

In your copy, write about your experience of the meditation. Did you find it a good way of praying? Why?

Contemplation

Contemplation – When we use no words but simply sit and concentrate on God.

Another type of prayer that is similar to meditation is called **contemplation**. This is when no words are used at all and we simply sit and concentrate on God. We may do it by focusing on a picture or a burning candle or we may concentrate on a phrase in our minds such as, 'God is my rock'.

This can be a difficult way of praying, as it requires deep concentration and patience. But for those who use it, it can be a very spiritual and rewarding way of praying. It is based on the idea that we are in God's presence.

Difficulties with Prayer

Consider the following lyrics from the Garth Brooks song, 'Unanswered Prayers'.

Just the other night at a hometown football game,
My wife and I ran into my old high school flame
And as I introduced them, the past came back to me,
And I couldn't help but think of the way things used to be.

She was the one that I'd wanted for all times,
And each night I'd spend prayin' that God would make her mine,
And if he'd only grant me this wish I wished back then
I'd never ask for anything again.

Sometimes I thank God for unanswered prayers
Remember when you're talkin' to the man upstairs
That just because he doesn't answer, doesn't mean he don't care
Some of God's greatest gifts are unanswered prayers.

She wasn't quite the angel that I remembered in my dreams
And I could tell that time had changed me
In her eyes too it seemed
We tried to talk about the old days
There wasn't much we could recall
I guess the Lord knows what he's doin' after all.

And as she walked away and I looked at my wife
And then and there I thanked the good Lord, for the gifts in my life.

Sometimes I thank God …

What is this song saying about prayer? At times it can be difficult to pray, especially if we feel that God is not listening. But this song is telling us that we should put our trust in God when we pray because he knows what is best for us.

This is one example of a difficulty someone may have when they are praying. Others may include:

(a) **No time:** In our busy world people have very little free time on their hands. People work and study for longer periods of time than they ever did before. They may find it hard to set aside time for prayer.

(b) **No concentration:** There are so many distractions for people today. Television and computer games are just two

of the distractions that young people face on a daily basis. Shops are open seven days a week and people find it hard to just concentrate on one thing at a time or experience some quiet time.

(c) **No visual body:** Praying to a God that you cannot see physically can be very hard for some people, especially when we live in a world where science can provide evidence for most things.

Over to You

In groups, look at the difficulties with prayer mentioned above. What ideas can your group come up with that might help those having these difficulties. Share your answers with the rest of the class.

Prayer in Spiritual Traditions

Jesus praying with his diciples.

Prayer has always been very important in the Christian religion. People who wish to have a close and personal relationship with God do so through prayer. For many Christians it is part of their everyday life. They especially turn to it in times of difficulty or worry as a source of comfort and strength. It can give them hope and even provide them with answers.

They look to their founder Jesus as a model of someone who showed the importance of prayer. During all the significant times in his life Jesus turned to prayer:

- Before he began his public ministry he went out into the wilderness to pray to God for strength and guidance (Luke 4:1–2).
- On the Sabbath day he went to the synagogue to pray (Luke 4:16).
- After he performed miracles he prayed to thank God (John 11:41–42).
- Before he was arrested in the Garden of Gethsemane (Luke 22:42).

Jesus also gave people the gift of prayer when he taught them the Our Father.

Another person in the Christian tradition who understood the importance of prayer was Saint Maximilian Kolbe.

Saint Maximilian Kolbe

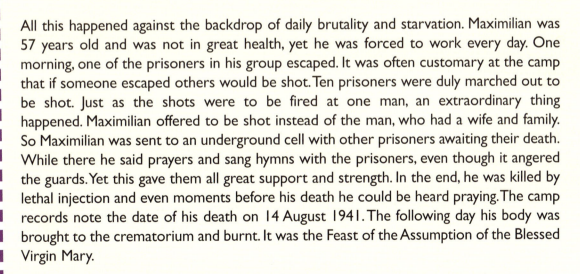

Saint Maximilian was born Raymond Kolbe in Poland in 1894. In 1910 he joined the Franciscan Order. As a priest, he had a deep devotion to Mary and published a monthly magazine to spread this devotion. In 1941 during the Nazi occupation of Poland he was sent to the concentration camp, Auschwitz. But he believed it was the will of God and his Blessed Mother that caused him to be there. There was nowhere else on earth he felt that was in such need of spiritual strength and encouragement. He was not just a visitor there: he was one of the prisoners taken from their homes to work in these camps. He wanted to be at the prisoners' disposal day and night. Many were astonished by him giving his dinner to a younger prisoner, but he believed that a young person should be given the opportunity to live. Many things he gave away; he took no gifts and accepted no special treatment.

After a while prisoners began to come to him from all over the camp. He spoke only words of love to those who despaired and those who were consumed by hate. He prayed with those that were losing their faith in God. His message was always the same. One must not give in to hatred no matter how awful things are. Hatred could achieve nothing and create nothing. Many were spellbound by his words. One priest who came to him for confession was asked to hear Maximilian's in return. The priest came away knowing he had met a living saint.

All this happened against the backdrop of daily brutality and starvation. Maximilian was 57 years old and was not in great health, yet he was forced to work every day. One morning, one of the prisoners in his group escaped. It was often customary at the camp that if someone escaped others would be shot. Ten prisoners were duly marched out to be shot. Just as the shots were to be fired at one man, an extraordinary thing happened. Maximilian offered to be shot instead of the man, who had a wife and family. So Maximilian was sent to an underground cell with other prisoners awaiting their death. While there he said prayers and sang hymns with the prisoners, even though it angered the guards. Yet this gave them all great support and strength. In the end, he was killed by lethal injection and even moments before his death he could be heard praying. The camp records note the date of his death on 14 August 1941. The following day his body was brought to the crematorium and burnt. It was the Feast of the Assumption of the Blessed Virgin Mary.

'Having loved his own, he loved them to the end.' His death was the logical end to his life. Everything that he had he had given away; the only thing he had to give was his life. But he did this with graciousness and love.

'A man can have no greater love than to lay down his life for his friend.' Maximilian knew that his days on earth were numbered, and it was through an act of evil that an act of total goodness shone through. Today he is a great example of a person for whom prayer played a central role in their life.

Over to You

1. What sort of life did Maximilian Kolbe lead in Auschwitz?
2. Describe the type of person he was?
3. Do you think he deserves the title saint?
4. Do you think it is significant that he was buried on such a feast day? Why/why not?
5. How do you think the man felt when he saw Maximilian take his place to die?
6. How do you think the man's family felt when they heard the story?
7. 'Having loved his own, he loved them to the end.' Discuss this statement in relation to the life of Maximilian Kolbe.

Exam Style Question

8. Write an essay on prayer, outlining the importance of prayer in the Christian religion. Make reference to the different types of prayer and the different ways people pray.

Section E – Key Definitions

Actions of significance:	An action has significance if it carries meaning for the person.
Celebration:	Ceremonies to mark a special event in your life.
Communal prayer:	When we pray with others.
Communication:	To share or pass on God's loving message.
Communicating experience:	To pass on the teachings of religion from one generation to the next.
Communication with God:	When prayer is used as a way of keeping our relationship with God alive.
Contemplation:	A type of prayer where we clear our minds to become one with God. *– when we use no words but simply sit and concentrate on God.*
Encounter with God:	To meet God or feel his presence around us.
Encountering mystery:	Experiences that make people wonder about the meaning of life.
Icon:	Sacred or holy images painted in a particular way that can help people to pray.
Identity:	The unique characteristics of a person or group.
Meditation:	*when we become quiet and focus our thoughts on God.* A type of prayer where we focus on God through deep thought.
Participation:	To become actively involved in something.
Penitence:	A type of prayer where we say sorry to God for any wrongdoings.
Personal prayer:	When we pray alone.
Petition:	A type of prayer that asks God for something.
Places of significance:	A place or building that has special meaning or importance for a group of people.
Praise and thanksgiving:	A type of prayer that gives thanks to God for all he has given us.
Reflection:	To think deeply about something.
Ritual:	A religious ceremony that involves a series of actions that are performed without any variation.
Sacrament:	A religious ceremony in which participants receive the grace of God.
Sacredness:	Something set apart as holy.
Sign:	An action, word or picture that gives a message.
Symbol:	Actions, words or gestures that can have a deeper meaning than a sign and evoke a response from people.

SECTION F

THE MORAL CHALLENGE

AIMS

- To explore the human need to order relationships at the personal, communal and global levels.

- To explore how this need can be expressed in a variety of ways.

- To identify how this need is expressed in civil and other legal codes.

- To show how religious belief is expressed in particular moral visions.

- To explore the moral visions of two major world religions, one of which should be Christianity.

- To analyse the impact of these visions on the lives of believers and non-believers in considering some current moral issues.

HIGHER LEVEL ONLY

- To introduce students to some aspects of the relationship between religion, morality and state law.

In this chapter,
you will become familiar with the following concepts:

- Morality
- Relationships
- Choice
- Society
- Action and consequence
- Freedom
- Influence

Chapter 23:

Introduction to Morality

Morality

The broken vase

Linda couldn't believe it! Her mother's favourite vase lay in pieces at her feet. She knew she would be in serious trouble now. If only she could turn back the clock. So many times she had been told not to touch the precious item, but she just loved picking it up to look closely at its beautiful patterns. How would she break the news to her mother?

Just as she was about to go and face the music she saw her brother Brian's ball in the corner. A plan began to form in her mind. Only yesterday he had been told off for playing ball in the house. She could sneak out of the room now and pretend that she knew nothing about it. Her mother would just presume Brian had done it and he could take the blame. It all seemed so simple!

But just as Linda was about to leave the room a little voice in her head made her stop. Would it be fair to Brian to let him take the punishment for something she had done? Even though it would make things easier for her, she just knew it wasn't the right thing to do. Taking a deep breath, she went to find her mother and tell her the truth.

Up for Discussion

Have you ever been in a situation like this?
Think about how this story could have ended differently.

Choice

Morality – Knowing what is good and bad behaviour and making decisions on this basis.

In the story Linda had a choice to make between right and wrong. Knowing what is good behaviour and what is bad behaviour and making decisions based on this can be described as **morality**.

In the story Linda decided to do the right thing because she knew it would not be fair on her brother. She felt guilty about doing wrong. This is what made her decide what was right or **moral**.

People can have different reasons for deciding what is moral:

 1. Feeling guilty

 5. Gut instinct

 2. Fear of being caught

 6. Following the crowd

 3. The laws of their country

 7. Obeying orders

 4. The laws of their religion

Society

We can therefore see that a person's sense of right or wrong depends upon many things. What one person sees as right or moral, another may see as wrong or immoral. A sense of morality is something which every person has, regardless of their age, race or religious background. Because we live in communities our morality affects those around us, so in this way we can say that our morality is **personal** and **communal**.

When making moral decisions we must remember that we have different kinds of relationships with people and our decisions can affect them in different ways.

Interpersonal
The relationships I have with certain individuals such as a parent, brother, sister or friend.

Communal
The relationships I have with a group of people, such as those who live in my area or members of a club I belong to.

Global
Even though we may not realise it, we have relationships with people of different races and religions from all over the world.

   We are connected to them simply because we all live on the same planet. Decisions made by individuals or groups of people can have a global effect such as damaging the environment or using nuclear weapons.

Human Relationships

Read the following article about how morality can have a global effect.

Bob Geldof: Reaching the World

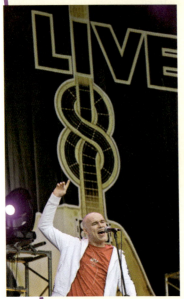

This Irishman's face is recognised throughout the world. While Bob Geldof is a talented musician, he is more widely known for his work in helping others. In 1984 he was moved by a BBC news item on famine-stricken Ethiopia in Africa. It made him want to reach out and do something practical to help those who were suffering. So he called on his famous friends in the music business to help. The result was a Christmas song, 'Feed the World', which was an instant number one hit and whose popularity helped raise both money and awareness for those in need. But the story didn't end there. The following year saw one of the biggest music concerts of all time, Live Aid in Wembley Stadium, which continued the good work.

However, the problem of poverty in the developing world didn't go away. So 20 years later, in July 2005, a concert called Live 8 took place in eight cities around the world. Its aim was to convince world leaders to make a **choice** to end poverty. By cancelling African debt and increasing the amount of aid to these countries, the politicians could make a huge change to our **society**. The idea was a huge success as more than $40 billion of debt owed by the African countries was cancelled.

People all over the world had been **influenced** by the example set by Bob Geldof. They reached out to help their fellow human beings.

Choice – A moral choice is making a decision about what is right or wrong.

Society – Human beings living together in community.

Influence – Something that affects our decisions.

Over to You – Exam Style Questions

1. Why did Bob Geldof decide to organise Live Aid?
2. What did the song 'Feed the World' achieve?
3. Would you describe Bob Geldof as a moral person? Why?
4. How does this article show what is meant by the term influence?

Action and Consequence

What Amanda did...

Amanda went to the disco with her friends
Cool was what she wanted to be
Together they drank some alcohol
Ignoring the fact she knew it was wrong.
One hour later she felt very ill
Nobody knew what to do.

Crying she made her way home
Opening the front door she knew her parents would be angry
No way was she going to a disco again, they said.
Saying she was sorry, she went to her room.
Everyone knew the next day in school.
Questions from everyone about what had happened.
Upset and
Embarrassed, she told them the story.
Never again would she drink.
Clearly it was the wrong choice to have made
Even though it felt right at the time.

This incident with Amanda tells us about the connection between actions and consequences. One action here had many consequences. What were they?

Everything we say or do causes something else to happen. Not only do our actions have consequences for ourselves but also for others.

 **Over to You**

Look at the following headline from a newspaper and describe the action and consequences for all those involved.

90-year-old woman badly injured in mugging by youth

Fill in the box showing the choice of action, influence and consequence of Amanda's night.

 **Over to You**

Choice
Action
Influence
Consequence

Freedom and Responsibility

When it comes to making moral choices people often say, 'I have the right to do as I please.' Everyone in the world has certain rights, in other words, things they are entitled to. As humans we are free to make choices in our lives. As Christians we believe that God gave us this right to have free will. However, with this right comes responsibility. We have already seen that our actions have consequences. We are responsible for these consequences.

Consider the following situation:

Right

Walking down the street I finish a bar of chocolate. I have the right to throw the wrapper on the ground if that is what I choose…

But

Responsibility

I have a responsibility to my local community to keep the place clean and to look after the environment.

Moral people are those who do not forget their responsibilities when making decisions about what to say or do.

Over to You

Can you think of a responsibility that would go with the rights listed?

1. I am playing my stereo in my bedroom at night. I have the right to turn the volume up high.
2. There is a water shortage in my area after a hot spell of weather. I have the right to water the garden.
3. I see a younger pupil in school being bullied. I have the right not to get involved.
4. There is a guest speaker in school giving a talk to my year group. I have the right to talk to the person beside me.

Influence and Behaviour

We learned earlier in the chapter that an influence is something that affects our decisions. At different stages of our lives the way we make our decisions are affected by different influences on us. How we behave at certain times can often be as a result of these influences.

Look at the following extracts taken from the diary of Suzanne over a number of years, beginning at the age of 10.

6 October 1997
Dear diary,
I'm so bored! All my friends are down at the old wreck playing hide and seek. It's only down the road but Mam and Dad won't let me go there. They think it's dangerous. My friend Ciara said I should just go anyway because my Mam will never find out. But I know Mam likes to know where I am when I'm out playing. Anyway, Dad always says he'd be very disappointed if I told lies. So I suppose I have to think of something else to do instead. Maybe Dad will help me practise my basketball.

30 March 2000

Dear diary,
There's a new girl in our class. Her name is Sarah. She seems a bit quiet. All the girls were going to the bowling alley today after school. No one wanted her to come because we're not sure if we like her yet. I didn't want her to come either. But I remember my first week in secondary school and how lonely I felt. Our school has a buddy system where an older girl becomes your buddy and helps you settle in. My buddy was really nice. Maybe I should talk to the new girl tomorrow and be a buddy to her? She might turn out to be really nice.

20 August 2001

Dear diary,
I can't believe it! Finally, the new Amber jeans are in the shops. I saw them today when I was in town with Sarah. We saw them in all our favourite magazines and everyone who's anyone is wearing them. I have to have a pair! Mam says there's no way she's paying that kind of money for jeans but she doesn't realise how much I need them. All the magazines said they're the 'must haves' of this season. My plan is to tell Mam I need the money for a birthday present for Sarah and I'll tell Dad I need new runners for basketball. I just hope they don't find out.

7 May 2003

Dear diary,
Help! I don't know what to do. Sarah and Ciara have said they are definitely going to skip school tomorrow. If I'm caught, I'll be in so much trouble with school and at home. Plus we've a big test next week in history. So I don't want to miss that class tomorrow in case the teacher says anything I need to know. The girls really want me to go with them. But I don't want them to think I'm afraid to do it. Sarah and Ciara think it will be easy to get away with it. I hope so.

1 July 2005

Dear diary,
Finally, the exams are over! I can't wait until Saturday. This time next week I'll be in India. I'm nervous but really looking forward to it too. I know it'll be hard work but I think it'll be worth it. When my parish priest told me about the volunteer programme run by the diocese, I wasn't sure if I wanted to go. But then Father Frank told me what a difference I could make to the people there. He reminded me that by helping others I'm helping God too. God has always been there to help me so it will be nice to give something back. Everyone in the parish has helped to raise money for the trip. I'm going to give a talk at Mass when I get back just to let them all know how it went.

13 January 2007

Dear diary,
I can't believe I'm up at eight o'clock on a Saturday morning! I should've gone to bed early last night. But it's all for a good cause. The whole neighbourhood has decided to help out getting the area ready for the Tidy Towns competition. I'm in the grass-cutting group. I suppose it could be worse. The whole town is really pulling together so that the place will look really nice. I can't wait to see how it'll look when it's finished. The residents' association organised the whole thing. They think we've a good chance of winning. Let's hope so!

From these diary extracts we can see that throughout Suzanne's life different people or groups had an influence on her decisions. The main influences we saw were **(a) family, (b) school, (c) the media, (d) friends, (e) our church, and (f) our community**. These influences can be positive or negative and can greatly affect our decisions.

Up for Discussion

1. Which influences in Suzanne's life had a positive effect and which influences had a negative effect on her decisions?
2. What are the biggest influences in your life when it comes to making decisions?

Over to You – Exam Style Questions

1. (a) Morality is _____

   (b) Fear of being caught is one reason that might make somone decide what is moral. Name two other reasons.
2. In your own words explain the connection between
   (a) action and consequences and (b) rights and responsibilities.

263

In this chapter,
you will become familiar with the following concepts:

■ Moral vision
■ Laws
■ Religious moral vision
■ Authority
■ Tradition

Chapter 24:

Sources of Morality

Paul's Dilemma

Paul and Seán had been friends since their first day in primary school. Lately, Seán began hanging around with Peter and Mike who were in their class. Paul did not like either of the boys as he felt they were always messing and making fun of other people. At times they even made fun of him in front of other lads in the class. Most of all he hated how small and stupid they made him feel.

One morning as Paul and Seán were on their way to school they met Peter and Mike outside the local shop. Neither Peter nor Mike had any homework done as they had been out late the previous night. So they decided to spend the day at Mike's house on the PlayStation. Both of Mike's parents worked so they knew that there would be no one home for ages.

On hearing this, Seán thought it was a great idea and immediately tried to persuade Paul to do the same. But Paul's brother had mitched school before and Paul remembered how much trouble he had gotten into from school and from home. He told this to Seán, much to the amusement of the other two boys. Now Paul knew he had to think quickly!

Over to You

1. Have you ever found yourself in a situation like the one described here?
2. What do you think Paul should do?
3. What do you think his parents and the school would say to him if he were found out?
4. Do you think he can remain friends with Seán if he decides not to spend the day with him?

Sources of Morality

To **source** something is to find out exactly where it has come from. Our morality comes from a number of sources that help to shape us into the people we are now and the people we will become. So what are these sources?

- Home and family
- The peer group
- The school
- Religion
- The State.

Home and family

The **home** and the **family** are two of the most important sources of morality. The family provides moral standards, education, religious background, love, security, customs and cultures. If we are taught good values in the home, we will learn to be respectful to others throughout life. Parents are the primary educators of their children. They instil in their children good values that will stand to them throughout life.

It is in the home that talents are nurtured and nourished. It is through the family that you learn about yourself and come to appreciate what is good. Stories are passed from one generation to the next which helps in the formation of your character. Every family is unique and has its own identity. Every family has a responsibility to look after each other, especially in times of difficulty and distress.

The love a family shows to each other is unconditional. In saying all this no family is perfect. This is evident in Luke 15:11–31, where the father welcomes his son home after he has squandered a lot of money.

The Prodigal Son

A man had two sons that he loved equally. The younger of the sons asked his father to divide the estate. When the father did this, the younger son left for a distant country where he squandered the money on having a good time.

When all the money was spent, he didn't know what to do. Eventually, he decided to go home to see his family. Knowing he had done wrong, he felt awful about his behaviour. As he came near his family estate, his father saw him in the distance and ran towards him. That night the father organised a big party to honour his young son.

Meanwhile, the elder son was working in the fields and heard that his younger brother had returned. Immediately he was angry that his father was holding a party for him. After all, he was the one who had looked after his father and worked hard on the estate when the younger brother had left. But his father replied, 'My son, you are with me always and all I have is yours. But it was only right we should celebrate and rejoice, because your brother here was dead and has come to life; he was lost and is found.'

Over to You

1. How is the home and family an important source of morality?
2. What values have been instilled in you that you would like to pass on to others?
3. Do you think the story of the Prodigal Son is a good example of family life today in the 21st century?

The peer group

The **peer group** can be seen as another source of morality. It can be defined as a group of the same age. All young people want to belong to a peer group and they feel anxious and different when they are excluded from activities of the group. Friends are important as they help us become better people. During adolescence, we often make new friends because as we grow and develop we know what type of people we want to be friends with.

Sometimes during adolescence young people become pressurised into doing things that the group decides. As seen in Peter's dilemma at the beginning of this chapter, it can be a difficult time. It is a time when we have to stand on our own two feet and make decisions for ourselves. Due to some of the decisions we make, we can be left out in the cold by our friends, laughed at and made feel different. Real friends treat each other with respect and listen and care for each other. They are supportive of one another.

Up for Discussion

1. What values have you learnt from your friends?
2. How important are friends to adolescents?
3. Describe how the peer group can be both positive and negative.

Up for Discussion

Check out your school's anti-bullying policy. Did a committee of people write it? What do you like / dislike about it?

The school

The **school** is a community that works together to help and support each other. Because young people spend a lot of time in school it is important that they work together to make this community great for all. This means showing respect for their fellow classmates, teachers and all who work in the school community.

At school we can be influenced by other people or we can be a source of influence for others. Therefore, school is a very important place that can shape the people we become in later life.

The religion

Another important source of morality is **religion**. Most world religions have a **moral vision**. A moral vision is to see the difference between right and wrong. For Christians the most important ideal is the teachings of Jesus Christ given to us in the sacred scriptures, such as the Bible. For members of Islam, they look to the Koran for spiritual guidance and support. Jewish people look to the Torah for their spiritual well-being.

For centuries Christians worldwide have been guided by the Church on moral issues, e.g. divorce, abortion, etc. By listening to the Church and following sacred scripture we become more informed and therefore can make correct decisions.

Read the following poem and answer the questions that follow.

One Solitary Life

Here is a man
who was born of Jewish parents
the child of a peasant woman…
He never wrote a book.
He never held an office.
He never owned a home.
He never had a family.
He never went to college.
He never travelled two hundred
miles from the place
where he was born.

He never did one of the things that
usually accompanies greatness.
He had no credentials
but himself…

While still a young man,
the tide of popular opinion
turned against him.
His friends ran away.
One of them denied him…
He was nailed to a cross
between two thieves.
His executioners gambled for
the only piece of property
he had on earth – his coat.
When he was dead
he was taken down
and laid in a borrowed grave
through the pity of a friend.

Nineteen wide centuries
have come and gone
and today he is the centrepiece
of the human race and the
leader of the column of progress.

I am far within the mark
when I say that all the armies
that ever marched,
and all the navies
that were ever built…
have not affected the life of a man
upon earth
as powerfully as has that
One Solitary Life.

Author unknown.

Over to You

1. What do you think of the title of this poem?
2. What effect has Jesus had on our lives to date?
3. How important do you feel religion is as a source of morality in the 21st century?

269

The state

Another source of morality for us is the **state**. In Ireland we live in what is called a democratic state. This means that every few years we elect people to represent us in parliament (Dáil Éireann). The elected government makes the laws for the country that each citizen must abide by. The laws of the country protect its people. In March 2004 the government introduced a law in Ireland preventing people from smoking in public places. Anyone who fails to abide by the law is fined. Most people do not want to be fined so they abide by all laws.

Over to You

1. What do you think of the smoking ban?
2. Can you think of some other examples of the laws of the state and how they shape our morality?

Ban on smoking in the workplace in Ireland

Since 29 March 2004 the Irish Government has implemented a ban on smoking in the workplace in Ireland. This means that with effect from that date (29 March 2004) smoking is forbidden in enclosed places of work in Ireland. This includes office blocks, various buildings, public houses/bars, restaurants and company vehicles (cars and vans). The ban is being introduced as part of the **Public Health (Tobacco) Act, 2002 (Section 47) Regulations 2003**.

Just under 25% of the Irish population smoke and the purpose of this ban is to offer protection to employees and the public who are exposed to the harmful and toxic effects of tobacco smoke in the workplace. Smoking has been identified as a major cause of heart disease and a significant contributor to lung cancer in Ireland.

Moral Rules and Guidelines

Principle – A law that one holds to be right.

Before we look at how formal and informal codes and principles came about, let us look at the following concepts to help us:

- Principle
- Code
- Law
- Moral vision

Code – A set of rules and guidelines.

A **principle** is **a law that one holds to be right**. Therefore, the principles that we live by help shape our behaviour and influence the moral decisions that we make. A principled person would not allow another in their class to be bullied because it is wrong.

Law – A rule that prevents us doing the wrong thing or making the wrong decision on a particular matter.

A **code** is **a set of rules and guidelines**. We regularly hear from our teachers about our code of behaviour in school. Do you know what your school's code of behaviour is?

A **law** is **a rule that prevents us doing the wrong thing or making the wrong decision on a particular matter**. In school there are many

laws in place to safeguard the well-being of each student in the school. One example of this is not to put graffiti on the school desks as it is unfair to other students. What laws do you feel are most important in your school?

Moral vision is a person's view of what is right and good. It is their outlook on life and how it should be lived. Their moral vision will shape the decision and choices they make. Our moral vision can often be influenced by our religious beliefs. Most religions have a moral vision. A moral vision is always the basis of any code or set of guidelines. The moral vision underlying the United Nations Convention on the Rights of the Child values the equality, dignity and freedom of all children.

Moral vision – A person's view of what is right and good.

When God delivered the Ten Commandments to Moses on Mount Sinai he promised to be always with his people and to always be their God. When we follow the Ten Commandments we show respect to God. By following these commandments we become happier and fulfilled in our lives and our relationships.

The Ten Commandments

1. I am the Lord your God. You should have no other Gods but me.
2. You should not take the Lord your God's name in vain.
3. Remember to always keep holy the Sabbath day.
4. Always honour your father and mother.
5. Never kill anyone.
6. Never commit adultery.
7. Never steal from anyone.
8. Never bear false witness against your neighbour.
9. Never covet your neighbour's wife.
10. Never covet your neighbour's goods.

It is often difficult to sum up one's moral code but the word **love** is a very strong one in the Ten Commandments. Here we are told to love the lord your God with all your heart, all your mind and all your strength.

Throughout scripture we hear Jesus telling us to 'love one another as I have loved you' or treat others the way you would like to be treated yourself. Jesus showed love to all sinners, outcasts and lepers. Love is a very strong theme for Christians and one that we should always live by. It is at the heart of the Christian moral vision.

Christina Noble: A Person with a Moral Vision

Christina Noble was born in 1944 in the slums of Dublin. Her father was an alcoholic and drank any money they had. As a result, she was often seen collecting scraps off the street to feed her three siblings. After her mother's death when Christina was 10, the family was broken up and put into separate orphanages. All Christina ever wanted was to be cared for and loved. The neglect she felt would later help her understand the pain of others.

At 18 she discovered that her brother had moved to Birmingham and she decided to follow him. She settled in England, married and had a family. One night in 1971 she had a dream about the children of Vietnam which would shape her life forever. Years passed and she decided to visit Vietnam. It was no holiday as everywhere she went she saw ragged children. Soon she began to reminisce about her own childhood and quickly realised that there was no difference between the gutter she had lived in as a child in Dublin and the gutter she saw in front of her in Vietnam.

The sight of the children made her cry. Her crusade for street children in Vietnam had begun. When she saw an orphanage she knew she could fulfil her destiny there. So she began to fundraise but her requests for money were repeatedly turned down in the city. Even with one generous donation the children's needs were still endless. It was then that she realised she needed official help, which eventually she got. Christina's dream had finally become a reality! The Christina Noble Children's Foundation was then established in 1989. Today she is often referred to as a Mother Teresa!

Laws

Formal codes

Some codes and principles are **formal**. They have been put together for a reason. Formal codes tend to be written down and must be accepted by everyone. For example, Health and Safety in the workforce is a formal rule as it safeguards every individual working there. Therefore, many workplaces are obliged to have regular fire drills so that each worker knows what to do in the event of a fire occurring. Formal rules also tend to be put together over a period of time, usually with trial and error.

Informal codes

Other codes are described as **informal** as they are often unofficial and not written down. A lot of the time informal rules depend on the goodwill of people. A youth club may have an informal set of rules that people may abide by. For example, the club may share its facilities so that everyone has a chance to use them. This is for the greater good of the club.

Moral vision

All laws are specific but each law is based on an underlying **moral vision**. For example let us look at the Road Traffic Act 1991, which requires the majority of people in Ireland to wear a seat belt. Each year in Ireland many people are killed or seriously injured on our roads. This is often attributed to speeding, drink driving or not wearing a seat belt. The penalty points system introduced in 2003 was to deter people from speeding. There is now an onus on drivers to wear their seat belt and to ensure that passengers less than 17 years of age are wearing a seat belt. If you are caught not wearing a seat belt, a fine and penalty points are given.

So what is the moral vision behind this law?

In protecting yourself and others by wearing a seat belt, not speeding or drink driving, you can see that lives can be saved. Putting others first is something that we have learnt from scriptures. Jesus taught us that we should treat others the way we would like to be treated ourselves. By following the laws of the State on our roads we are following this message.

Religious Moral Vision

A person who does not shape their moral vision by religion may not seem very different to someone who does. Both may have a social conscience, a passion for justice and a love of one's neighbour. But the non-religious person may only be acting out of social concern. On the other hand, the religious person understands and appreciates that each of us are made in the image and likeness of God and each of us are unique to Him. Because religious people feel this way there is a yearning to live by God's message of 'Love your neighbour as yourself'.

Sister Stanislaus Kennedy: Living by God's Message of Love

One person who is testament to living by God's message of love is Sister Stanislaus Kennedy or Sister Stan as she is called. Born in Lispole on the Dingle Peninsula in 1940, she joined the Irish Sisters of Charity at the age of 18. In fact, she was one of a hundred women that entered the novitiate that year. All she ever wanted to do was to work with the poor. So her life's work has been based on the belief that each person is equal and therefore deserves respect.

In time she persuaded her religious superiors to allow her to study a degree in Social Science. Following her degree and postgraduate work she began to put the knowledge she had learnt to good use. In Kilkenny she started to work with Bishop Birch. In 1983 when Bishop Birch died she commenced the next phase of her life, working with the homeless of Dublin.

For many years she lived with homeless women in a dilapidated building in Eustace Street. She hoped to give these women back their dignity and sense of self-worth. During this time she also learned much about herself and it was from this experience that she founded Focus Point, now known as Focus Ireland. Its mission was to find accommodation and renew the self-worth of homeless women.

Sister Stan's religious moral vision is deeply rooted in scripture. The respect and love she shows to those who have no voice in society is evidence of this. She lives her life as God wants us too. As St John's Gospel 4:40 says 'All love invites love, God calls us to love'.

Sister Stan remains Life President of Focus Ireland but is not as involved as before. In recent times she has founded the Sanctuary, a holistic spirituality centre in Dublin. Also, she has been instrumental in the founding of the Young Social Innovators Programme for transition year students. This programme is an imaginative response to social needs in the 21st century.

Over to You

1. What was Sister Stan's mission in life?
2. How do you think her dream was fulfilled?
3. How significant was the work of Focus Ireland when it was set up?
4. Can you think of another person or persons who have a religious moral vision? Tell their story.

Authority

Another aspect to codes and principles is authority. To have **authority** means to have a certain power or to be highly knowledgeable about a certain subject. Many people look to their religion as an authority to help and guide them when making moral decisions or forming a moral vision. For Christians this authority comes from two sources.

1. **Scripture:** Religious people see their sacred text as a direct link with their god and because of this they see it as a special authority. Therefore they look to their sacred text to find out what it says about a particular moral issue.

2. **Religious Leaders:** When Jesus' time on earth was over he gave his apostles a special authority to continue his work on earth. Of all the apostles, Jesus gave Peter a special authority. He said Peter would be the rock on which he would build his church. Peter went on to become the first pope of the Church. This authority given by Jesus has been handed down to each pope right up to today. Religious people look to the authority of their leaders when making a moral decision. Popes and bishops often write letters to their communities of followers to advise them on moral issues. The followers see these as a source of authority.

Over to You

Can you name the religious texts of the following religions?
Judaism
Islam
Buddhism
Hinduism
Christianity.

Tradition

Another aspect to codes and principles is **tradition**. Tradition is never seen as something outdated, but as a continuing process through which the church reflects on and passes from one generation to the next. An example of tradition in the Catholic Church is to give up something for Lent. For many people they give up cigarettes or alcohol, for others they give up sweets. Tradition grows and develops over time. Today the Christian church lives by the teachings of Jesus Christ 2000 years after his birth and is guided by the Holy Spirit.

Over to You

1. Do your family have any traditions passed on from previous generations?
2. How important do you think traditions of the Church are?

Over to You Crossword

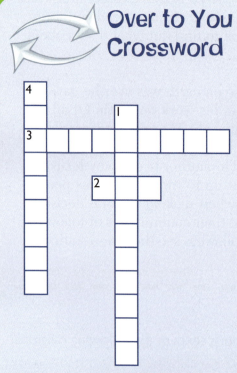

1 (down): A person's view of what is right and good.

2 (across): A set of rules that prevents us doing the wrong thing.

3 (across): To have a certain power or a knowledge on an issue.

4 (down): Something that is handed down from one generation to the next.

Answers on page 299.

Growing in Morality

Moral Growth

Saint Ignatius Loyola

Ignatius Loyola

Inigo de Loyola was born into a wealthy family in Spain in 1491. When he was young he loved gambling and fighting. This continued until he was seriously injured in a battle with the French when he was 30 years old. During his convalescence he began to read some religious books that made him begin to question his life. Soon he began to feel at peace with himself. When he had fully recovered he set out on a pilgrimage to the monastery at Montserrat, near Barcelona. During his stay there he devoted himself to prayer, fasting and works of piety. Finally, he decided to devote his life to the service of God.

In his desire to serve God, he realised that he needed more education in philosophy and theology. As a result, he went back to school to learn Latin. After some time he set up a group of priests called the Companions of Jesus and he began to call himself Ignatius. In Rome the group was welcomed by the Pope. They took vows of poverty, obedience and chastity and vowed to travel wherever they were needed. In 1622 Ignatius was canonised a saint. The Jesuits as they are called today are involved in the education of young people all over the world.

Over to You

1. What sort of person was Ignatius at the start of the story?
2. What inspired him to change his ways?
3. Do you think Ignatius grew as a person in the story? If he did grow, in what way did it come about?
4. Find out more information on the work of the Jesuit order today.

Stages of moral growth

Children

Like with Saint Ignatius Loyola all moral growth is gradual. As children we learn very quickly that something is either right or wrong. When we do something that is good, like put our toys away, we are rewarded. When we do something bad, like hit our brother or sister, we are punished. In the early days we learn a lot from our parents or guardians as they are our primary educators. We as children want to please because we know that our reward is something like sweets or toys. The fact that we learn this as children influences our behaviour at the time, but also in later life.

Adolescence

As we move into adolescence we understand very clearly the difference between right and wrong. In a lot of ways we have matured from the days of hitting a family member. We seek the approval of others: at school, at home and in our peer group. The peer group has a major significance in our life because its approval of what we do is fundamental to our being.

The school and home have rules that we must obey too because if we don't we are punished. Staying out at night past our curfew often leads us into conflict with our parents because they don't know where we are. As adolescents we want to be trusted and so feel the need to assert our independence. This often spreads to the classroom where an adolescent might daydream due to tiredness instead of doing classwork. Quickly adolescents learn what behaviour is correct and that throughout their lives rules and laws are an important influence on their behaviour.

Moral Maturity

Society expects people to grow in maturity as well as physically, emotionally and intellectually. But this does not always happen. Not everyone at 40 years of age is at the same stage of moral development as their neighbour of the same age. Sometimes a child of 10 years may make a moral decision better than an adult might make. When you reach moral maturity you move from selfishness to altruism. To be altruistic means that you think of others before yourself when making a decision.

This is very important for our society to work well. If we all stayed at the level of a small child whose behaviour is self-centred, there would be even more suffering in the world. People would want to simply satisfy their own needs and not care for anyone else. Remember, a child's morality is often based on reward and punishment. If people continued at this level of moral maturity they might be motivated by fear and choose to do wrong in situations where they felt they could escape punishment. Equally they might do wrong simply to gain the approval of others. A morally mature person is aware of their responsibility to respect the rights of others and think of the consequences of the decisions they make. They are less influenced by factors outside of themselves.

Moral maturity – A person who takes into consideration the feelings of others and bases their morality on what they hold to be true.

Up for Discussion

Imagine for a moment there has been a natural disaster like an earthquake. Many shop windows have been smashed and there are no security people around to protect the stock.

1. (a) What would the morally mature person do in this situation? Why?
   (b) What would the morally immature person do in this situation? Why?

2. What would the effects of both their actions be for others in the community?

James and Ronan: Morally Mature or Not?

One December night James and Ronan made plans to meet a group of friends in the park. At 15 years old they were too young to go to the local pub so the off-licence and park was their best alternative. It was raining and James had been debating whether to go out at all. But with his parents at home watching television he knew the park was a better option. On his way out he told his parents that he was going over to Ronan's house and would be back by eleven. His parents liked Ronan so they happily waved their son off.

The friends met in the park at about eight o'clock. Earlier they had sent one of the older lads into the off-licence as he never had a problem being served. Less people showed up in the park that night because of the rain so there was more drink to go round.

Very quickly Ronan got drunk and decided he was going for a drive in a car parked at the entrance to the park. Though he had 'hot wired' a car once before, he had never gone joyriding. At first James tried to persuade him not to go joyriding as he had had too much to drink, he was underage and what would he do if he were caught. Earlier James had heard his Dad telling his sister about all the Garda checkpoints he had seen the previous night on his way home. But still Ronan couldn't be persuaded not to do it. As he felt sober, James decided he would go with Ronan so that he could watch out for anything that might happen.

The two set off in the car and Ronan began to accelerate faster and faster. James asked him to slow down and to pull over because no one would know they had taken the car. However, Ronan wouldn't listen. He just went faster and faster, going around corners at high speed. By now James was very scared and nervous. Minutes passed and suddenly there was an eerie silence in the car. Then a thud. What had he hit? Both boys looked at each other as Ronan stopped the car. Nervously, James got out first and in front of him a woman was lying very still on the road. He shouted at Ronan to get out of the car. Slowly Ronan got out and people began to gather around. All he wanted to do was run away but he knew it was too late as people would recognise him.

Over to You

1. In the story do you think James tried hard enough to prevent Ronan driving the car? Explain your answer.
2. Why do you think James wanted to flee the scene?
3. Do you think both boys should be punished equally?
4. What do you think happened when the Gardaí came?
5. How morally mature was James in relation to Ronan?
6. Do you think an incident like this might lead someone to moral maturity? Explain your answer.

Conscience

The word **conscience** is derived from the Latin word 'to know'. A lot of people describe their conscience as their inner voice telling them what to do in a situation they find themselves in. Others say 'always let your conscience be your guide', thus giving them inner peace. One must be careful with this theory of the inner voice as it might tell us to do something wrong, e.g. 'If he wants to spread rumours about me, I will spread rumours about him!'. Conscience therefore needs to be more than just a voice inside of us.

The catechism of the Catholic Church teaches us that conscience is a law that we must obey because it is written on our hearts by God. From this we are encouraged to show love to others and to do good rather than evil. Conscience is our ability to know, using our judgement and knowledge, what is the right and wrong thing to do in a situation. Having an informed conscience means that one has all the facts on the matter before a decision is made. There are different ways we can inform our conscience. A person might decide to look to the experts and read up on the matter. They may try and talk to someone who has been in a similar situation. A religious person would inform their conscience by reading their sacred text or by speaking to a leader from their religion. This means that they have tried to get all the information before they make their decision.

Over to You

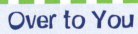

1. What does the word conscience mean to you?
2. What do you think of the saying, 'Always let your conscience be your guide'?
3. Write about an incident where you used your conscience when making a moral decision.

- Decision-making
- Truth
- Justice
- Peace
- Life
- Stewardship
- Respect
- Integrity
- Forgiveness
- Reconciliation
- Sin
- Judgement

Chapter 26:

Religious Morality in Action

In Search of Truth

The Blind Men and the Elephant

It was six men of Indostan,
To learning much inclined,
Who went to see the Elephant
(Though all of them were blind),
That each by observation
Might satisfy his mind.
The First approached the Elephant

And happening to fall
Against his broad and sturdy side,
At once began to bawl:
'I clearly see the elephant
Is very like a wall!'

The Second, feeling of the tusk,
Cried, 'Ho! What have we here,
So very round and smooth and sharp?
To me 'tis mighty clear
This wonder of an Elephant
Is very like a spear!'

The Third approached the animal,
And happening to take
The squirming trunk within his hands,
Thus boldly up and spake:
'I see,' quote he, 'the Elephant
Is very like a snake!'

The Fourth reached out his eager hand
And fell about the knee.
'What most this wondrous beast is like
Is mighty plain,' said he;
''Tis clear enough the Elephant
Is very like a tree!'

The Fifth, who chanced to touch the ear,
Said: 'Even the blindest man
Can tell what this resembles most;
Deny the fact who can,
This marvel of an Elephant
Is very like a fan!'

The Sixth no sooner had begun
About the beast to grope,
Than, seizing on the swinging tail
That fell within his scope,
'I see,' quote he, 'the Elephant
Is very like a rope!'

And so these men of Indostan
Disputed loud and long,
Each in his own opinion
Exceeding stiff and strong,
Though each was partly in the right,
And all were in the wrong!

**John Godfrey Saxe
(1816–1887)**

Moral Decisions

Making moral decisions can be described as a process. Like the blind men of Indostan, called Hindustan today, when making a moral decision we must take into account all aspects of the decision, not just part of it. There are two parts to this process:

Asking questions

What are my options?
What might be the consequences for myself?
Who will I affect by my decision?
How might others be affected?

Finding answers

What does my conscience tell me?
What would my parents and friends think?
What does my religion tell me?
What does the law say about it?

Sarah: Decision-making

Sarah knew her parents would not be happy with her new habit. It was costing her a lot of money but she didn't care. All her friends smoked, it was no big deal. The only problem was her pocket money wasn't enough.

On her way out the door one morning she noticed her mother's purse on the kitchen table. Her mother had just been paid, so she wouldn't miss a couple of euro.

Decision making – The ability to make a decision on a matter whether it is the right one or not.

283

ASKING QUESTIONS		FINDING ANSWERS	
Options	**Take the money?**	**Conscience**	**Does she feel guilty?**
	Leave the purse alone?		Is it the right thing to do?
Consequences	**Being caught and punished**	**Parents**	**Family rules and morals**
	Harming her health	Friends	Surprised at her actions
Who is affected	**Mother**	**Religion**	**Thou shalt not steal**
	Shopkeeper		Honour thy mother and father
How affected	**Mother angry hurt disappointed**	**Law**	**Stealing is wrong**
	Shopkeeper fined		Illegal to smoke under age of 16

Over to You

Think of another situation where someone has to make a moral decision. Apply the process outlined above to your example.

Justice and Peace

Justice – to act justly and fairly towards others.

The struggle for **justice** and **peace** is one of the most important ideals of any Christian moral vision. It unites people together in a shared learning goal. This is vital to our lives as Christians. However, it is not exclusive to Christianity, as it is shared by all churches who work continually for justice.

In Ireland, leaders north and south have spoken publicly about the struggle for justice and peace. They have condemned the unmerciful killing of innocent people.

On 8 November 1987, a bomb went off in Enniskillen. In the bombings, Gordon Wilson lost his daughter Marie. Afterwards he spoke publicly

284

about her death and his forgiveness towards those who had planted the bomb. He did not want retaliation where other innocent people would lose their lives. 'I bear no ill will. I bear no grudge. Dirty sort of talk is not going to bring her back to life.' He encouraged the process of reconciliation.

Throughout scripture, we are asked to follow the teachings of Jesus Christ and to act justly towards our neighbour. Jesus' teaching on justice is rooted in the writings of the prophets: Amos, Job and Jeremiah. The prophets continually speak of the love that God shows to all, especially the poor and downtrodden.

The teachings of the Old Testament were given a new and deeper meaning by Jesus who saw his mission to fulfil the will of God. Jesus clearly identified with the poor, sick, women and the downtrodden during his ministry. At all times he preached: 'You must love the Lord your God with all your heart, with all your soul, with all your strength … You must love your neighbour as yourself.' (Mark 12:30). There can never be real love of God without loving others. It is clear from scripture that justice should be central to all our lives.

The dove is a symbol of peace

Over to You

1. Find out some examples from scripture where justice is at the forefront of Jesus' teaching.
2. Can you think of an example where you put justice at the forefront of a decision you had to make?

Glencree: Centre of Peace and Reconciliation

'If we wage peace with the intensity with which we waged war, there would be no wars.'

One such organisation that puts peace and justice to its forefront is the Glencree Centre. Its motto is: 'If we wage peace with the intensity with which we waged war, there would be no wars.'

The Glencree Centre was founded in 1974 in reaction to the violent conflict in Irish society. People wanted to believe there was a better way than violence and vandalism, intolerance and sectarianism. Concern for what was happening in the North of Ireland in the 1970s was not enough. Reconciliation was the key. The achievement of a peaceful society is of interest and value to us all.

The Centre for Peace and Reconciliation welcomes all traditions in Ireland that have the same hopes in peace-building. It is a non-governmental organisation. Its people see peace-building as a way to understand the nature and meaning of conflicts. It also gives a chance to resolve them without using violence. The Centre's programmes are based on the belief that new ways can be found to deal with diversity and conflict in a democratic society. In Glencree the job of reconciling very old differences requires enormous effort and courage, as well as time and patience.

Since its foundation, Glencree has been the scene of important events and projects. These have been in the fields of education, recreation, fundraising, work camps and hosting a flow of visitors.

Over to You

1. What do you think of the slogan 'If we wage peace with the intensity with which we waged war, there would be no wars'.
2. What do you think is responsible for the success of the Glencree Centre?
3. Find out more about the Glencree Centre. You may find their website helpful at www.glencree.ie.

Stewardship

Being a **steward** means looking after and protecting all of creation. It calls on us to be responsible for the decisions we make about how we use the earth and its resources. We must be aware that the choices we make about our environment will affect the generations coming after us. We must be caretakers of the earth and of each other.

A Christian religious moral vision calls on us to be stewards of creation because we believe that God created the world in his own image and likeness. As a result, we are called to act as stewards to all living things and to show respect to all forms of life.

We have already looked at what it means to have a religious moral vision. Our religious beliefs and the teachings of our church can a have huge effect on the decisions we make about many different issues. We are all familiar with the following slogan:

Reduce, Reuse, Recycle

You may wonder what this statement about the environment has to do with religion. In order to find out, let us look at each of the five world religions and see what they have to say about this issue.

Respect – To have a high regard for something and so treat it with consideration.

Stewardship – Being responsible for caring for all of God's creation.

Judaism

The Jewish sacred texts tell us that God created the earth and every living thing on it. The Book of Genesis contains the creation story which explains how God created the world in seven days. In it we see that God created the land, the water, the plants and the animals. After he had created each thing he 'saw that it was good'.

God also created human life to live side by side with these creations and so humans are seen as a part of nature. God tells man to work in the Garden of Eden and to watch over it. Jewish scholars have said that God's commandment to watch over the garden characterises the land as God's property, not ours.

After his work of creation on the seventh day, we are told that God 'rested on the seventh day after all the work had been done. God blessed the seventh day and made it holy, because on that day he rested after all his work of creating'. (Genesis 2: 2–3). This day of rest became the Jewish Sabbath which allows all of God's creation to take a break. No work on the land or jobs done by farm animals is allowed on this day. Not only that but every seven years, the Sabbath year, Jewish farmers have to let their land rest. This not only helps the soil but reminds Jewish people that the land belongs to God. The land and the people depend on each other.

Christianity

Christians share the same creation story as the Jewish religion. Therefore they see God as the one who gave us the earth. One of God's natural creations, water, plays a huge part in Christian worship, especially in the sacrament of baptism. In his parables and teachings Jesus often spoke about nature. His life was based on the idea of living in harmony with all of God's creations. In recent years Christian leaders have spoken about our responsibility to care for God's creation. In 1998 the Catholic bishops of the Philippines published the first pastoral letter on the environment called 'What is happening to our beautiful land?'. We can therefore see that care for the environment is a big part of Christianity's moral vision.

Islam

It is estimated that there are 500 verses in the Islamic sacred text, the Qur'an. It gives guidance on how Muslims should view the natural world. 'It is He who has appointed you viceroys in the earth' (6. 165). Muslims see humans as having a privileged position as guardians of the earth. Islam has a strong sense of the goodness and purity of the earth. If water is not available for **wudu** (the ritual washing before prayer), then clean dust may be used. In fact, the colour green is the most blessed of all colours for Muslims.

Buddhism

According to Buddhism, all life is precious and all life is connected. Buddhists believe that all beings on the earth share the same conditions of birth, old age, suffering and death. This means that they have compassion for all living things. In fact, their founding story features a tree! One of their leaders, the Dalai Lama, said: 'The world grows smaller and smaller, more and more interdependent … today more than ever before life must be characterised by a sense of universal responsibility, not only human to human but also human to other forms of life.' Buddhists strive to live in harmony with one's body, nature and other people.

Hinduism

The Vedas, Hinduism's sacred texts, contains imagery that values the power of the natural world. This polytheistic religion has Gods connected to the earth, sky and water, which mean that they see these things as sacred. They also have a huge respect for trees and rivers. The River Ganges plays an important role in their beliefs and worship. Their doctrine of dharma emphasises a need to act 'for the sake of the good of the world'. One of the most famous Hindus is Mahatma Gandhi who preached about the importance of living a simple life in harmony with the earth.

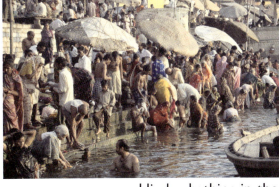

Hindus bathing in the River Ganges

We can see that all of the major world religions have a similar religious moral vision when it comes to the earth. It could be said that this vision is based on the principle of **stewardship.**

Over to You

1. 'God saw all he had made, and indeed it was very good.' What does this quote from the Book of Genesis tell us about how we should view the world?
2. What is the idea behind the Jewish Sabbath year?
3. Water is a symbol from nature used a lot in Christian worship. What other symbols from nature are associated with the Christian religion?
4. Why is the colour green very important for Muslims?
5. What might happen if we are not good stewards of creation?
6. Imagine your school is having a 'Green Week'. Produce a booklet telling people why it is important to care for the environment. Give them ideas about how they might be good stewards of creation in school, at home and in their community.

Sin

In rugby when players commit an offence (break a rule in some way) they are sent to the 'Sin Bin' for ten minutes. When we do something wrong we are committing a sin. There are different types of sins just like there are different reasons for a rugby player to be sent to the 'Sin Bin'.

1. We can sin by doing something wrong. For example, if I bully someone this is called a sin of commission – I have committed the sin.
2. We can also sin by not doing something. For example, if I see someone being bullied and I don't do anything to help, this is a sin of omission – I have omitted or not done the right thing.

Sin has traditionally been divided into two types. The less serious sin is called venial sin. While this is wrong it is not as grave as the type of sin called mortal sin. This refers to when we commit a sin that is seriously wrong, for example, murdering someone. When we sin we turn away from God and damage our relationship with him. If we sin against another person we damage our relationship with them too. However, if we genuinely want to change our ways and rebuild our relationship with God and others we can turn to the sacrament of reconciliation.

Reconciliation

Forgiveness and reconciliation

For Christians reconciliation is much more than the simple process of forgive and forget. Just because we do not hold grudges towards another person, it does not mean we are living up to the true Christian ideal of reconciliation. Pope John Paul II is testament to this in both his words and actions. True reconciliation is not achieved by just tolerating those who may have hurt us, but by actively embracing them in love and welcoming them back into our lives.

There are many examples from the Bible that show us that the God we know and love is a forgiving God. So forgiveness of sin should be at the heart of all Christian being. The greatest example of forgiveness is when Jesus was nailed to the cross on the Hill of Calvary with criminals on either side. In St Luke's Gospel we are told that nearing his death Jesus calls out to his Father, 'Father, forgive them; they do not know what they are doing'.

In the Jubilee Year in 2000, the Pope's mission for his followers was reconciliation. Not only had Pope John Paul preached on forgiveness and reconciliation, he had manifested it too. The Pope throughout his life lived by the message of St Paul to the Corinthians (2 Corinthians 5:18). 'It is all God's work; he reconciled us to himself through Christ and he gave us the ministry of reconciliation.'

Restoration of relationships

For reconciliation to fully happen there has to be an action. The relationship that has been broken needs to return to where it was before the offence took place. Reconciliation is the restoration of relationships. It welcomes the offender back into the life of the offended just as God has welcomed us back into His life.

The story of the Prodigal Son in chapter 26 is testament to this. The father always remained faithful to his son, even though the son left and showed no respect for his father. On his return with nothing left, the father welcomed the prodigal son with open arms and held a feast in his honour. God forgives all the wrong things we do and embraces each of us back into his family. He does not keep us at arm's length but places us in the middle of the table with the Father, Son and Holy Spirit.

This may be one of the most difficult things we are asked to do as Christians. We may be able to forgive but can we forget? Can we move on to invite the person that has sinned against us back into our lives, as if nothing has happened?

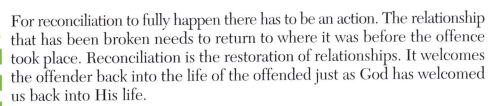

Up for Discussion

1. Can you think of examples where you may have been asked to reconcile with someone? Write about that time.
2. Do you think it is a difficult thing to do?

291

Pope John Paul II

Karol Wojtyla was born in Krakow, Poland in 1920. As a young man he excelled at sports and had a great love for the theatre. For some time he even considered acting as a career. However, he was ordained a priest in 1946. By 1964 he was a cardinal. In 1978 he was elected as Pope taking the name John Paul II. Because he was so dynamic and approachable, he signalled a new era in Catholic affairs and was recognised as a world leader of the Catholic Church. During his ministry he travelled extensively, visiting Ireland in 1979. There he appealed to the men of violence to give up their arms and return to a time of peace.

Above all, John Paul wanted to be the people's pope and his insistence on getting close to the crowd almost cost him his life in May 1981. Leaning out of his vehicle in St Peter's Square, he was shot and seriously wounded by a Turk called Mehmet Ali Aga. Mehmet had committed a sin that he would have to be punished for. The Pope spent a long time recovering from his injuries. Afterwards, he visited Mehmet Ali Aga in his prison cell where he forgave and embraced him. He welcomed him back into the family of God, thus reminding the whole world that God has welcomed us back. Pope John Paul was a man of integrity. His moral vision was steeped in the faith of Jesus Christ.

Over to You

1. Do you think Pope John Paul II fulfilled his dream of being a 'people's pope'?
2. When the Pope visited Mehmet Ali Aga in prison what do you think both men said to each other?
3. Do you think Pope John Paul was advised to visit the prison or did he go of his own accord?
4. Do you think Catholics today have embraced the message of reconciliation left by the Pope?

Although he remained in poor health, he made many journeys around the world to spread the Good News. Often the places he visited had political as well as pastoral problems, but he always felt the need to reach out to all. When he visited his native Poland to see the graves of his parents and brother, vast crowds of people turned out to see the man they believed was a living saint. Throughout his life he worked tirelessly to maintain the dignity of all humankind. In the Church's Jubilee Year he encouraged everyone to embrace the ministry of reconciliation.

Sacrament of Reconciliation

When we hurt or upset someone that we really like, we feel unhappy and guilty. We think about what we have done. We long to take back the hurt we have caused. When the person forgives us unconditionally, we feel great because they have not made us feel small. We are very thankful and promise ourselves not to hurt that person again.

Healing of relationships

Reconciliation is about bringing the Christian community closer together and closer to God. Reconciliation heals any hurt that people feel and in doing so makes it easier for people to love again without any barriers.

In the sacrament of reconciliation we are given the opportunity to meet the risen Christ. Through his forgiveness we are encouraged to move forward in harmony with ourselves and our neighbours. By doing this, God's love can be seen in the world around us. The sacrament can therefore be seen as a healing of the relationships that one has broken. Through sin we turn away from God, but through reconciliation we are allowed to turn back into the palm of his hand.

Confession

The priest who hears our confession represents the community of believers. He offers us forgiveness on behalf of the community. This sacrament can take place individually in a confession box where the priest hears confession privately. The confessor first acknowledges their sinfulness and the length of time it has been since their last confession. The Act of Contrition is then recited whereby the confessor thanks God for all the love he shows us and promises not to sin again. After this the priest gives an absolution and the person is cleansed from their sins. When the penitent leaves they are given a penance which normally involves a few prayers being said.

Today many Christians worldwide attend penitential services. Here the community gathers together to pray for forgiveness. Confession is held not in a box but in a quiet area in the church.

Reconciliation service

A prayer of confession

You are our God. We are your people.
But in today's world we can find ourselves in a place of unbelief.
We find ourselves in a world where too many people have despaired.
In a world where too many people do not know or do not care
that their brother or sister, with whom they are one, is crying out for help.
Too many of us do not practise what we preach.
Too many of us are too proud to apologise.
Too many of us judge too quickly.
Too many of us forget the message which you preached so
eloquently and for all ages.
My Lord and my God, look at us standing before you.
You alone can see deep down into our hearts.
You know us.
We stand before you together, help us to see the truth.
Help us to understand ourselves as you understand us.
So we may forgive ourselves as you forgive us.

Read one of the following scripture readings on forgiveness:
Luke 15, Luke 23:32–46, Luke 5:17–26.

Examination of Conscience

1. For the times I have not taken you seriously God,
   for the times I have not been aware of your love or
   have not spoken to you in prayer.
   (Pause)
   Response: Have mercy on me God; I am sorry.

2. For the times I have caused suffering to others
   by my unkindness, thoughtlessness or my neglect.
   (Pause)
   Response: Have mercy on me God; I am sorry.

3. For the times I have turned my back on those who
   who needed my friendship, help or sympathy.
   (Pause)
   Response: Have mercy on me God; I am sorry.

4. For the times when I have refused to forgive others
   in the same way as you forgive us.
   (Pause)
   Response: Have mercy on me God; I am sorry.

In this chapter, you will become familiar with the following concepts:

■ State law
■ Personal morality
■ Pluralism
■ Religious fundamentalism
■ Libertarianism

Chapter 27:

Religious Morality and State Law

■ (Higher Level)

State Law

A law can be defined as a set of rules or guidelines. In our society the people in charge, usually the government, establish the laws by which we live. These laws allow people to live in a safe and secure environment with each other. Often these laws are concerned with issues of morality. They inform the people about what is acceptable behaviour in a country or state. Very often these laws reflect the laws of our religion. They complement our personal morality. For example:

STATE LAW	RELIGIOUS MORALITY
It is against the law to take another person's life	'Thou shall not kill' (The Ten Commandments – Christianity)
It is against the law to slander another's good name	Right speech (The Eightfold Path – Buddhism)
It is against the law to take another person's possessions	'Thou shall not steal' (The Ten Commandments – Judaism)

The rulers of a country use a set of guidelines to help them when making the laws of the land. This is known as the constitution of the state. The Constitution of Ireland is called Bunreacht na hÉireann and contains guidelines on how the country should be governed, what rights people living in the state have, the status of religion and how laws are made and enforced.

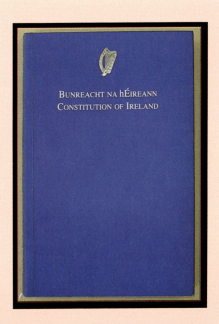

BUNREACHT NA hÉIREANN
CONSTITUTION OF IRELAND

Personal Morality vs State Law

We have already looked at how a person's morality is shaped by factors such as their family, friends, education and religion. But what happens when someone's personal morality and the law of the state or country they live in clash?

Sometimes conflict does occur between personal morality and state law. At times the individual can choose to ignore the clash. An example of this would be if a person's religious morality led them to be anti-abortion, yet the country they live in allows or legalises abortions. In this case the individual's personal morality would mean that they choose to have nothing to do with the abortion process in their country even though it is legal. But sometimes it is not that straight forward. Sometimes not getting involved is not enough.

Dead Man Walking

You may be familiar with a nun named Sister Helen Prejean whose extraordinary story is told in the film *Dead Man Walking*. This woman was a servant of God who found her personal morality colliding with state law when she became a penpal to an inmate on death row called Patrick Sonnier in 1982. Sonnier had been imprisoned for killing two teenagers. As a result of becoming his spiritual adviser, Sister Helen was there to witness his execution by electrocution in April 1984. Before the execution took place she told him: 'You look at my face. Look at me, and I will be the face of Christ for you.'

When asked why she would get involved with such people, Sister Helen's reply goes back to the person of Jesus Christ: 'Look at who Jesus hung out with: lepers, prostitutes, thieves – the throwaways of his day … and there are no more marginated … people in our society than death row inmates.'

Sister Helen strongly condemns the death penalty, which is still used in America, China and Israel today. She objects to it because 'Jesus Christ, whose way of life I try to follow, refused to meet hate with hate and violence with violence. I pray for the strength to be like him'.

Her reason for getting involved with people on death row is that she responded to the call of the social Gospel of Jesus, especially the poor.

Nearly all of the 3,000 people on death row in America are poor. As well as it being morally wrong, Sister Helen feels that the death penalty system is grossly unfair as it is a punishment usually reserved for poor, coloured people. She also questions the right of anyone to take away another human life, 'Who deserves to kill this man?'.

A still from the film 'Dead Man Walking'.

Sister Helen reflects on her experience of accompanying three men to their executions: 'You are in this building in the middle of the night, and all these people are organised to kill this man. And the Gospel comes to you as it never has before: Are you for compassion or are you for violence? Are you for mercy or are you for vengeance? Are you for love or are you for hate? Are you for life or are you for death? And the words of Jesus from the Gospel kept coming to me that night: "And the last will be first" and "This too is my beloved son, hear him"'. For Sister Helen, this convicted criminal had what God has given to all his people, dignity.

Before Patrick Sonnier died, Sister Helen made a promise to him to tell his story to others in the hope that it would allow people to see the immorality of the death penalty. Ever since she has worked tirelessly to have the death penalty abolished. The UN Declaration on Human Rights states that all humans have the right not to be tortured or killed. According to her, 'allowing our government to kill citizens compromises the deepest moral values upon which this country was conceived: the inviolable dignity of human persons'.

Over to You – Exam Style Questions (Type 1)

1. Why did Sister Helen Prejean become involved with death row inmates?
2. How did her personal morality clash with state law?
3. Do you agree with her opinion? Why?
4. Would you describe Sister Helen as a morally mature person? Why?
5. What do you think was Sister Helen's moral vision?

Over to You – Exam Style Questions (Type 2)

1. Research and write an essay on how personal morality and state law may be in conflict on one of the following issues: abortion, divorce or apartheid.
2. The story of Sister Helen Prejean has shown us how someone's personal morality may clash with state law. Some people feel that religious morality should shape or influence state law, while others feel that they should be two separate issues. What do you think?

Pluralism

Pluralism – The belief that groups belonging to different races or different political or religious beliefs can live together in peace in one society.

KEEP CHURCH AND STATE SEPARATE! LET DIVERSITY RULE!

A **pluralist** is someone who holds the view that the laws of the state should not be influenced in any way by the laws of a religion. They believe that society is made up of people from all different races, cultures and religions and each should be as important as the other. No one group of people should have the right to influence the laws of a country over another group.

A pluralist would strongly oppose a theocracy, which is a system where the laws of a religion become the law of the land. They feel that just because one group of people may be against something because of their religion or culture, it does not mean that other people living in the same country should be affected by these views. They believe religion and state law should be kept separate.

Up For Discussion

What do you think are the advantages and disadvantages of living in a pluralist society?

Religious Fundamentalism

Fundamentalism could be described as the opposite of pluralism. Fundamentalists are people who believe that the beliefs, teachings and writings of their religion should be taken word for word or literally. They believe no one should try to interpret the teachings in any way. These teachings should not only be the laws of their religion but also the law of the land.

Some countries in the world practise religious fundamentalism by living in a theocracy. One example would be in Afghanistan in 1931, when the constitution was based on the laws of Islam. In 1964 the constitution was changed to allow secular law as long as it did not interfere with the values of the Islamic law. Some people would say that religious fundamentalism can become dangerous when taken to extremes.

Up For Discussion

What do you think are the advantages and disadvantages of living in a fundamentalist society?

Libertarianism

A libertarian is someone who values the freedom of the individual above all else. They do not agree with the state having any influence in the moral lives of its citizens. They see state involvement as limiting the liberty of individuals.

Up For Discussion

What do you think are the advantages and disadvantages of living in a libertarian society?

Answers to the crossword on page 276

1. Moral Vision

2. Law

3. Authority

4. Tradition

Section F – Key Definitions

ACTION AND CONSEQUENCE:	The things we do or say (actions) cause something else to happen (consequence).
AUTHORITY AND TRADITION:	To have authority means to have a certain power or to be highly knowledgeable about a certain subject.
CIVIL LAW:	The rules of a country, which are put in place by those in charge.
CHOICE:	A moral choice is making a decision about what is right or wrong.
CONSCIENCE:	The ability to know what is right and wrong using judgement and knowledge.
CONSTITUTION:	The guidelines used by the authorities when making rules of law.
DECISION-MAKING:	The ability to make a decision on a matter whether it is the right one or not.
FORGIVENESS:	To stop feeling angry towards someone and more towards reconciliation.
FREEDOM:	We are free to choose when making a moral decision but are limited by our responsibilities to others.
INFLUENCE:	Something that affects our decisions.
INTEGRITY:	Being modest and morally upright.
JUDGEMENT:	The ability to make a sound decision.
JUSTICE:	To act justly and fairly towards others.
LAWS:	A law prevents us from doing something wrong. The government makes laws for the country.
LIBERTARIANISM:	The belief that everyone should be free to do as they choose, so long as they do not interfere with the rights of others.
MORAL GROWTH:	This is a gradual process moving from childhood through to adolescence and into adulthood.
MORAL MATURITY:	When someone is morally mature they take into consideration the feelings of others and base their morality on what they hold to be true.
MORALITY:	Knowing what is good and bad behaviour and making decisions based on this.
MORAL VISION:	To see the difference between something that is right and wrong.
PEACE:	To be free of violence.
PLURALISM:	The belief that groups belonging to different races or different political or religious beliefs can live together in peace in one society.
RECONCILIATION:	Actively embracing the person that has sinned against us and welcoming them back into our lives.
RELATIONSHIPS:	The connections we have to other people.

Section F – Key Definitions

RELIGIOUS FUNDAMENTALISM:	Believing what the sacred text or laws of your religion say, word for word, i.e. literally.
RELIGIOUS MORAL VISION:	The ability to see that we are made in the image and likeness of God and this helps us shape our moral decisions.
RESPECT:	To have a high regard for something and so treat it with consideration.
SIN:	An act that breaks a religious code.
SOCIETY:	Human beings living together in a community.
STEWARDSHIP:	Being responsible for caring for all of God's creation.
TRADITION:	knowledgeable about a certain subject. Tradition is something that we pass on from one generation to the next.
TRUTH:	The state of being true to oneself and others and not telling a lie.

The Journal

As well as completing a written exam in Religious Education you must also produce a piece called **journal work.**

This is worth **20% of your final** mark so it is worth doing well!

Each year there will be a list of official titles given and you must work on one of these titles.

Your teacher will guide you as you do this but remember it must be **your** work.

Writing a journal is different to simply doing a project. You may do a project as part of it but at the end it is the actual journal you will be marked on and not the project.

You will fill out an official booklet or journal, which will be sent to your school.

Journal work is about investigating a topic in a certain way and then reflecting on how you did this.

It may be useful to keep a journal work diary to have a record of events, as this will help when it comes to writing up the journal booklet.

In the official booklet there are **five different sections**, which you must fill out and each one contains what we will call lead statements.

It may help to write up a draft journal before you fill out the actual booklet.

You only have a small amount of space to write in your answers so remember to keep to the point. There's no room for waffle!

Introduction

Section One

To begin this section you must write down the prescribed title of your journal work. If you're not sure check this with your teacher. You also have to tick a box to show whether you did journal work on your own or as part of a group. Remember, even if you do it as a group you must write up the journal on your own. You are then asked for a personal title for your journal. This is sometimes easier to do at the end when you have had time to reflect more on your title. Try and make it original but remember to keep it relevant to the prescribed title. Look at the example below.

The prescribed title of my journal is … An investigation of the elements involved in the celebration of a sacrament.

The personal title of my journal work is … Baptism — my introduction to this introductory rite.

The next lead statement asks you why you chose this title. Think about why an investigation into this topic would be interesting or relevant to you.

I chose this title because … As a Catholic I have been baptised so I would like to find out what this actually involves. I was a baby when it happened so I don't remember! Also it is the first sacrament Christians receive so it must be important and I want to see why. Finally my aunt just had a baby who will be baptised soon and I would like to know what is going to happen.

The final lead statement in this section asks you what you hope to achieve, learn or find out by doing journal work on this title.

By doing journal work on this title I hope to … learn the meaning behind the celebration of baptism. I want to find out if there is any preparation involved and what exactly happens during the sacrament for everyone who's there. I hope to produce a booklet on baptism to help new parents in my parish who are having their babies baptised.

Getting Started

Section Two

This section is about the planning that you or your group do for your journal work. You should give a detailed description of the work you hope to carry out.

To prepare for doing my journal work I ... decided that we would look up information on baptism in the library. We would also see what we could find on the internet and hope to be able to download pictures of the sacrament. I would interview my aunt and find out what questions she had about the upcoming baptism of her baby. Another member of the group would interview our local parish priest and ask him about baptism in general and how we celebrate it in our parish. We all came up with one question we could ask him. Another member of the group would begin to design the booklet on baptism and we would try to arrange for an adult in our parish who was recently baptised to come in and talk to our class on his experience.

Work

Section Three

Here you must detail what work you actually did. It may be similar to what you said in the previous section but remember things might not go exactly as you planned. If you do your journal work as part of a group you should mention your role as well as the others in the group. Make sure you relate what you say back to the title.

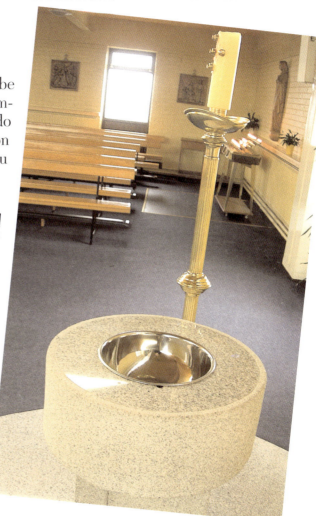

To do my journal work I … When we went to the library we found that it was difficult to get a book on baptism but there was one on sacraments and we could use some chapters in this. The Internet had too much information so it was hard to know what to use. We interviewed Fr Lynch from our parish and he gave a lot of information and told us there was a baptismal team in our parish, which we didn't know, so we arranged a meeting with them. Unfortunately the adult who had been baptised was away on holidays so we couldn't interview him. I interviewed my aunt and she told me why she was having her baby baptised and what questions she had. Someone else in our group went to our church and took photos of the baptismal font. They also got a copy of the leaflet used in the ceremony. We bought the materials needed for our booklet.

The next lead statement is asking you about the methods you used to do journal work. You should say why you chose this way of doing journal work.

I included this in my journal work because … We decided to interview Fr Lynch because he has celebrated a lot of baptisms in our parish. We met with the baptismal team because they are in charge of meeting parents who are bringing their babies to be baptised and so would know what is involved. The photos of the baptismal font helped us to see where it took place. Interviewing my aunt would help us to get a personal view of the sacrament of baptism.

The last part of section three is about your reaction to doing this work. You could include what part you found the most interesting or difficult. Remember to mention the group's reaction as well as your own.

My reaction to doing this work was … I thought the meeting with the baptismal team was the most interesting part because I didn't know there was one in my parish and they do a lot of very important work. The group also liked this as we got to meet people who work in our parish. Finding books on the sacrament of baptism was the hardest part, as we couldn't find any that just deal with baptism. The group and I thought the interview with Fr Lynch was very helpful as he knew a lot about the elements involved in baptism and he was very interesting.

Discoveries

Section Four

This section looks at the information you learned, the skills you used and how your journal work links in with the rest of your religion course.

The first part asks about what you learned. You probably learned a lot, so you may have to decide to include only the main points as there won't be room to write everything. Try asking yourself what the three most interesting things you learned were.

I learned … that baptism is a sacrament of initiation. It is a formal ceremony where the church welcomes its new members. The parents of a child being baptised usually choose godparents who will help to bring the child up in the faith of their church. There is a reading from the New Testament. Some of the symbols used are water, oil, a candle and a white shawl. The baby is formally named and the parents and godparents make baptismal promises on behalf of the child.

The next part of section four asks you about the effect doing journal work had on you. Do you have a new awareness, new opinion or different attitude about the topic now?

As a result of what I have learned … I am looking forward to going to my cousin's baptism, as I now know what it's all about. I really appreciate the work the baptismal team do in my parish and I hope to get involved in it when I'm older. I now understand why we are baptised as babies and I think it is a very important sacrament. I hope our booklet will help parents who want to get their child baptised.

You are now asked about the skills you used when you did your journal work. You must pick two skills out of the six listed; enquiry skills, observational skills, problem-solving skills, research skills, reflective skills and organisational skills. Pick two of these skills and explain how you used them. Ask your teacher if you're not sure what any of the skills mean.

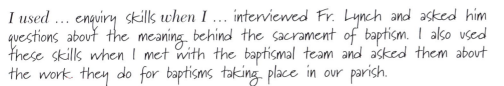

I used … enquiry skills when I … interviewed Fr. Lynch and asked him questions about the meaning behind the sacrament of baptism. I also used these skills when I met with the baptismal team and asked them about the work they do for baptisms taking place in our parish.

I used … research skills when I … went to the library to look for books on the sacrament of baptism. I also used research skills when I went on the internet to see if I could get any pictures of a baptismal ceremony.

The last part of section four asks you to link what you did in journal work with other topics you learned about in religion class. Think back over the work you did in class. It may help to look back over your old books and copies. Remember not to just say you learned about the topic already. Try and link it with a different topic. You must make two links and explain them.

My journal work reminded me of studying … communities … because … when we studied communities we looked at what makes a community work, the characteristics of it. In the journal work I saw a community working well together when I met the baptismal team. They had the characteristics that I had learned about before; cooperation, communication and sharing. They were a good example of a community of people working together who shared the same beliefs.

My journal work reminded me of studying … symbols … because … we looked at why symbols are used and some examples of symbols used in religious ceremonies. One of the most important symbols used in baptism is water and it symbolises the gift of life and the cleansing that takes place during baptism. I came across this symbol when we studied other major world religions too.

Looking Back

Section Five

The last section is about reflecting on the whole experience of doing journal work. It asks you to comment on what you think went well or what you would do differently if you were doing journal work again. You can also say what advice you would give to someone else who was doing journal work on the same title.

Looking back at my experience of doing journal work on this title …
I think my journal work went very well. The interviews went really well and were interesting as well as helpful. If I were starting again I wouldn't bother looking on the internet as it's very hard to know what information to use as there's so much. I would also think of more questions for the interview with Fr Lynch as he knew so much about it and was happy to help us. If someone else were doing this title for journal work I would advise them to check if there is a baptismal team in their parish as meeting them was one of the best parts of the whole project. I would also advise them to plan well in advance as you might be waiting to interview someone and this could slow you up. Overall I thought the journal work was a really fun way to learn about the sacrament of baptism.